9x6|12

A Comrade
Lost and Found

ALSO BY JAN WONG

Red China Blues: My Long March
from Mao to Now

A Comrade
Lost and Found

A Beijing Story

Jan Wong

HOUGHTON MIFFLIN HARCOURT

Boston · *New York*

2009

First published in Canada as *Beijing Confidential* by Doubleday
Canada, a division of Random House of Canada Limited in 2007.

Library of Congress Cataloging-in-Publication Data
Wong, Jan.
A comrade lost and found: a Beijing story / Jan Wong.
p.   cm.
1. Wong, Jan—Travel—China.   2. Beijing (China)—
Description and travel.   I. Title.   II. Title: Beijing story.
DS795.W67   2009
951'.156057092—dc22   [B]   2008023788
ISBN 978-0-15-101342-5

Set in Perpetua

Printed in the United States of America

VB 10 9 8 7 6 5 4 3 2 1

For Colleen

Contents

A Comrade
Lost and Found

China

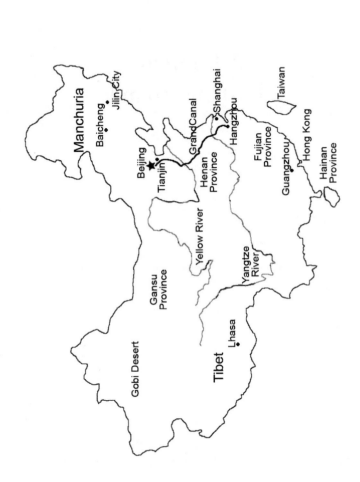

Map by Ben Shulman

City of Beijing

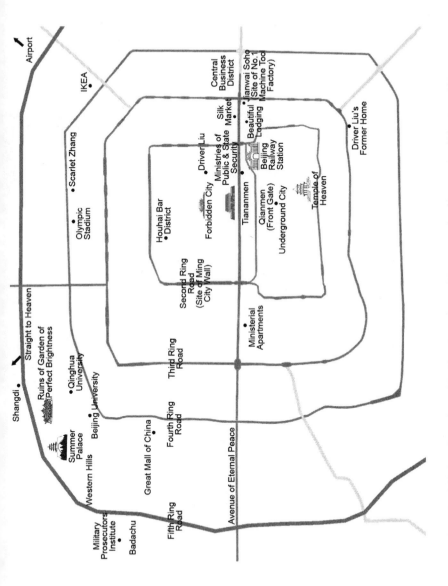

Map by Ben Shulman

Mission Impossible

On the tarmac at Newark International Airport, a heat wave makes the August air dance. Inside our Boeing 777, a black flight attendant sings out the standard Chinese greeting. "*Ni hao,*" she chimes, mangling the tones. Nevertheless the passengers, mostly mainland Chinese, seem pleased. When even this American female is trying to speak their language, it reinforces their view that the Middle Kingdom is, once again, the center of the world.

My husband, Norman, and I lived in Beijing for years during the 1970s, 1980s and 1990s. On this trip back, we are bringing two reluctant fellow travelers, our teenaged sons, Ben, sixteen, and Sam, thirteen. As usual these days on flights to Beijing, every seat is taken. The Chinese passengers in their knock-off Burberry outfits are more self-assured than the handful who left the mainland during Chairman Mao's Great Proletarian Cultural Revolution. In the 1970s, the Chinese who traveled abroad were members of official delegations, kept on short leashes, tight schedules and tiny cash allowances.

Foreigners heading to China faced obstacles, too. Beijing rarely issued visas to Americans, but Norman was deemed to be "friendly." His father, Jack Shulman, had been an aide to William Z. Foster, longtime head of the Communist Party USA. In 1965, Jack had gone to Beijing to polish English-language propaganda at Xinhua, the state-run New China News Agency. To the Chinese, it was natural for a son to join his father. Filial piety, however, wasn't Norman's motivating factor. The Vietnam War was. At twenty-two, he was looking for an interesting place to dodge the draft.

In 1966, his journey from New York City to Beijing would take days. The United States had no diplomatic relations with China. To obtain a visa, Norman had to fly to London. From there, the only air route to mainland China was a twice-monthly Pakistan International Airlines flight to Canton, now known as Guangzhou. PIA normally refueled twice en route, in Karachi and Dhaka. At the time, India was at war with Pakistan, so Norman's flight was rerouted through Colombo, Sri Lanka. When his flight finally landed in Canton, he was a jet-lagged wreck. But the arrival of a foreigner was a rare chance to feast at government expense. Hungry local officials insisted on feeding him a ten-course banquet, after which they bundled him aboard a three-hour flight to Beijing.

Forty years later, Continental Airlines flight 89 takes thirteen hours. With the Cold War over, it zips across the Arctic Circle and the former Soviet Union. Our tickets are a bargain, too, 80 percent less expensive in real terms than when I first went to China in 1972. The Middle Kingdom is still on the other side of the world, but it's no longer far away.

• • •

Ben and Sam spent their earliest years in Beijing. They were born during my six-year posting as China correspondent for the Toronto *Globe and Mail*. Sam was one when we moved back to Canada in 1994. He remembers nothing. Ben, who was four, has fragmented memories. He recalls making little cakes from Play-Doh with Nanny Ma. He remembers wandering into the kitchen to sit on Cook Mu's lap.

In 2003, the year severe acute respiratory syndrome, or SARS, broke out in Beijing (and Toronto), Norman and I figured the Great Wall might not be too crowded. After the all-clear, we took the boys back for the grand tour. Along with the Wall, we visited the Forbidden City, the Temple of Heaven, the terra cotta warriors in Xi'an, the Shanghai Bund and the Yangtze River. We picked grapes in Kashgar and sledded down sand dunes in the Gobi Desert.

Now, when I propose a holiday in Beijing, my sons both groan. Ben would rather hang out in Toronto with his girlfriend, Tash, and go mountain biking with friends. Sam prefers to play road hockey and chat on MSN. The boys grow markedly un-enthusiastic when I mention I also plan to hire a Chinese tutor in Beijing so they can start each day with private Mandarin lessons.

"Um, do I have to go?" Sam asks politely, hoping good manners will get him off the hook.

"Yes," I say.

"Why do I have to go?" Ben asks belligerently, hoping attitude will get *him* off the hook.

"Because," I reply enigmatically, "I need you."

I promise the boys we won't go sightseeing. I promise I won't make them visit a single museum. I swear we will not re-climb the Great Wall. I bill the trip as a once-in-a-lifetime opportunity to live, briefly, in a crazy, amped-up city. Indeed, that's why I've persuaded myself to come back. I already know the city well, or at least I think I do. But the ancient capital I knew is disappearing fast. If I blink, it might vanish. So on this trip back I want to write about the city I loved and about the new, modern, shiny one that is obliterating the old. I figure it's now or never.

We have exactly twenty-eight days in Beijing. August is brutally hot, but earlier in the summer the boys were busy with hockey camp, invitations to friends' cottages and mountain biking at Whistler in British Columbia. In September they have to go back to school—and I have to go back to work.

Now, as we settle into our seats on the plane, Ben asks, grumpily, for the umpteenth time, "Why do I have to go?"

"Because I need you," I reply, for the umpteenth time.

I need Norman, too. A software developer, he prefers to sit at home and read technical journals. He already lived in Beijing for twenty years, and unlike me, the journalist, he sees no need to spend yet another month there. But his deep experience is a big reason I want him with me there. He first arrived in China in 1966, on the eve of the Cultural Revolution. He saw the Ming-dynasty city walls come tumbling down. He cut ice from the lakes in winter to store for use in summer—before the advent of air-conditioning and refrigeration. He knows Beijing better than I do. And his spoken and written Chinese is excellent. Norman even has a real Chinese name: Yulu. Jack, as the patriarch, named him after Jiao Yulu, a rural official lionized as a model Communist. Like any good peasant's name, Yulu combines the dual dream of wealth and job security. *Yu* means riches; *lu* means an official's salary in ancient China. Norman has always objected to my translation: Fat Paycheck.

• • •

As the plane rumbles down the runway at Newark, I'm acutely aware that I still haven't explained to my boys why I need them. The fact is I'm too afraid to go alone.

Being chicken isn't characteristic of me. In 1972, the first time I went to China, I went by myself. I had just finished my third year at university, majoring in Asian history and student sit-ins. I was nineteen and believed I was invincible. Canada had diplomatic relations with China, but in the midst of the Cultural Revolution, Beijing was issuing few visas. It did, however, make exceptions for ethnic Chinese, most of whom were too scared to go. I wasn't.

When I arrived in China, I confused everyone, including myself. I was a Montreal Maoist who looked Chinese but couldn't speak Chinese. The authorities could not wrap their minds around the fact that I was a Canadian, and a third-generation one at that. My grandfather had arrived in Canada in 1881, one of thousands of coolies who built the Canadian Pacific Railroad. My other three grandparents had arrived at the turn of the last century, and had paid the discriminatory head tax on Chinese immigrants.

Miraculously, my solo jaunt through China ended with an invitation to study Mandarin at Beijing University. As part of the Maoist curriculum, I worked in a factory, dug ditches and hauled pig manure. Along the way, I narrowly avoided getting expelled—this is true—for contact with another foreigner. Looking back on the mystery of it all, I believe I was accepted at Beijing University because I was in the right place at the right time. After six years of Cult Rev xenophobia, Beijing was trying to thaw relations with the West. In 1971, it had invited the U.S. table-tennis team to Beijing. In 1972, I was the logical next step, the first Canadian to study there since the Cultural Revolution.

No one knew it, but in another year Beijing was planning to restore international student exchanges. The regime needed to start sending its own students abroad to study foreign languages. But after so many years of isolation, it was understandably cautious about Western teenagers. I was about to become a guinea pig in China's revolution in education. But I wouldn't be completely alone.

Unbeknownst to me, Erica Jen, a Chinese-American teenager from Yale University, had just been accepted at Beijing University, too. In the 1920s, her China-born father had roomed with Zhou Peiyuan at the California Institute of Technology. Zhou was now the chancellor of Beijing University and in a position to do a favor for his old roommate: enable his American-born daughter to study Chinese. The authorities apparently feared it might be too hard for Erica to be the lone Westerner at Beijing University. Serendipitously, I was the perfect companion: a lone, teenage feminist and wannabe Maoist who was dying to learn Mandarin. Even better, I was not American. Beijing did not yet have diplomatic relations with Washington, and accepting *two* Americans would send the wrong signal. A Canadian was a kinder, gentler version of a Yank, without all the imperialist baggage. Canadians also happened to be popular after Chairman Mao wrote an essay, "In Memory of Norman Bethune," canonizing a swashbuckling doctor from Gravenhurst, Ontario, who had died of septicemia in China in 1939 while tending to wounded Communist soldiers. What's more, Ottawa had established diplomatic relations with Beijing way back in 1959. And in October 1971 the Canadian delegation to the United Nations joined with other nations to recognize the People's Republic as the only legitimate representative of China at the UN, a vote that effectively expelled the Taiwanese delegation.

The offer to study came out of the blue. My inability to speak Chinese initially surprised the authorities, but they finally had allowed me to glom on to an English-speaking tour group. On July 18, 1972, I was sightseeing in Beijing when the guide gave me the news. She refused to provide any details at all, including which school I'd attend or when I'd start. She also said I had to make up my mind right away, without consulting my parents. I asked for ten minutes. I walked once around the block, took a deep breath and said yes. Then I sent a telegram home: I'M NOT COMING BACK. SEND MONEY.

Later, as a reporter in Beijing, I hadn't been afraid of much, either. Like lots of resident Western journalists, my phone had been tapped, my mail opened. The secret police tailed me, interrogated my sources and sometimes arrested them. In 1989, a few days after the massacre at Tiananmen Square, plain-clothes police mistook me for a student and tried to kidnap me. I fought back, screaming—in English. The agents stopped trying to stuff me in the back of the unmarked car. Still shaking on the sidewalk, I belatedly realized that if only I had gone along with them, I would have had a great story.

About the same time, someone stole the *Globe*'s aging Toyota hatchback. Fat Paycheck discovered that the thieves were the Beijing police when, a year later, he caught them red-handed using it as a squad car. They had even strapped red flashing lights over the roof. I wasn't afraid. I hustled right down to the station and made the police give me back my car. Now *that* was a great story.

But on this trip I'm nervous, because I'm returning to Beijing for another reason. I am not only planning to chronicle the future of this great city; I also need to come to terms with my own past. For this, I want moral support. I need my family to reassure me that I'm not a horrible human being. Or that, if I am, they love me anyway. Thirty-three years ago, in one thoughtless, misguided moment, I destroyed someone's life. This is what I did: in 1973, I ratted out a stranger at Beijing University who wanted to get to America. At the time I did not give it much thought. I certainly did not understand the enormity of what I had done. I recorded the incident in my diary, and forgot about it. A month or two later, I left Beijing and shipped my diaries home, where they lay unread for years in my mom's basement in Montreal.

In the ensuing years, I graduated from McGill University and returned to Beijing University for another degree in Chinese history. In 1979, I became the first news assistant in the Beijing bureau of the *New York Times.* After earning a master's degree in journalism at Columbia University, I worked as a business reporter for the Montreal *Gazette,* the *Boston Globe,* the *Wall Street Journal* and the Toronto *Globe and Mail.* In 1988 the *Globe and Mail* appointed me its thirteenth China correspondent.

Before I left Canada, I retrieved the dusty box from my mom's basement. I wanted my diaries with me in Beijing—for what, I wasn't sure. For six more years, I never looked at them. Then, in 1994, when I was ending my posting, I paged through the small three-ring binders. In 1973 my handwriting had been girlish and neat, each letter painstakingly formed with a fountain pen in blue ink. Some pages I'd typed, using a battered Hermes portable left behind by a British visitor. The paper was cheap and lined. I had hole-punched the sheets by hand.

After a day's reporting and writing stories for my newspaper back in Toronto, and in between making arrangements to pack up our household, I would hole up alone with my old diaries in the *Globe*'s whitewashed office in Beijing. I read about my struggle to integrate into a hermetically sealed society, about wielding a pneumatic drill at the Number One Machine Tool Factory, about my ludicrous efforts to overcome my bourgeois affinity for rock and roll. I had been an enthusiastic participant in my own brainwashing. The Chinese used the term *xi nao,* "washing the brain," approvingly. After all, you wash something to cleanse it of filth. Reading about my misguided youth, I occasionally smiled. More often I winced. Then I read an entry about a stranger who had invited me and Erica for a stroll around No Name Lake. With a sinking heart, it all came back. How could I have ever forgotten?

In 1972, Erica's and my studies had been approved at the highest levels of the Chinese government. As the first foreign students, we had our own teachers, our own cook and our own dormitory. Everyone who befriended us had been carefully vetted by the Communist Party. Beijing University even moved in hand-picked female students to fill the emptiness of the foreign-student dormitory. Looking back, I liken it to the 1998 hit film *The Truman Show.* Truman Burbank, Jim Carrey's happy-go-lucky character, thinks he's living in a picture-perfect small town. In fact, the town is fake and all the others are actors reciting rehearsed lines. Similarly, at Beijing University, everyone around us spouted Communist Party propaganda. And we were too naive to see through it.

Erica and I had been there nearly a year without one spontaneous encounter. So we were delighted when someone new approached us. The young woman had no inkling Erica and I were both starry-eyed Maoists. As we walked around the campus lake, she peppered us with questions. How much money did a worker make in America? Did every American have a refrigerator? What kind of class background was required to attend university? When we told her how much workers earned, she gasped. We grudgingly acknowledged that everyone had a fridge. And we conceded that there were no class-based restrictions on university attendance.

Suddenly she said, "I want to go to America. Can you help me?"

We were shocked. Our roommates had never expressed the slightest interest in the West. For nearly a year, our teachers had taught that China was a proletarian paradise. But perhaps I shouldn't have been surprised. Only a few months earlier, I had personally experienced the dark side of paradise. I had nearly been expelled from Beijing University for an innocent friendship with another foreigner, a young Swedish diplomat in Beijing. When the crisis was resolved, I had simply resumed classes. But it was my first experience with thought control. Everyone—my teachers, my classmates, the officials in the Foreign Student's Office—all pretended it had never happened. Only Erica assured me I wasn't delusional.

That incident had shaken my faith. Yet I still stubbornly, desperately wanted to believe that socialism was superior to capitalism. I was still in love with China, and falling out of love would be a long, slow, painful process.

Erica was even more left-wing than I was. That night, we discussed what to do. Helping the young stranger leave was out of the question. We reasoned that the workers and peasants had paid for her university education. Anyone who accepted this privilege was duty-bound to stay in China and help develop the country. Also, we wanted to save her from a fate of panty hose and shopping malls. We could have done nothing. Certainly, we both felt squeamish about tattling. Then we decided our discomfort was just another manifestation of the bourgeois Western sentimentality we were trying to overcome. Chairman Mao had exhorted us to "let politics take command." Any other considerations were superfluous.

"We didn't do it to earn brownie points," Erica, a research professor in mathematics at the Los Alamos National Laboratory in New Mexico, told me years later. But maybe I did. Having almost been cast out myself, I now wanted desperately to be accepted, to be part of what I then called "New China." Perhaps this was an opportunity to prove my revolutionary fervor. A radical classmate back at McGill—now a family physician in Vancouver—recently told me that my letters to her at the time had sounded "ferocious." She sent me a photocopy of a letter she'd saved from 1972. In it, I talk about the constant struggle to transform myself. I suggest, quite seriously, that "propaganda work really needs to be done." I actually quote Mao. I write about "making revolution."

I was that very dangerous combination: fanatic, ignorant and adolescent. In 1973 I thought I knew everything about China, but I actually knew very little. I knew that it was unacceptable to express a desire to leave the motherland, but I didn't know there were labor camps for dissidents. I didn't know that China during the Cultural Revolution was a crazy place where someone could be ruined, imprisoned or beaten simply for accidentally ripping up a newspaper that happened to contain a photo of Mao. China's human rights violations weren't common knowledge then. To outsiders, Beijing projected an image of harmony, happiness and clean living, like the town of Seahaven in *The Truman Show*. Insiders knew it was a police state, but that same police state so tightly controlled access to the dark side that few outsiders got a glimpse. In 1973 China, reporting was so rudimentary that John Burns, one of my predecessors in the *Globe*'s Beijing bureau, would write about a simple train ride. Burns, who would later become one of the *New York Times*'s great foreign correspondents, even wrote glowingly about the Red Flag Canal, a showpiece Maoist project: "The work produced many heroes, paraded now before the constant stream of visitors to the canal. Their stories are too . . . long . . . , but there is enough substance in them to show that great courage and initiative were involved."

Erica and I assumed that Communist Party officials would give the young woman a tongue-lashing. That was the system we'd been shown. I'd been criticized many times that year for reading old copies of *Newsweek* that my mother sent, for slacking off on homework, for leaving my dorm room unlocked (thereby tempting class enemies). I'd been scolded for tap dancing on the stone floor of a Ming tomb when the guide launched into a boring discourse on fifteenth-century class struggle. And yet, given my near expulsion, Erica and I should have been more cautious. We weren't.

The next morning, we told our respective teachers about Yin's American dream.

By 1994 I had lived in China, off and on, for a dozen years. I had covered Tiananmen Square. I had written about dissidents, human rights, labor camps, torture and secret execution grounds. Before that, I had witnessed the outpouring of bitterness after the Cultural Revolution ended upon Mao Zedong's death in 1976. I learned how colleagues had turned on one another, how neighbors had ratted each other out, how children had snitched on their parents—all in the name of the Revolution.

By 1980, the Chinese began calling the 1966–1976 Cultural Revolution the "Decade of Disaster." When I read my diary in 1994, of course I had no more illusions. I knew with blinding clarity what I had done. At the age of twenty, I had thoughtlessly destroyed a young woman I didn't even know. In my diary I had recorded only her surname, Yin. Anxiously, I sought out my old roommate, Scarlet. She remembered. She said that Yin, a history major, had been expelled at a department-wide meeting. Scarlet said she wasn't sure what had happened to her after that. Nor did she quite remember Yin's full name. "I think it was Yin Luoyi," she said.

At that point I stopped asking questions. There was no way to trace Yin, and no time. In a few weeks I would be leaving China. I didn't have time to chase down my past. At least that's what I told myself. Deep down I was afraid to look for Yin. What if I found her? Worse, what if I didn't?

I spent my first year back in Toronto writing a memoir, *Red China Blues.* I considered omitting any mention of the young stranger. If I didn't write about her, who would know? If I did write about her, I'd be pilloried for sure. Still, as a journalist, I've always demanded honesty in others. If I wanted to write truthfully about China, if I wanted to show the true face of Communism, it was essential to come clean myself. I had harbored no ill will toward Yin. I didn't even know her. And yet I had betrayed her. Why? I wasn't even sure myself.

I wrote about Yin in *Red China Blues,* and people have attacked me for it ever since. They often get the details wrong. They say that I turned in my roommate, or another classmate. Yin was not my classmate. I didn't know her at all. And obviously she didn't know me. If she had, she would have run screaming in the opposite direction. But writing about Yin did not lay my demons to rest. As the years passed, I tried to forget her. I couldn't. I kept thinking about her. I wanted to know what had happened to her, and yet I was afraid to find out. I reasoned to myself that anyone who wanted to leave that badly must have gotten out. I comforted myself with the fantasy that she was alive and well and living in Las Vegas. Then doubts would set in. She must have suffered terribly. Perhaps she was dead. Then I hoped she might have had a child—a daughter, perhaps— whom I could help in some way. Perhaps that daughter might want to come to Canada.

There was only risk in finding out. It was easy to do nothing. In the ensuing twelve years, I returned to Beijing four times— twice on reporting stints for my newspaper, once on the grand tour with my family, and once to complete research on my second book, *Jan Wong's China,* and to make a documentary film, *Jan Wong's Forbidden China.* The documentary's producer, Robin Benger, suggested I look for Yin during that trip. He thought it would make for gripping footage. I squirmed. I hung my head. I changed the subject. I was a coward. I told Robin it would be impossible to find her.

Still, Yin has haunted me for many years. I need to understand why I threw myself so enthusiastically into the Cultural

Revolution. If I can figure that out, I might understand why so many Chinese did, too. At a moment in history when Beijing is emerging on the world stage and its stability remains uncertain, any clarity might help prevent a future convulsion. Of course, I am seeking answers from a relatively privileged position. My life is not here in Beijing. I am dropping in for twenty-eight days, and after that I can conveniently leave any messiness behind. Deep down, perhaps, I am praying that I won't actually find Yin—but at least I can tell myself that I tried.

Aboard flight 89, the flight attendants serve a choice of New Jersey dim sum or overcooked chicken and mash. The in-flight entertainment include *She's the Man, The Shoe Fairy, Benchwarmers* and *Mission Impossible III*. I watch *MI III* while chewing on dried-out chicken. Here's the plot: the hero thwarts a plan to sell a destructive secret to an unnamed enemy nation where everyone speaks Chinese. It's supposed to be a thriller, but I laugh out loud. The bloopers include the inability of Tom Cruise's character to get a cellphone signal in downtown Shanghai. Anyone who's been to China knows you can get a clear signal anywhere, including the Gobi Desert and the grasslands of Inner Mongolia. Then there's the car chase through downtown Shanghai. Like Beijing, Shanghai is clogged with traffic night and day. No one gets anywhere fast. And finally, there's the climactic shoot-out in a picturesque warren of Qing-dynasty homes. But Shanghai has razed everything old, except the riverside Bund and the hallowed spot where Mao and others founded the Chinese Communist Party in 1921.

When the movie ends, I contemplate my own mission

impossible. How will I find a stranger in a country of 1.3 billion? I have four weeks and no plan of action. All I know is I'm fifty-three now and I am running out of excuses. It's time to find Yin, apologize and try to make amends. The bittersweet irony is that, thirty-three years after I turned her in, I am on a planeload of mainland Chinese returning home of their own free will.

Life as It Has Always Been Lived

I n 1949, when the People's Liberation Army marched into Beijing, China had no common spoken language. To rule effectively, control the populace and disseminate propaganda, the Communist Party needed a single dialect. Mandarin was the obvious choice. It was the dialect of Beijing, which had been the capital of China for nearly nine hundred years. Yet within the Party, there was debate.

Mao resented Mandarin, the court language of imperial China. At the time of the Communist victory, he was nearly fifty-six. Despite tutoring, he was too old to learn China's official language. (He also studied English his whole life, with similarly dismal results.) A native of the south, he spoke the guttural dialect of Hunan province. At twenty-four, he had taken a lowly job at Beijing University, proudly telling his family he had "a position . . . as a staff member." In fact, his assistant librarian's salary of eight Chinese dollars a month was half what a rickshaw coolie earned. In the 1930s, he confessed to Edgar Snow, the American journalist and author of *Red Star over China,* "My office was so low that people avoided me. One of my tasks was to register the names of people who came to read newspapers, but to most of them I didn't exist as a human being. Among those who came to read, I recognized the names of famous leaders . . . I tried to begin conversations with them on political and cultural subjects, but they were very busy men. They had no time to listen to an assistant librarian speaking southern dialect."

After the Communist victory, the new mandarins eventually settled on Mandarin. Curiously, there is no Chinese word for "Mandarin." The English word derives from the scholar-officials who ruled the Chinese empire. The defeated Kuomintang had called it *guoyu,* "the national language." Emphasizing their proletarian leanings, the Communists called it *putonghua,* "the common speech." By banning local dialects in public schools, and aided by radio, television and film, the government managed to popularize Mandarin. (It also set all the clocks in China to Beijing time, except in Tibet. That exception ended with the Cultural Revolution. Now, when it is 9 a.m. in Beijing, it is also 9 a.m. in Tibet, four thousand kilometers to the west. Tibetans compensate by showing up at the office around 11 a.m., an hour after sunrise.)

In unifying spoken Chinese, the Communist Party succeeded where the greatest emperor had failed. In 221 BC, Qin Shihuang standardized written Chinese. To facilitate trade, he established uniform weights and measures, created a common currency and decreed a standard length for wagon axles. He built the Great Wall to keep out marauding nomads. His greatest legacy was unifying seven warring states into a single country. His kingdom of Qin, pronounced *chin,* would give this nation its enduring name, China.

But the dozens of dialects and thousands of subdialects in China stymied even the First Emperor of Qin. For the next two millennia, the Chinese would speak the tongue of the village or hamlet where they were born. When they ventured afield, the literate would communicate using a kind of sign language. With an index finger, they would swiftly trace the written character on their palm. The other person could then read what was said. The illiterate were out of luck.

On October 1, 1949, Mao stood on the rostrum overlooking Tiananmen Square and bellowed through a microphone in his Hunan brogue, "The Chinese people have stood up!" The masses cheered hysterically, although it is unclear whether they understood a word he was saying. (Authorities have since imposed subtitles on documentary footage of that historic moment, screened in a continuous loop at the Capital Museum in Beijing.)

Mandarin is the dialect my teacher, Fu Min, pounded into my skull. She was a doctrinaire Communist Party member. Secretly I called her Fu the Enforcer. From her, I learned the four distinct tones. The first tone rings like a note on a bronze bell, the second rises gently like yeast, the third swoops like a hawk and the fourth clatters like a stone on a marble floor. The language is chaste and spare, full of sibilance and crisp consonants. If I close my eyes, I can conjure up mandarins in the Forbidden City, whispering behind silken sleeves. Alas, by the time of the Cultural Revolution, many of the antiquated linguistic courtesies had been purged. The polite response to a compliment, for instance, is, *nali, nali,* literally "Where? Where?" (presumably with puzzled swiveling of the head and a modest wave of one's silken sleeve). Fu the Enforcer never taught me that. Instead, she drilled me on such felicitous phrases as "running dog of imperialism," "the East is red" and "Chairman Mao is our great savior."

With Mandarin, polite or political, I could go anywhere in China. If the other person didn't know Mandarin, someone could always be found to help out. Beijingers ruled.

Beijing's history dates to the beginning of humankind. In 1929, archaeologists found remains from 500,000 BC southwest of the city. This was *Homo erectus pekinensis,* or Peking man. Five thousand years ago, modern man farmed and domesticated animals here. Three thousand years ago, a small city emerged on the present site. In the twelfth century, Beijing became a capital for the first time. When medieval London was bustling with eighty thousand people, Beijing's population was already one million, making it the biggest city in the world. Unlike many great capitals, Beijing was not by a sea or river. It was at the far end of the North China Plain, hard by the Mongolian foothills and vulnerable to invasion. Some of those invaders—barbarian tribes from the north—established cities on this site. The Khitan called theirs Yanjing. The Jurched called theirs Zhongdu.

In the thirteenth century, the Mongols, led by the grandson of Genghis Khan, razed Zhongdu. The victorious Kublai Khan, the founder of the Yuan dynasty, established his own capital here, calling it Dadu, or "Great Capital." In Mongolian, it was simply known as Khanbaliq, or Khan's Town. By then war and conquest had cut the city's population to a half million. The devastation created an opportunity as expansive as a blank sheet of paper. In 1271, on the flat, featureless North China Plain, Yuan-dynasty planners designed a pure rectangle centered on the north–south meridian.

Befitting the largest empire the world had ever seen, Kublai Khan undertook three megaprojects: the imperial palaces, a fortress-like city wall with moats, and a waterway strategically

linking the capital to the existing Grand Canal, the longest artificial river ever built. The scale and pace of the work in the thirteenth century foreshadowed the construction convulsing
Beijing in the twenty-first. Kublai Khan's imperial palace was
completed in just three years. Marco Polo, who served Kublai
Khan for seventeen years, describes the imperial palace in his
memoir, *The Description of the World:*

> You must know that it is the greatest palace that
> ever was. The roof is very lofty, and the walls of the
> palace are all covered with gold and silver. They are
> adorned with dragons, beasts and birds, knights
> and idols, and other such things. The Hall of the
> Palace is so large that six thousand people could
> easily dine there, and it is quite a marvel to see how
> many rooms there are besides. The building is al-
> together so vast, so rich and so beautiful, that no
> man on earth could design anything superior to it.
> The outside of the roof is all colored with vermil-
> ion and yellow and green and blue and other hues,
> which are fixed with a varnish so fine and exquisite
> that they shine like crystal, and lend a resplendent
> luster to the palace as seen for a great way around.

The perimeter of the city walls was thirty kilometers. The
planners filled in the rectangle with an efficient grid of roads
and streets. Paris would not do the same until the 1850s, when
Emperor Napoleon III ordered his engineer, Baron Georges-
Eugène Haussmann, to replace the medieval chaos with wide
boulevards radiating from central points. Dadu's main streets
were twenty-four paces wide. Side streets and lanes were half as

wide. The planners filled in the spaces with *hutongs,* Beijing's famed residential laneways. The Chinese word *hutong* is a transliteration of the Mongolian *hottog.* Lacking a word for "alleyway," the nomadic Mongols chose *hottog,* or "water hole," a traditional gathering spot on the grasslands.

The third megaproject connected the capital with the Grand Canal, an achievement as significant for its time as the Panama Canal would be later. With the completion of the Tonghui Canal in 1293, Kublai Khan created a secure north–south trade route. For the first time, emperors could easily make inspection tours of the south, protected from sea pirates and coastal typhoons. Each year, barges arrived laden with the riches of the fertile south—tax grain, tea, rice, porcelain, timber and silk. Poled by boatmen, the barges would climb 140 feet above sea level through sophisticated locks—a Chinese invention—two thousand kilometers north to the capital.

The construction of Dadu or Khanbaliq took twenty-six years. Marco Polo observed that only persons of rank lived within the Chinese capital he called Cambaluc. For that reason, certain services could only be procured outside the city walls: ". . . And again I tell you another thing, that inside the town dare live no sinful woman (unless it is secretly) as is said before, these are women of the world who do service to men for money, but I tell you that they all live outside in the suburbs. And you may know that there are so great a multitude of them for the foreigners that no man could believe it, for I dare tell you in truth that they are quite twenty thousand . . . who all serve men for money, and they all find a living."

Yuan-dynasty records fail to mention Marco Polo, leading some historians to dispute whether he ever actually made it to China. Frances Wood, head of the Chinese, Manchu and

Mongolian collections at the British Library, is one such skeptic. In her book *Did Marco Polo Go to China?* she theorizes he might have picked up gossip from Persian merchants in caravan stops along the Silk Road. Polo does describe porcelain, paper money and the use of coal, all unknown to Europeans in the thirteenth century, yet he fails to mention tea, also unknown in Europe at the time, Chinese writing, chopsticks, acupuncture or even the Great Wall.

Either way, his memoir was greeted with disbelief, even as it became one of the most widely read books on the continent. Few Europeans would accept that theirs could be a second-rate civilization. Perhaps Polo felt constrained to omit some of the more incredible details. The phrase "It's a Marco Polo" came to mean an embellishment. On his deathbed in 1324, Polo refused to recant, saying, "I have not written down the half of those things which I saw."

In 1368, the Ming army captured Dadu, overthrowing the Mongol Yuan dynasty. The new rulers changed Dadu's name to Beiping, or "Northern Peace." The Ming, an ethnic Chinese dynasty, established the capital in the more secure south, in Nanjing, which means "Southern Capital." Thirty-five years later, when Yong Le usurped the throne from his nephew, he established the Ming capital near his supporters in the north, in the former Yuan capital. He called it Beijing, or "Northern Capital."

Like Kublai Khan, Yong Le decided to rebuild the city. The Beijing that has been bulldozed for the 2008 Olympics is essentially the imperial city created by one of the greatest emperors in Chinese history. In 1406, Yong Le set his capital on the meridian, using a perfect symmetry that dazzles city planners today. Like the Yuan planners, Ming officials established precise measurements for roads. They shifted the original Yuan wall south and enclosed the southern suburbs within a separate set of walls.

The heart of the new capital was Yong Le's imperial palace. In 1417, Yong Le set 200,000 laborers and artisans to work building it. The Forbidden City was completed three years later, matching Kublai Khan's speed record. Legend has it that its layout was based on a dream Yong Le's tutor had: an unearthly city where the Son of Heaven lived in harmony within a series of perfect rectangles, aligned north to south along the Pole Star. Apocryphal or not, the palace was indeed built on these lines, and so was the entire city. Yong Le called it Zi Jin Cheng, an allusion to a constellation revolving around the Pole Star. If China was Zhong Guo, the Middle Kingdom, then the emperor was its axis, the center, the one constant around which the cosmic order revolved. *Zi* usually means "purple," but not in this instance. It is essentially untranslatable. *Jin* means "forbidden to enter." *Cheng* means city. Hence the name in English, "Forbidden City."

Even the Communists respected the invisible line that was the Ming-dynasty meridian. When Mao enlarged Tiananmen Square for mass rallies, he retained its symmetry, flanking it with two monolithic Stalinist structures: the Great Hall of the People and the Museum of Revolutionary History. He hung his own giant portrait on the Tiananmen rostrum, right on the axis. And when he died, the Communist Party set his mausoleum and embalmed corpse precisely on the meridian.

The Manchus, who followed the Ming, founding the Qing dynasty in 1644, left the city alone. Instead they devoted themselves to building lavish summer retreats in the suburbs. The vast Yuan Ming Yuan (Garden of Perfect Brightness) rivaled Versailles as a masterpiece of landscape architecture. Another retreat, Yi He Yuan, the Summer Palace, was the largest imperial pleasure ground in China. After Pu Yi, the last Qing emperor, abdicated in 1912, Beijing was successively ruled by warlords, foreign invaders and a president who attempted to crown himself emperor. Meanwhile, the beleaguered government nervously shifted the capital from Canton to Wuhan to Nanking to Chungking, until 1949, when Chiang Kai-shek and his Kuomintang army fled in defeat to Taiwan.

War and upheaval failed to destroy Beijing. The Kuomintang general, Fu Tso-yi, patriotically surrendered the capital to the Communists without a fight. During the Cultural Revolution, Red Guards burned books, paintings and antiques, but the temples and palaces survived because they were closed to the public.

Nothing preserves a city like a century of economic decline. With the exception of ten major public buildings erected by the masses in 1958 during Mao's Great Leap Forward, the essential architecture and layout of the city remained intact. By 1972, when I arrived in Beijing for the first time, Mao's various economic debacles had done more to save the city than the most energetic preservation society. The streets still followed the invisible grid determined by the four points of the compass. Many residents lived in traditional gray-brick homes surrounded by walls. Each compound was actually a series of separate pavilions sociably facing a central courtyard. Originally designed for a single multigenerational family, the walled courtyard home was called a *siheyuan,* or "four-harmonies courtyard."

The *hutong* reflected the shape of the courtyard homes within. As homes expanded, the alleyway would twist and turn, like a maze of high blank walls. The narrowest surviving *hutong* today is reportedly just forty centimeters (sixteen inches) wide. The front gate of each house was usually painted bright red and was always split in two. When the gate was opened, privacy was ensured by a "spirit screen," a stand-alone wall erected to block evil spirits, which were deemed incapable of making turns. But privacy vanished during the Cultural Revolution. A severe housing shortage meant that a dozen or more families typically squeezed into a single home, rendering the spirit screen useless. Families shared a single cold-water tap. The public latrines, many without plumbing, were down the alley. Fights were inevitable. A friend of mine suffered a breakdown because she could never talk to her husband without the neighbors hearing.

Beijing's streets, however, remained peaceful. With virtually no cars, only the occasional truck and the tinkle of bicycle bells at rush hour, the city of eight million was mostly silent. To wander the *hutongs* in 1972 was to sense the beauty of the city. Fall, Beijingers would agree, was the best time there. The crystalline sunshine accentuated the brilliant greens, lapis, golds and reds of the palace eaves. Fat Paycheck and I often biked for picnics into the Western Hills, where the maples and sumac turned flame red. Peddlers sold candied crabapples threaded on wooden sticks, practically the only sweet available.

Winter most suited the sea of courtyard homes. With the trees bare, the capital resembled a Chinese ink-brush painting, in muted strokes of charcoal and slate. When a rare snowfall blanketed the city, people rushed out with twig brooms to sweep the sidewalks. They hung padded quilts over their doors as insulation and huddled by little iron stoves fed by cakes of poor-quality coal dust. In a shady corner, residents stacked Beijing cabbage, a long-leafed, white variety tipped with pale green. It was virtually the only available vegetable of the entire winter, and as time passed, the aging cabbages would give off a musty, none-too-appetizing smell.

Beijingers heralded spring early, in January or February during Spring Festival, at the lunar New Year. They grew narcissus in water, balancing the bulbs in shallow earthen dishes filled with pebbles. When the flowers bloomed, their heavy perfume filled the courtyards. By March the harsh northwest winds would start howling. Overnight, we would awaken to miniature sand dunes from the Gobi Desert on our windowsill. Sand fell into our mugs, ruining our tea. Our teeth felt gritty. Bicycling was a torment. But by April the winds subsided and the locust trees dripped with fragrant cones of white flowers that people stuffed into *jiaozi,* the traditional boiled dumplings of Beijing.

In summer the sun burned against a sky so intensely blue it seemed unreal. Sleep became fitful. For relief, we laid *xizi,* thin bamboo mats, atop our mattress. Fat Paycheck and I would join a handful of swimmers, all male, in the canal near the Purple Bamboo Park. Shade was abundant, provided by willows, poplars with rustling leaves and leafy plane trees with bark like camouflage. Sidewalk vendors sold mountains of ripe tomatoes for pennies a catty, a measure equal to half a kilo. I never got used to the Beijing taste—tomatoes sprinkled with granulated white sugar. I preferred mine with salt, which disgusted the Chinese no end.

Life spilled out into the *hutong.* Elderly women with bound feet would fan themselves on tiny bamboo chairs. Toddlers would scoot around, bare-bottomed, in pants slit up the crotch. Families would take their rice bowls and chopsticks outside, hoping to catch the breeze. This was life as it had always been lived.

On the eve of the Communist takeover, Beijing had 1,330 *hutongs*. Most dated from the Ming and Qing dynasties. In the 1990s, many were replaced by broad boulevards and expressways. Brick Pagoda (Zhuan Ta) Hutong, often mentioned in Yuan dramas, is one of the few original *hutongs* extant today. The effort to create a new Beijing for the 2008 Olympics has demolished entire neighborhoods. On our last trip here, we were too busy running through museums. This time I want Ben and Sam to see the ancient *hutongs* before they disappear.

Continental Airlines flight 89 lands on time at Beijing International Airport. Through the plane window, I watch straw-hatted men sweeping an adjacent runway with twig brooms. In the distance, worker ants swarm over a dusty battlefield, the construction cranes like ancient catapults, red flags aflutter like medieval standards. This is the site of Beijing's new airport, slated for completion by the 2008 Olympics. Its four-year construction schedule is, as the *Guardian* points out, "somewhat less time than lawyers have spent arguing over London's Heathrow Terminal 5." And only one more year than Kublai Khan and Emperor Yong Le spent building their imperial palaces. At the moment the new airport is the world's largest construction project. Designed by British architect Norman Foster, when finished it will be energy efficient and will handle an unprecedented 60 million passengers a year. Work is proceeding at breakneck speed. Nothing slows it down, not even the occasional discovery of dinosaur bones or ancient stone carvings. Seven days a week, 45,000 laborers work three shifts a day, each earning about seven dollars a day.

In 1972, Beijing's airport was a modest sandstone building. It had a single reception area and a couple of VIP rooms furnished with armchairs covered in lace antimacassars. In 1988, when I returned as a foreign correspondent, Beijing had built a second airport. This one had cracked walls and crude metal windows. The gift shop sold boxes of dried persimmons and pickled vegetables. The current Beijing airport, the third incarnation, is as instantly forgettable as any other international terminal. It has marble floors, conveyor-belt walkways and stores selling expensive silk ties. Most cities would be proud to have one like it.

We hurry past a SARS checkpoint and get into a long line at the border control. While I wait, I read the Chinglish signs. They make sense only if you translate the English back into Chinese, and they remind me of the hit movie *Borat: Cultural Learnings of America for Make Benefit Glorious Nation of Kazakhstan.*

A big computerized sign says, "Laws are fully enforced and service for passengers warmly." My personal favorite is "Inspectors must service passengers." A little sex after a long flight might be therapeutic for jet lag. After all, the border-inspection process can be tense, especially for a writer sneaking into China. Unfortunately, the unsmiling border official doesn't look all that sexy. I'm sure I'm not attractive to him, either. China doesn't like Western reporters, especially those who can pass for locals. Beijing assumes we're all spies because it sometimes uses its own reporters that way. After NATO bombed the Chinese embassy in Belgrade in 1999, the United States apologized profusely, blaming an outdated CIA map. But a joint report from Britain's *Observer* and Denmark's *Politiken* contends that the bombing was intentional. The report said the embassy was relaying radio signals from the Yugoslav military. Whatever the truth, all three fatalities were Chinese journalists.

China requires foreign journalists to have special visas. This means extra scrutiny, cliffhanger delays and, often, denial. If you do get one, you might as well have a scarlet letter on your forehead. You must show your passport to buy plane tickets or rent hotel rooms. The "journalist" visa marks you wherever you go. Of course, journalists can avoid this agony by sneaking in on tourist visas, but that can be nerve-wracking. To calm myself at the border, I count security cameras. At Toronto's Pearson International Airport, I've noticed just one camera in the immigration area. Here there are dozens embedded in the ceiling, including four aimed at each inspector's booth.

When it's our turn, I push the boys forward. Fat Paycheck is right behind me. We've been through this drill before. Ben and Sam know not to say a word. The border officer types our names into a computer. We wait in silence. I try to estimate how many Wongs there are in China. Perhaps the computer is choking. Or does the delay mean something more sinister? The officer stares at our passport pictures and then back at us. He does not smile. Then he pushes our passports back. We're in.

We collect our luggage and head outside. The terminal is awash with people pushing carts mounded with luggage. Tour groups swarm behind flag-waving, shouting guides. Young men and women hold up hand-scrawled signs that say "Ford/Mr. Beckman" or "Palace Hotel/Miss Weizl." I scan the crowd. An old contact, a Chinese Canadian architect, has promised to meet us at the airport. I walk around the chaotic greeting zone twice, searching every face. He isn't there.

We give up and get in a taxi line outside. The humid, polluted air overwhelms us. We each have a carry-on and a checked bag. In addition, we have two bulging suitcases that belong to a Toronto friend who is relocating to China. I breezily offered to help him bring back a few things. One suitcase had broken wheels. The other burst its zipper en route. I'd forgotten most Beijing taxis are subcompacts. It becomes obvious that the four of us, four carry-on bags and six suitcases can't fit into one taxi. But I'm worried about separating. Suddenly, I spot a Red Flag, the limo once favored by Chairman Mao. It's not red, actually, and the Mao-mobile has definitely shrunk. Once the size of a Lincoln Continental, it's now no bigger than an ordinary Toyota sedan, and that may be generous. But it looks marginally bigger than the regular taxis, and I'm desperate. The driver looks dubious as he heaves my friend's two suitcases into the trunk, followed by two big backpacks. He jams our own suitcases in the back seat, which leaves a narrow space for Ben, who is clutching two more backpacks. Somehow I squeeze in beside Ben, our hip bones digging into one another, ankles at unnatural angles. Fat Paycheck takes the front passenger seat, with thirteen-year-old Sam on his lap and another backpack on his feet. At this point I waive my parental seat-belt rule. In a crash, we're wedged in so tight that only Sam would fly through the windshield. And as I keep telling my second-born, he's the spare.

The taxi driver pulls onto a magnificent new six-lane toll expressway. The old airport road was two lanes wide, unlit and clogged with horsecarts. The trunks of the poplar trees flanking the road were painted white with insecticide, an added advantage for night-time driving. As Ben and I shift painfully in the back, I compliment the taxi driver on his Red Flag. He tells me that the city recently ordered thirty thousand old taxis off the roads to meet pollution-control standards. I ask him if some distant town or village received the old taxis.

"Nah, they were wrecks," he says. "They were trashed."

Police states are awfully convenient. No debate, no time-consuming scientific studies, no silly electoral votes. Someone at the top says the old taxis have to go, and that's that. As we speed into downtown Beijing, I crane my neck to look at the sky. It is a strange grayish hue, the color of soiled cotton balls. It is not even close to the pure blue I remember. The sun is invisible.

3

You Can't Get There from Here

My legs are numb by the time the Red Flag turns onto Reconstructing China Road South. The street lives up to its name: the pavement is torn up, high-rise towers on each side are under construction and there is a gaping hole in the road. A sign, stuck in a mound of dirt, points ahead to our apartment-hotel: "Luxury Serviced Residence." In Chinese, it's called "*Li She* Serviced Flats," apparently because *li she* in Cantonese sounds like "luxury" in English. A better translation is "Beautiful Lodging."

The Chinese language used to be self-sufficient. With few exceptions, such as *hutong,* it disdained transliteration. Its richness could always accommodate the new. But now globalization, the Internet and China's own passionate embrace of the West have introduced impurities. For instance, Mandarin has several good words for "exhibit" or "show," but a fashion show has become now a fashion *xiu.*

We arrive at the driveway to Beautiful Lodging. Strangely, a sidewalk cuts off access. After outpacing the world in urban design in the thirteenth century, Beijing is now falling down on basic city planning. Buildings are thrown up willy-nilly. Sidewalks are an afterthought. Pedestrians must pick their way through mud, loose bricks and sand. Undeterred, our taxi driver barrels through the driveway of an adjacent restaurant, across its parking lot and into the circular drive for our hotel apartment. We still can't get in. A horizontal red and white pole blocks our way. A young security guard peers uncertainly into our taxi. He's wearing a white and navy uniform with epaulets and fake brass buttons. When he sees Fat Paycheck, he lifts the pole to let us in.

The Chinese gatekeeper is a remnant from ancient times when servants were part of the established order. At grander homes, he—for it was always a man—would scrutinize all comers and decide who could pass, which peddler of fresh bean curd, which hawker of candied crabapples. He would not retire to bed until the last member of the household had returned. The Chinese had traditional locks, of course, but until the modern era, human ones were cheaper. By Mao's time, the gatekeeper was an integral part of the state's security system. He (and now sometimes she) would force visitors to fill out little forms in triplicate. With every building and compound surrounded by a wall, it was easy for the Communist Party to control the people. Nowadays, as businesses throw open their doors to lure in customers, the Chinese guard's job is essentially meaningless; he is as decorative and useless as a brass door knocker.

Friends recommended Beautiful Lodging. I researched it on the Internet and paid in advance for a two-bedroom suite. Such convenience wasn't possible even a few years ago. But right after I coughed up my Visa number, I began to worry. My friends told me that if demand is high, hotels sometimes resell your room at a higher price before you arrive. Happily, our apartment is waiting for us. Like the gatekeeper under Mao, the smartly suited concierge copies down our passport details in triplicate, including the numbers of our Chinese visas. This will be entered into a state-security database so Big Brother will know where everyone is.

"Welcome to Beautiful Lodging," the concierge says in Chinese, handing over four electronic key cards. "You need these to get into the elevator lobby, to go up the elevator and to get into your apartment."

The lobby looks sleek and modern, but I can't shake my journalist's paranoia. I note three surveillance cameras, plus a fourth outside the elevator and a fifth inside. "There's no thirteenth floor," says Ben, as the granite-clad elevator takes us to the sixteenth floor. Four and fourteen are missing too. Years after Mao banned superstition, numerical nuttiness is making inroads. Westerners, of course, think thirteen is unlucky. Chinese think anything with four is bad because *si*—four—is a pun on "death."

If you do the math, our sixteenth-floor apartment is, horrors, actually on the thirteenth floor. But it doesn't look particularly unlucky. It looks Scandinavian. There is blond-wood trim, an IKEA-style glass table and trim upholstered chairs. The old Beijing style favored oxblood varnish, hulking armchairs and beige slipcovers primly pleated at the hem. Ben and Sam start whooping. They've spotted a DVD player and *two* flat-screen televisions. At home we get basic cable on a 1983 clunker. Here we get CNN, TSN and HBO. If it weren't for several dozen Chinese channels, we could be in Manhattan.

The apartment is air-conditioned. The living-room windows soar two stories high and have remotely controlled electric blinds. The main floor has a bedroom, powder room and living/dining room. In the kitchen, the made-in-China gas stove and exhaust fan are better than mine at home. The LG refrigerator, oddly, is in the living room, like in the early 1980s, when the first Chinese to acquire a fridge proudly displayed it for all to see. Upstairs, there's a full bathroom, a second, larger bedroom, a spacious loft and a huge walk-in closet. No one had closets in Mao's day. They used *guizi,* armoires of cheap varnished wood, and even those required a ration coupon. My roommate, Scarlet, and I shared a *guizi.* We stacked our quilts in it, leaving only a small space to hang our clothing. That was okay because cloth was also rationed, so we never had much to hang.

The rent at Beautiful Lodging includes twice-weekly maid service, linen changes, a twenty-four-hour reception desk and an in-house plumber. There is a fitness room, a sauna, a business center, coin-operated washers and dryers in the basement, an in-room safe and another new Beijing phenomenon: an underground parking garage. I had almost rented ordinary Chinese housing, which I thought would be a more authentic experience for the boys—whitewashed walls, cement floors, leaky windows, infernal heat and squat toilets. My Beijing friends told me I was hopelessly out of date. They asked me who I imagined was living in the thousands of luxury condos rising all over the city. Then I realize that many of the guests in our building are local Chinese. Beautiful Lodging isn't Manhattan after all. It's the new Beijing.

A young woman with a clipboard arrives to jot down readings on the gas and electric meters. Our month-long rental contract includes an energy cap. If we exceed 500 yuan ($65) in water, electricity and gas, we have to pay more. I have no idea how much water, electricity and gas 500 yuan buys, but I'm sufficiently alarmed to tell Ben he can't take extra-long showers the way he does at home. You'd think Beautiful Lodging would start saving energy by stripping the granite from the elevators. Still, I'm glad Beijing is trying to conserve. Experts predict that China will soon become the biggest source of greenhouse gases in the world. Living here, it's easy to see the danger. If we turn off the air-conditioning for fifteen minutes, we start to suffocate. The air outside is too polluted to open the windows.

From our north-facing apartment, we should see all the way to the Temple of the Sun Park, a ten-minute walk away. But when I climb onto the sofa to look out our two-story windows, the cityscape blurs into a pastel mist. It's a surprisingly attractive, panoramic view of . . . smog. I can see how the Impressionists like Monet and Turner created beauty from the poisoned air and foul waters of the Industrial Revolution. Beijing, however, wants to leave a better impression. In the run-up to the Olympics, it accomplished something possible only in a totalitarian regime: to clean up the air, it exiled the city's heavy industry, including Capital Steel, the Beijing Petrochemical General Factory and other major polluters, to outlying counties. I wonder what has happened to the Number One Machine Tool Factory, where Fu the Enforcer and I worked during the Cultural Revolution.

It's too early for supper and too hot to walk around. Our guest privileges include the use of the health club at the nearby, strangely named Sci-Tech Hotel. It was built in the 1990s when China began equating wealth with science and technology. The name is even stranger in Chinese. *Sai Te,* the two Chinese characters, do not mean "science" and "technology"; they merely sound like the English words. In Chinese, *sai te* means "competition special," not a very restful name for a hotel. Our concierge tells us the health club is close by. He waves his hand above his head, pointing behind him. Then he points forward and sideways. I'm confused.

"It's very close," he says.

It would be close, were we birds. Outside, I see Sci-Tech's neon sign to the northwest. But we have to head east, out the only exit from Beautiful Lodging. Going from point A to point B is never simple when walls are a national obsession. Once we're out of Beautiful Lodging, we turn north. We try to head west but keep encountering more walls, more barriers, more dead-end compounds. Eventually we encounter a huge development. We take a chance and head inside the compound. Hallelujah! The property is so big it straddles two streets and has a *second* gate. The Sci-Tech Hotel is now right in front of us. Its only entrance, however, is on the far side of the compound. And the hotel, naturally, is surrounded by an enclosed parking lot with an accordion-style metal fence, a low brick wall and, for good measure, a meter-wide swath of shrubs. Even if we hurled ourselves over the metal fence, steeplechase-style, we'd land in the bushes.

I've had it with all the great walls of China. The Great Wall never saved China from the barbarian hordes, who ended up founding the Jin, Yuan and Qing dynasties. Just think how much this country could save in bricks, mortar and labor if it just stopped walling itself in.

We've been up nearly thirty hours. We're jet-lagged and hot. The boys are getting cranky, or maybe I'm getting cranky and I just think they are. Happily, there are only a handful of swimmers at the pool. One swims laps. Several cling passively to the edge. Unlike a decade earlier, when only foreigners had access to health clubs, these are all local Chinese. And unlike in my canal-diving days in the 1970s, four are female. Refreshed, we explore the rest of Sci-Tech, which has a deserted bowling alley, an empty indoor tennis court, some table-tennis tables and—the boys' favorite—a pool room. Ben and Sam stop complaining about being dragged to China.

On the way back to Beautiful Lodging, I suggest to everyone that there must be a better route home. The kids are willing to try. Fat Paycheck, with his years of living in Beijing, is dubious. Heading south, we enter a narrow *hutong* bordering the west side of Beautiful Lodging. Logically, it should lead us directly home. We pass tumbledown shops—a barber shop, a scallion-pancake vendor, two grimy convenience stores. A plump woman in a loose sleeveless blouse squats on the ground, trimming some leeks. A younger woman scrubs a bedsheet in a small enamel basin. The alley is rutted, with mud puddles and garbage. This isn't how I remember the fabled Beijing *hutongs.* This one reeks of urine, feces, sweat and rotting vegetables. I tell the boys to breathe through their mouths. Sam, who knows I never want to miss a thing, helpfully points out that someone has vomited by the edge of the road.

I call a halt to our stumbling procession. I have forgotten that the Chinese approach to architecture is defensive. Everything is separated, protected, walled off. When Beautiful Lodging was built, it insulated itself from the noxious reality of old Beijing. Fat Paycheck was right. You can't get there from here. We end up making a huge circle around Beautiful Lodging until we finally get back to the east—and only—entrance.

4

No One Left Behind to
Say Who Went Where

The next morning, Norman and the boys are sleeping off the jet lag when I slip out to forage for breakfast at the 7-Eleven across from Beautiful Lodging. Like bamboo shoots after a spring rain—to use a Chinese cliché—the convenience-store chain has sprung up all over Beijing. "*Huanying guang lin!*" a young man at the cash sings out. "Welcome your approaching luminous presence!" Two women clerks chime, "Welcome your approaching luminous presence!" Their perkiness startles me. It's six in the morning. And I'm used to the sullen clerks of the Cultural Revolution.

A flat-screen monitor explains that the chain was founded in 1927 in Oak Cliff, Texas, and that its name derives from its opening hours: 7 a.m. to 11 p.m. This must be confusing to Chinese customers. The 7-Elevens in Beijing are open 24/7. This store doesn't offer Big Bite hot dogs, Go-Go Taquitos or Bloody Zit Slurpees. It doesn't even sell coffee. The breakfast staples include hot soy milk, congee and steamed *baozi* stuffed with pork or spinach. There's also something I haven't seen before in Beijing, *hao dun*—literally, good stew. A stainless-steel vat, compartmentalized like a Hong Kong street cart, is filled with simmering anise-scented broth packed with hard-boiled eggs, golden-skinned bean curd, lotus root and daikon turnip. For one dollar, I buy enough hot soy milk and *baozi* to feed a family of four.

Back upstairs, I spread out the breakfast on our round glass dining-room table and casually mention my plan to the boys. Fat Paycheck already knows I want to find Yin. He's resigned to accompanying me on this mission impossible. The boys have heard about Yin before, but now I reveal my intentions. "You remember that person I turned in a long time ago when I was a student at Beijing University?" I tell them. "I'm going to try to find her." Ben, whom I've dragged out of bed, is too tired to answer. Sam is indifferent. He begs to stay in and watch television. Neither thinks that looking for Yin is an extraordinary quest. They've become inured to my crazy ideas.

I first told Ben about Yin when he was six. I had just finished writing *Red China Blues,* and I wanted him to understand that adults make mistakes. But when I tried to put tattling in a context a little kid could understand, I fell into a swamp of relativity. What was the difference between telling on someone and being a helpful bystander? If Molly punches Fred, and Ben witnesses it, should he tell? What if he knew that, an hour earlier, Fred had teased Molly for being fat? Did Fred get what he deserved? Consequences mattered too. If the punishment was no recess for a day, maybe you'd tattle. But what if Molly's punishment was a whipping? What if she'd be expelled from the school? What if you didn't even *know* what the consequences would be? It was too much for a six-year-old.

I gave up when it came to Sam. By the time he was old enough to understand, I had stopped talking about Yin. Then a month before we left for Beijing, I mentioned her and what I'd done. He thought about it for a moment. "I guess you were just stupid, and you ruined the person's life," he said, with the clarity of a thirteen-year-old. "You were young. You didn't know what you were doing."

Now, having flown with me halfway around the world, the boys aren't the slightest bit interested in joining in the search. "We're tired," says Sam, finishing the last steamed *baozi*. He looks hopefully at his older brother.

"Yeah. We'll see you later," agrees Ben. At sixteen, he has finally stopped obeying my every command.

As a reporter's offspring, the boys have grown both wary and weary of my adventures. When Sam was in kindergarten, he helped me stake out the Ontario premier's suburban cul-de-sac home for a story. Because loitering was conspicuous on a dead-end street, Sam pretended he was learning to ride his bike. He even took a few pretend tumbles for verisimilitude. A few years later the whole family endured a quarantine after I was exposed to the SARS virus while trying to track down the first victims in a Toronto hospital. They suffered through a death threat after I wrote about a college shooting in Quebec. Sam got punched in the mouth by a classmate after I wrote about his father, a municipal politician. (The boys are now friends, no thanks to me or the dad.) More recently, for a story on the minimum wage, Ben and Sam moved with me into a basement apartment. While I worked undercover as a maid, the boys lived on macaroni, mopped our little hovel and helped me wash my rags at night. Meanwhile, Norman was thrilled to have the house to himself for a month.

Over breakfast at Beautiful Lodging, I tell Ben and Sam and Fat Paycheck that it will probably be impossible to find Yin but that I want to try. Sam has great faith in me. "You're so good at finding people," he says solemnly. "I know you are going to find her."

The problem is I have no idea where to start. Beijing has 16 million people, and there is no reason to presume she lives here. China has 1.3 billion, and she might have left. I don't articulate the last possibility—that she might not be alive. Fat Paycheck chews a *baozi* and drily suggests the obvious. "Why don't you start with your classmates?"

Unfortunately, I don't have current phone numbers and addresses. I can't even find the old ones. Some reporters are organized. My *Globe* colleague Peter Cheney can unearth a contact from five years earlier and email it to me within seconds. I'm not like that. While I'm working on a story, I *am* organized. Everything is at my fingertips, even though my desk is a mess and I'm elbow deep in scraps of paper. In fact, I index notebooks and number each page. I make outlines of notes, and outlines of outlines. I write chronologies and brief biographies of the main players. I color-code facts, observations and telling quotes. When I finish, I move on. With my editors impatient for the next story, I have no time to organize the phone numbers. I must ask Peter how he does it.

I also have a really terrible memory. I like to think it's because I am so focused on the present that my brain, which seems to have a fixed capacity, like a hard drive, ends up deleting the past. If you ask me what stories I worked on last month, I have to stop and think. On the other hand, maybe I just have a lousy memory. I can invite a couple to dinner at my house, have a wonderfully stimulating evening and a decade later forget I ever met them. I can watch a thriller for the second time—I'm basing this on Fat Paycheck's assurances that I have indeed seen the movie before—and be as riveted as the first time because I can't remember how it ends. I am in awe of people who memorize poems. After a three-week vacation, I can't even recall my computer password at work. As a reporter, I've learned to take voluminous notes. If I don't, I am lost. That's why I didn't remember turning in Yin until I read my diary years later. Or maybe I didn't remember because I wanted to forget. After all, I do remember, quite vividly, other parts of my experience at Beijing University. Selective amnesia, perhaps, is a peculiar affliction of the victimizer.

I should start my search with Scarlet, the only person I know for sure remembers Yin. Unfortunately, I don't have her phone number. I last saw her nine years ago when she was living in a high-rise housing complex near the Beijing Science Center. We met by the Science Center's iconic giant silver ball and then walked a few minutes to her home. I know where the silver ball is, and where the high-rises are in relation to it. I just don't remember which building she lived in. Two years ago, when I was briefly in Beijing, I tried unsuccessfully to find Scarlet at her work place, the Beijing Library, a vast organization akin to the U.S. Library of Congress. Her office would not divulge any information. Gloomily I think, *If I can't even find Scarlet, how am I ever going to find Yin?*

A police state used to be so helpful. In 1972, when I visited my ancestral village of Taishan, I didn't have a single name or address of any of my distant relatives. The government did. My parents had visited nine months earlier and, naturally, the authorities kept records on everyone they had seen. That was then. In the twenty-first century, everyone in China is on the move. People change jobs, cities, professions. Their homes are bulldozed. Neighborhoods vanish and people scatter, with no one left behind to say who went where. Kathy Wilhelm, a former correspondent for the Associated Press in Beijing, tells me she lost touch with several friends after the Tiananmen Massacre.

"We had to cool off a bit, so we didn't have contact, and now I can't find them," says Kathy, who now works as a lawyer for an American law firm in Beijing.

Imagine if Toronto had no phone books or directory assistance. Imagine if, over the past ten years, everyone changed phone numbers seven times and moved three. Imagine if every building a decade old or older had been razed, excepting only the CN Tower. Then try to find an old classmate—or someone you talked to briefly thirty-three years ago. Oh, sure, Beijing has phone directories. But no one I talk to ever uses one or is listed in one. With a nod to privacy uncharacteristic of a police state, residential numbers are published *only if the customer grants permission.* And because it is a police state, most customers decline. Lately there's another reason they prefer anonymity: telemarketing, the scourge of the West, is now ruining dinners all over Beijing.

China has 400 million cellphone users—all unlisted. To keep up with the latest technology, according to the *People's Daily,* many people replace their cellphones—and cellphone numbers—every three to six months. Disaster strikes when people lose their cellphones, along with all their stored numbers. They can't call anyone they know, and friends can't call them.

Surnames are another logistical nightmare. About 40 percent of the population shares ten surnames. That averages out to 52 million people per name. My own name, Wong (Huang in Mandarin), is seventh most popular; there are 30 million of us. Imagine if everyone in Canada (population 32 million) was named Wong—and most were unlisted. Luckily, Yin is an extremely uncommon surname. Unluckily, there are two ways to write it and I'm not sure which is hers. It's going to be tough enough finding Scarlet Zhang. Hers is the third most popular surname in China, after Li and Wang. One hundred million people are surnamed Zhang.

In Mao's time, it was ridiculously easy to find someone. People remained in one *danwei,* or work unit, for life. Housing, assigned by the state, was linked to the work unit. The Communists also embraced an imperial system of residence permits, call *hukou,* as a ready-made twentieth-century tool of civilian control. The *hukou* system built virtual walls around every city, town and hamlet, tying peasants to the land and Beijingers to Beijing. Without state permission, you could not relocate to another city. Enforcement was unnecessary. If peasants from the Pearl River delta managed to sneak into Beijing, they would starve. Ration coupons ensured that only Beijingers could eat in Beijing, only Shanghainese could eat in Shanghai and so on. The coupons, tiny bits of paper that looked like food stamps, controlled all essential foods: rice, wheat flour, corn meal, sorghum, cooking oil, bean curd, eggs, meat and peanuts.

You could always move *down* the food chain. If city-dwellers were foolish enough to marry beneath them, they could shift to rural areas. But peasants could not take up residence in the city, even if they married someone there. And of all the city permits in China, the capital's *hukou* was the most coveted permit of all. Despite these draconian restrictions, Beijing's population still doubled every few decades. In 1949 it was four million. In 1972 it was eight million. By 2006, it was sixteen million.

. . .

Ben and Sam stay behind while Norman and I venture out to handle the first order of business: obtaining Chinese currency. Beijing is now dotted with bank machines, but many won't accept a foreign card. Luckily, Fat Paycheck has pinpointed a Citibank ATM a twenty-minute walk away. When we step outside Beautiful Lodging, I gasp. It feels as though someone has thrown a hot, dirty towel over my head. At mid-morning it's scorching hot. The sky is gray and I can't spot the sun. I look down. There are no shadows.

We trudge through the construction site that is Reconstructing China Road South. Cars honk and swerve past us, pouring out exhaust. The heat and smog press down on my lungs. My feet drag. Midsummer is the hottest time in Beijing, which is on the same latitude as southern Italy. When I covered the 1996 Olympics in Atlanta, the athletes struggled desperately with the humidity and heat. At the 2008 Beijing Olympics, the athletes will face the same obstacles, plus one: the capital ranks among the most polluted cities in the world.

The setting doesn't help. Beijing sits in an alluvial basin, far from the sea, with mountains to the north and west. Each year westerly winds blow in tons of Gobi Desert sand. Although authorities have shut down virtually all heavy industry in the capital, the volume of new cars has more than canceled out the environmental gain. Every single day, about a thousand new cars hit the road in Beijing. Nowadays, university professors, restaurateurs, web designers and architects can all afford cars. The cheapest one costs just 28,000 yuan (about $3,600). The capital already has three million cars. By the time the Olympics arrive, Beijing will have three and a half million.

During the Games, the government vows to force drivers to keep cars at home. And this being a police state, it will succeed.

Beijing has already phased out leaded fuel and made catalytic converters compulsory in new cars. It is rapidly expanding subway and light rail lines. During the Games, it plans to spray roads to dampen dust and to send up planes and rockets to seed clouds for rain.

Before condemning China's car craze, I remind myself that American motorists remain the single biggest consumers of petroleum in the world. They use more than nine million barrels of gasoline a day, one-third more than China consumes of all types of petroleum in every home, car and factory, according to *BusinessWeek*. Unfortunately, Beijing is using the Los Angeles model to solve New York–style problems. It considers cars a sign of modernity, a new and irresistible status symbol. The government remains obsessed with building roads, axing mature trees to widen streets. Replacement saplings provide scant shade.

For years now I've carried a folding fan for instant relief in Beijing's summers. The fan's design is unchanged from a thousand years ago—polished caramel-colored slats of bamboo topped by unadorned sturdy black paper. But on this trip, when I fan myself, I just feel hotter. Meteorologists here serve the interests of the state. In the 1970s, workers were supposed to get a holiday whenever the mercury hit 37 degrees Celsius (99 degrees Fahrenheit). It never did—except on our own thermometers. Today's *China Daily* is reporting a high of 32—90 on the Fahrenheit scale. I don't know where the state meteorologist is sticking the thermometer, but it isn't downtown Beijing. It has to be hotter than that.

As we trudge along, Norman and I have the same debate the whole world is having about global warming. He disagrees with me. Perhaps he's right. In 1900, red-sashed peasants laid siege to Beijing's Foreign Legation Quarter in what came to be known as the Boxer Rebellion. Sterling Seagrave, in *Dragon Lady: The Life and Legend of the Last Empress of China,* writes, "The weather did not help. It was midsummer, over 100 degrees Fahrenheit, dusted with sand borne on a hot wind from the Gobi. Flies were everywhere, corpses crawled with maggots. The stench was infernal."

I'll bet it's actually 100 degrees today. I certainly can identify with maggot-infested corpses. I feel half-dead by the time we reach the shiny new Citibank tower, which occupies the site of the Ming dynasty's Imperial Examination Hall. The examinations, held every three years in late spring, once sustained the fabled Chinese meritocracy. Hundreds of candidates flocked here from all over the empire, vying for a government sinecure—a fat paycheck. Each candidate was assigned a cell. To curtail cheating, they had to change into assigned gowns. The doors to the cells would then be sealed and not reopened, for any reason, until three days and two nights later.

At Citibank, the automated revolving door blasts us with cold air. The central core is decorated by a garish, gorilla-sized bouquet of fake orange and yellow flowers, sparkling with gold glitter. I end up in a slot almost treading on the heels of two strangers. They don't seem to mind. Based on unscientific observations, I've noticed that a culture's personal space is inversely proportional to its population density. Take Finland, which has only one-third as many people as the entire city of Beijing. On a recent trip there with Sam's hockey team, I saw a Finnish man waiting impatiently—*two meters* behind a Canadian dad—at a salad bar in Lohja, population 41,400. The Canadian took his sweet time filling his plate, unaware someone was waiting for access to the pickled herring. In Canada, the salad-bar norm is about two bowls' distance. In China, the person behind you would be digging into the *same* bowl, then leapfrogging you in the line.

The bank's ATM lobby has white armchairs and marble floors. There's also a water cooler with paper cups, a luxurious touch in a country where drinking water must first be boiled. ATMs are supposed to cut down on labor costs, but a security guard stands watch. Or perhaps he's guarding the free water. Norman inserts his Citibank card into the machine. I hold my breath. The ATM whirs and clicks, expelling a wad of red hundred-yuan Chinese banknotes.

Flush with cash, we head back to Beautiful Lodging. Outside the bank, smog covers Beijing like an Tupperware lid. It's past eleven, but the sun remains invisible. We walk along Jianguomen Nei Da Jie, which means "Inside Building-China-Gate Big Road." For years, I never considered why so many street names contained the word "gate." Eventually I learned that only a few years before I first arrived in Beijing, there had been actual gates and a spectacular city wall. The suffix -*nei* meant "inside the gate"; the suffix -*wai* meant "outside the gate."

Beijing had been a city of cells within cells, moats within moats, walls within walls. Each walled building was surrounded by more walls. Knowing this, it is easy to understand why the city remains obsessed with gates and gatekeepers. The Chinese character *cheng* means both "wall" and "city." The innermost walled sanctum was the Forbidden City, called Da Nei, or the Big Within. The palace, with 8,700 rooms, was home to the emperor, his minor children and an entourage of empresses and concubines. The only adult males allowed to spend the night were the eunuchs.

The imperial palace was surrounded by a moat, still extant today, and by another walled enclave six times the size of the Forbidden City. This was the Huang Cheng, or Imperial City. Princes, eunuchs and palace officials lived here. Here too were the imperial storehouses, guild workshops, archives, armories, vegetable gardens, orchards, stables and sheep farms. The Imperial City was, in turn, surrounded by a second moat, the one Kublai Khan's planners linked to the Grand Canal. Around this the Mongols built a third walled enclave, called the Tartar City. It was a near-perfect square, with walls reaching as far south as the present-day Avenue of Eternal Peace. Ten magnificent gates punctured the Tartar City wall. As the first foreigner to rule all China, Kublai Khan was preoccupied with security; he built yet another moat around the Tartar City wall. He even had nearby fields plowed so that the furrows in the fields impeded, rather than aided, invading horsemen.

In the mid-fifteenth century, the Ming shifted the entire Tartar City several kilometers to the south. The new Ming wall, built of hardened gray bricks, encircled the city. It loomed fifty feet high and was wide enough on top for a dozen horsemen to gallop abreast. Like a medieval fortress, it was crowned by parapets. Nine massive gatehouses pierced it at precise intervals, each with an archery tower, barracks, a barbican and administrative offices. Architecturally stunning, the gatehouses were built of fine gray brick, capped with tiled roofs, the elaborate eaves painted in red, cobalt, leaf green and white.

South of the Tartar City, the Ming established another walled enclave, with seven gates. After the Ming, the Manchu invaders who established the Qing dynasty would exile ethnic Chinese here. Eventually it would become known as the Chinese City, a kind of Chinatown within China. This walled city contained both the most sacred and the most profane elements of the capital. The Temple of Heaven, crowned with a triple roof of lapis-blue tiles and surrounded by concentric marble balustrades, remains the most beautiful temple in China. The Chinese City was also home to the boisterous Vegetable Market, which doubled as a public execution ground, and to a sizable Muslim community. Even today, real estate is cheaper in the Chinese City than elsewhere.

At night, each city gate was ceremoniously shut, not to reopen until dawn. Each had an auspicious name and ritual role. In ancient times, imperial troops would leave Beijing from Xuanwumen, the Gate Proclaiming Military Strength. They would return through Deshengmen, the Gate of Virtue Victorious. Today only three gates remain. The others live on as the names of subway stops. Beijing's magnificent city walls stood for more than five hundred years—until Mao decreed them an obstacle to progress. In 1965, he ordered them demolished. Despite sixteen years of totalitarian rule, Beijingers fearlessly fought to save it. Historians, architects, writers and ordinary citizens wrote letters and signed petitions. Some suggested making it a greenbelt where people could stroll around the city.

To no avail. Norman's father, Jack, helped dismantle the wall on his lunch break. Soon after he arrived in Beijing, Fat Paycheck witnessed People's Liberation Army soldiers tearing down one of the great gates. "I saw the keystone of Chongwenmen drop," he says, referring to the Gate of Venerating Culture. "There was a big PLA soldier with a sledgehammer. The keystone just fell. That was the beginning of the end for the gate."

By the time I arrived in 1972, the city wall had vanished. Below ground, workers began constructing a subway circle line that matched the circumference of the city wall. Aboveground, the blank imprint became the Second Ring Road. (Beijing has no First Ring Road; an early plan to build a ring road around the Forbidden City was abandoned after city planners conceded that too much of the ancient city would be destroyed.) Today, the Ming wall continues to leave its ghostly mark on the new Beijing. As the capital expands, new ring roads are built—a Third, Fourth, Fifth and Sixth—each echoing the now-vanished wall in ever-larger concentric circles.

The only extant fragment of the original Ming wall appears to be the section from Chongwenmen to Dongbianmen, which means East Convenience Gate. Except it's not. It's a fake, a twenty-first-century Communist Party creation, as authentic as King Tut's "tomb" in Las Vegas. The first time I saw the stunning gray-brick expanse, in 2005, I was taken in. Then I began wondering why I had never seen the ruins when I had biked around Beijing in the 1970s. I checked maps from seven different eras. Beijing had indeed pulled a fast one, fooling even established guidebook publishers, who dutifully repeat that the wall has been "restored." Some books add this embellishment: that the restoration uses original Ming bricks retrieved from nearby residents who had used them to build latrines after the wall was demolished.

For all his antipathy to feudal walls, Mao felt he needed them to separate him from the masses. He left them intact at his own compound at Zhongnanhai, now the headquarters of the Chinese Communist Party. Today, People's Liberation Army soldiers guard the compound's red and gold front gate. A huge spirit screen, ensuring total privacy, is inscribed with Mao's calligraphy: "Serve the People."

5

You Aren't Allowed to Call Anyone an Idiot—in English or Chinese

On our way home from Citibank, Fat Paycheck and I try to cross the intersection at Inside-Building-the-Nation Gate. Just to confuse matters, there was never a gate here, or an archery tower or a barbican. It was merely a cut in the wall, which is why it isn't marked on old maps. Now a highway interchange, it's so dangerous that we embed ourselves in a clump of pedestrians to cross to the other side. In this car-mad city, the pedestrian is the true proletariat of the road: we have nothing to lose but our limbs.

By chance I notice a simple, vertical, black and white sign outside a bland new office building. It's the Chinese Academy of Social Sciences. With a start, I realize that two of my classmates used to work there. Perhaps they still do, and perhaps they might know something about Yin. It's worth a try. At the very least, it's a good omen at the beginning of my search. We approach the main entrance. The gatekeeper swings out his arm to stop me.

"Go to the reception office," he orders, pointing to a small building. Inside, I'm swept back to Maoist times. There's an enamel washbasin, a grimy towel slung over the rim, and three red thermal containers for tea. The only modern touches are a small microwave oven, the black granite counter and the dyed auburn hair of the middle-aged clerk. "I'm looking for Gu Weiming and Wen Liming," I shout through the glass partition. "They both work in the History Institute."

The clerk shoves a notepad toward me. Each page, perforated down the center, is printed on both sides with a red serial number. I have to fill in my date of birth, workplace, address and phone number twice. I also have to say whom I want to see and who they are. Although China now has cellphones and the Internet, this antiquated Maoist system is intact. With cheap labor, it is entirely possible to keep track of a billion people on bits of paper. In 1973 I was almost expelled from Beijing University that way. I'd signed in to see a British teacher at the ironically named Friendship Hotel, a walled residential compound for foreign experts where ordinary Chinese rarely venture. I didn't know that my forbidden Swedish friend had just signed in to see the same Brit. Anders Hansson was a friend of a friend, the cultural attaché at the Swedish embassy and one of the few Westerners I knew in Beijing. Our friendship was innocent, although I hoped it would lead to something more. Anders was twenty-eight and I was twenty, and that made Zhou Peiyuan, the elderly chancellor of Beijing University, very nervous. He ordered me to stop seeing Anders. I reluctantly obeyed because, well, I thought it was the revolutionary thing to do, sort of like renouncing rock and roll.

Thanks to those scraps of paper, within days Chancellor Zhou found out about our chance encounter. In most countries, a meeting between a Canadian and a Swede at a Brit's apartment would elicit zero interest. To my shock, I was given sixteen days to leave China. I desperately wanted to stay. After my parents and a McGill professor with close ties to the regime rushed to the Chinese embassy in Ottawa, Beijing University rescinded the order. Four months later I would turn in Yin for seeking my help in leaving China.

At the Chinese Academy of Social Sciences, I fill out the forms using a cheap ballpoint pen tied to the counter with a length of pink raffia. I don't know which department my classmates work in. I'm not even sure they still work here. I push the half-finished paperwork back under the partition. "What are their phone extensions?" the clerk yells through the glass.

"I don't know," I shout back. I explain that Future Gu and Wen Liming are classmates from Beijing University. I tell the clerk I've come all the way from Canada to see them. Perhaps she can check her computerized database? She shakes her head. There is no computerized database. There isn't even an Academy phone directory.

"Can you call the History Institute for me?" I plead.

"Is that the Modern History Institute or the Ancient History Institute?" she asks.

I hesitate. Future spent years archiving Red Guard newspapers. That would be modern history. Wen Liming is the grandson of Wen Yiduo, a famous scholar who was assassinated in 1946 for opposing Generalissimo Chiang Kai-shek. Wen naturally was always more interested in modern Chinese history.

"Modern History," I say.

The clerk looks up the number and dials. I hear it ring and ring. She hangs up and glances at the clock on the wall. It's ten past eleven. "They've all gone to lunch," she says with a shrug, and then she turns to the next person waiting to fill out a form. I scribble a note to Wen and Gu and shove it under the glass partition. I ask her to pass it on, but since I don't even know whether they actually work here anymore, it seems futile. Fat Paycheck and I trudge back in silence to Beautiful Lodging.

Back at the apartment, Ben and Sam are ready to go exploring. Since I've promised them a museum-free vacation, I figure we might as well go completely crass. Beautiful Lodging is a ten-minute walk from the Silk Market, a paradise of pirated DVDs and counterfeit designer clothes. Shopping was once a Maoist ordeal of rationed goods. Now it's the opiate of the masses.

On the way, we pass a McDonald's. Sam clamors for a Big Mac. I veto eating there on our first full day in Beijing, but I let them take a peek because we've made it a habit to check out McDonald's around the world. It's an entertaining way for the boys to learn about globalization and national marketing strategies. We've sampled lobster rolls at a McDonald's franchise in New Brunswick and tacos at one in Mexico. In Rome, the McDonald's sold shrimp salad, fresh-squeezed blood-orange juice and espresso. This Beijing franchise sells purple-hued taro pies, red bean sundaes and deep-fried chicken wings.

I persuade the boys to eat at a nearby Chinese fast-food restaurant, which is half empty. We order *xiao long bao.* These "small-basket dumplings" are hand made by wrapping pasta around minced pork and cabbage and, miraculously, hot broth. The trick is to pluck one out of the bamboo steamer basket with your chopsticks, dip it into a small dish of rice vinegar scented with slivered ginger and convey it to your mouth without (a) breaking the thin casing, (b) dropping it on the table or (c) dribbling broth down your chin. Luckily, the boys have had ample chopstick training at home.

The tables and chairs here are screwed to the floor, just like at fast-food restaurants in Toronto. The Chinese designer has ingeniously filled the gap between two chairs with a small, low shelf, the perfect place to stash your purse (briefcase, laptop or shopping bags). In the West, we set our purses on the dirty floor or tuck them uncomfortably behind us. Or we take up an extra seat, which isn't very profitable for the restaurant owner.

Inexpensive solutions to everyday problems are a gauge of a culture's ingenuity. Decades of Maoism have paradoxically energized people, spurring its economy to double-digit growth. For the next month, I am going to be on the lookout for what China does better than we do. I'll discount anything based on cheap labor, though frankly that's one of China's biggest advantages. I'll ignore the exquisite head-and-shoulder massages that come free with haircuts. I won't count free same-day delivery by bicycle courier of theater and opera tickets. I can't include efficient mop-ups of supermarket spills. At my favorite Toronto supermarket, someone usually plunks down a yellow you-can't-sue-us "caution" sign. In Beijing, the staff run to mop up the spill, then fan the damp floor with a broken sheet of Styrofoam until it is safely dry.

In our collective memory, China has always been the Sick Man of Asia. In Montreal my mother warned me to clean my plate because children in China were starving. They *were* starving in the 1950s. But neither Mom nor anyone else mentioned that for much of recorded history—fifteen of the last seventeen centuries—China had the biggest economy in the world. In the eighth century, Changan, the terminus of the Silk Road, had a population of nearly two million. In the thirteenth century Marco Polo noted that China already had an advanced system of paper currency, backed by silver bullion. In the fifteenth century a Muslim eunuch named Zheng He commanded the Ming dynasty's navy on seven epic voyages as far west as Africa. It would be another century before Christopher Columbus arrived in the Americas and Vasco de Gama reached India. All their ships combined could have fit on the deck of Zheng He's flagship.

The Industrial Revolution is late in coming here, but China is catching up fast. After having invented gunpowder, the compass and a few other essentials, it is now gunning its economic engines. It is the world's largest consumer of coal and steel. It gobbles up half the cement produced on earth. Its voracious appetite for iron ore has prompted Australia to reopen defunct mines. China has become the world's largest maker of computers, cameras and cellphones. Forty percent of office employees in China work ten hours overtime a week. And 7 percent of the population works more than sixty hours a week. In 2006, China became the world's second-biggest market for cars, behind the United States. Any day now China will begin exporting cars to North America.

At the table next to us, a customer orders a can of Coke and a steamer basket of dumplings. She pulls a black and white frock out of her shopping bag. To my astonishment, she starts trying on her new dress. She wriggles it over her clothes. Everyone stops eating to watch. The waitress comes over to help. "It's a little tight," the waitress says, herself resplendent in a purple brocade vest and matching bowtie.

"It's a little bit long, too," says the customer, frowning. The waitress hikes up the shoulders. "You could shorten it here." A second waitress comes over to inspect the dress and asks, "How much did you pay?" The customer tells all of us, and the murmuring consensus among the diner-onlookers is that she got a bargain.

After lunch, Fat Paycheck, who hates shopping, heads back to the apartment. The boys and I head to the Silk Market. When the Silk Market was a chaotic outdoor bazaar behind the U.S. embassy, I'd go whenever I needed to confer with reporters from *The Times* of London or the *Washington Post*. We'd pretend to shop, or would actually shop, while discussing secret documents or organizing an unauthorized trip into Tibet. As I said, men hate shopping. It drove the (mostly male) secret police nuts. After 9/11 and a couple of anti-American demonstrations following that unfortunate bombing of the Chinese embassy in Belgrade, Beijing closed the outdoor market. In its new home, a five-story, air-conditioned building, the Silk Market has become a tourist destination. The government has even posted etiquette rules. You aren't, for instance, allowed to call anyone an idiot, in English or Chinese.

The government's real headache isn't the lack of market-place manners, but counterfeiting. Though the latter problem has flourished for years, now that China has joined the World Trade Organization, it must comply with international copyright laws. At the entrance to the Silk Market, a large sign in English and Chinese promises that vendors will no longer sell fake brand-name goods. They absolutely will not sell North Face, Polo, Hugo Boss, Kate Spade, Gucci, Chanel, Prada, Nike, Omega, Rolex, Cartier, Tiffany, Burberry, Tod's, Louis Vuitton, Swiss Army, Samsonite or Callaway. Inside the market, all the above brands are being sold, all fakes. Sam acquires a white and orange "Nike" shirt. A saleswoman spies my "Prada" purse, purchased on a trip to Shanghai a year earlier. "You like Prada!" she shrieks, waving a black nylon bag. "I have another one just like it." It is indeed identical to mine, except it's missing the little black and silver triangle logo. When I point that out, the saleswoman glances left and right. "I can get you one," she says, pulling open a drawer filled with Prada logos. Ben and Sam load up on pirated DVDs of *24, CSI* and a dozen movies. They're so thrilled that they forget they're supposed to be angry about spending their summer vacation in Beijing.

On our way back to Beautiful Lodging, a tout thrusts a discount coupon for a restaurant into my hand. Beijing once had only six hundred restaurants for eight million people, fewer Chinese restaurants than New York City in the 1970s. Now the Chinese capital has a restaurant for every four hundred people. Competition is so fierce, prices have actually dropped.

I can't resist a discount. We go back to Beautiful Lodging to fetch Fat Paycheck for dinner. The tout should have been a warning sign. We discover the restaurant is deserted inside, but when I see how hopeful the staff is, I don't have the heart to walk out. As in Paris, Beijing restaurants attract clientele by identifying with a specific *terroir*. This one claims to be Cantonese. Except for sweet and sour pork, the menu has no Cantonese specialties. It does have donkey, which is emphatically not a Cantonese specialty. The last time I had donkey was in Gansu, one of China's poorest provinces, where the *terroir* is a cuisine of extreme necessity. At a banquet, I sampled donkey penis, sliced thin and served naked at room temperature. It was, ah, okay.

Fat Paycheck knows about the donkey dick—I told him at the time—but Ben and Sam remain blissfully ignorant. When Fat Paycheck suggests the appetizer of "Five Spice Donkey Meat," the boys agree to try it. They weren't always adventurous eaters, but when they were picky as toddlers, I'd snatch the food off their plates, crowing, "Good! More for me!" They learned to eat everything. This parenting technique is now backfiring; when the donkey arrives, it is pink, soft and unpleasantly salty.

"Tastes like Spam," says Sam.

"Maybe donkey is the secret ingredient in Spam," Fat Paycheck says.

Frankly, the penis tasted better, but I keep that thought to myself. We all sample the Spamkey. We all hate it. I do not snatch the leftovers off the boys' plates. The rest of the meal—braised eggplant, a tomato omelet, sweet and sour pork—is mediocre. On the way out, I see a sign in Chinese in the window: "Two cooks wanted."

6

Is That Why They Call It Chai-Na?

I wake up in the middle of the night. My heart is pumping. I must be insane. I don't really want to find Yin. Everyone else in China has put the Cultural Revolution behind them. I should too. Besides, this is hopeless. If I can't even find my roommate, how can I find a woman I don't actually know? I'm sure the note I left at the Chinese Academy of Social Sciences will lead nowhere. As I drift off to sleep, I realize I have to go to Beijing University. Practically everyone I once knew there is gone, but it's the last place—and only place—I saw Yin. And I haven't got a better idea.

When I get up the next morning, I do have a better idea. As the saying goes, when you need help, ask a journalist. Chinese journalists have quasi-police powers, investigative clout that reporters can only dream of in the West. Half their mandate is producing sanitized stuff for the state-run media. The other half is figuring out for the government what's really going on. This, the hot stuff, goes into eyes-only reports for senior officials. So when Chinese reporters start sniffing around, few dare obfuscate or cover up. You never know: they could be making inquiries on behalf of the Politburo.

By chance, I know Tao Jie, the deputy director of the All-China Journalists Federation. Nine months ago, he led a high-powered delegation of fourteen journalists to Canada, including the deputy director general of Xinhua News Agency, the director general of the *Economic Daily* and the chief reporter for international news for China Central Television. When no one at the *Globe* responded to his emails requesting a tour, our Beijing correspondent, Geoff York, asked me to save our newspaper's collective face. I emailed Tao Jie and told him I would be pleased to arrange a newsroom tour. I reserved the boardroom and booked five senior editors and a former Beijing correspondent into twenty-minute Q&A slots. I also persuaded the publisher's secretary to cough up money for juice and cookies.

At the appointed time, I stood on the sidewalk in front of the *Globe*. To wait at my desk for them to phone up, as I normally do with visitors, would be rude. The delegation showed up exactly on time; tardiness is a breach of protocol too. The Chinese journalists had prepared a list of eleven questions. "Do reporters use their real names when they publish their stories?" (Absolutely, we're all glory hounds.) Another question: "Once it had happened in China, in a rainy day a reporter squatted near by [*sic*] a big mud puddle waiting for the pedestrians' falling down [*sic*], so he could take some news photos. How do you regard this kind of behavior?" (Brilliant; we'll steal the idea.)

Over chocolate-chip cookies and cans of ginger ale, my editors explained how we run corrections, what makes a successful feature story, whether we take bribes. I tried to keep the presentations honest. When our visitors asked about pressure from major advertisers, an editor started spouting the party line, until I reminded him of a recent case where we'd had to bend. The visitors were fascinated to learn that *Globe* reporters are members of Local 87-M of the Communications, Energy and Paperworkers Union of Canada. I explained that our base salaries, overtime pay and holidays were public information, published in a 207-page red book. I asked a colleague to fetch a copy. When the Chinese fought over *our* little red book, I sent the same colleague running through the newsroom to scavenge enough copies for each guest.

So I am fairly sure Tao Jie will remember me. I compose a two-page fax in Chinese, asking him to help me find Scarlet, Future and Wen Liming. I omit Yin. Even the All-China Journalists Federation can't do much without the correct Chinese characters for her name.

That morning, the boys' tutor arrives for their first lesson. Wang Zheng, a gentle, bookish woman in her thirties, is the translator and fixer for a Canadian television journalist who is away in Afghanistan reporting on the war against the Taliban. He has kindly allowed her to moonlight during August, provided she keeps the office running. She tells me her personal name, Zheng, is now quite unfashionable. It means "march," as in the Long March, the epic 1934 retreat that saved Mao's ragtag Communist forces from destruction by Generalissimo Chiang Kai-shek.

"Luckily, it also means to overcome, or succeed," she says, "so it's good for the new millennium, too."

To our kids' dismay, Long March (sorry, I just can't get over the Cult Rev) will come for an hour or so every morning. Two days a week, she'll take them after class on an outing to practice their Chinese. Linguistically torturing offspring is an overseas Chinese tradition, the solemn duty of the Chinese diaspora. In

Montreal, my Canadian-born parents signed my three siblings and me up for lessons in Cantonese, our ancestors' dialect. After school on Fridays, they'd drag us down to Chinatown, where our teacher, a stern nun who smelled of ginseng and incense, drilled us in polite, filial phrases such as *Mama, sic fan,* which means "Mother, eat rice," which we were supposed to murmur at the start of each meal to indicate that our mother had first dibs on the food. We hated those lessons, and learned next to nothing. The only reason we agreed to go was that our mother bribed us with chocolate bars and chow mein in Chinatown after each class.

In contrast, Ben and Sam were fluent in Mandarin when we left Beijing in 1994. Well, Ben was. Sam, a year old, couldn't say much of anything, but he understood. Cedes, the wonderful nanny we hired in Toronto, was Filipina Canadian. We soon lapsed into English, the household's only common language. The boys went to school in French, played in English and promptly forgot all their Chinese. As a Chinese Canadian parent, I dutifully ensured that they, too, suffered through pointless years of Friday afternoon Mandarin lessons in Toronto. Each year they begged me to stop. Each year I said I would, and I really meant to. But then the other ethnic Chinese parents at their school would go to work on me, and somehow I would re-enroll Ben and Sam for yet another year. The boys learned next to nothing.

From the upstairs loft, I eavesdrop as Long March Wang drills Ben and Sam in basic pronunciation. It brings back painful memories of Fu the Enforcer, my private teacher at Beijing University. She didn't speak any foreign language. Once she spent an inordinate amount of time trying to explain the concept of a verb. When I finally figured out what she was trying to tell me, I explained to her that English had verbs, too. She was astonished.

Learning vocabulary was stressful. We had no dictionaries. During the Cultural Revolution, they had all been withdrawn. When Fu tried to introduce a new word, her pedagogical technique was to say it louder and louder, with sighs and much rolling of eyes. When I simply couldn't fathom what she was saying, I'd knock on the wall to alert Erica, who was in the next room. A moment later, Erica, who spoke Mandarin at home, would shout back the meaning in English.

After the boys' lesson ends, I ask Long March to help me contact the Beijing Library. When I explain that I've lost touch with my old roommate, she nods. She herself has moved four times in the last ten years and changed her phone number three times. But when I tell her my roommate's name, she bursts out laughing. In Chinese, Scarlet's name is Zhang Hong. Zhang, of course, is the third most common surname. But Hong, which means "red," was the most popular female name for twenty-seven years between 1949 and Mao's death in 1976. When she finally stops laughing, Long March furrows her brow. "It's going to be hard to find her," she says. "But I will try."

That weekend, we visit Ben Mok, a Canadian friend in Beijing. Ben and I have been friends since McGill, where we masterminded a Maoist takeover of the Chinese Students Society from beer-guzzling engineering students in 1974. I was elected president and Ben was treasurer, and that's about all I can remember because I bailed out to return to Beijing University for a second time. Now Ben runs Coca-Cola's operations in North China. His turf includes Inner Mongolia, Tibet and Tianjin, a city of 11 million people east of Beijing. He and his lovely Chinese wife, Ke Naiai, and their two young sons, Jay and Ping-Ping, live near the airport, just north of Beijing. Every Monday morning, Ben commutes ninety minutes via chauffeured Toyota Land Cruiser to Tianjin.

Their gated community, Bright Capital, was built on paddy fields. Designed in the 1990s to attract foreign executives, it has the feel of a country club, except for the voracious mosquitoes. The compound has three swimming pools, multiple tennis courts, a couple of basketball courts and even the occasional sidewalk. Local Chinese own most of the houses, which can cost about one million dollars. "They don't always live in them," Ben says. "They may live in ordinary housing elsewhere, but they buy them as an investment." At a glance, the houses look like monster homes in Palo Alto, California, with lawns, garages and more bathrooms than bedrooms. But they aren't especially well built. Ben's roof is already leaking.

While his kids and mine go swimming with Fat Paycheck, Ben and I lounge by the pool. We don't need sunblock; the sun can't penetrate the smog. Ben, who has thinning, slightly wavy hair and an easy laugh, agrees that the air is getting worse every year. Before he joined Coca-Cola, he was in charge of Electrolux's China operations. In 1989, as a test, he sent his sales force selling vacuum cleaners door-to-door in Shanghai. Their success rate was a stunning 50 percent, a company record. Even though most customers didn't even own rugs, they ended up buying because they were so touched that a salesman had bothered to come to their home.

Every time I return to Beijing, Ben updates me on the latest trends. "There's a new mindset," he says, speaking a mix of English and Mandarin. "The Chinese don't think every foreign thing is necessarily better now. And they can accept criticism. They're not so sensitive."

The linguistic power balance in Beijing has changed too, according to Ben. He tells me that the days are over when a foreign manager would work through an interpreter. "Unless you're a very senior manager, you have to speak Chinese. I won't hire any foreigner that doesn't speak Chinese."

Fat Paycheck's fluency in Chinese used to be rare. In the 1990s, when Norman worked for a major American computer company, it valued him more for his accent-free Mandarin than for his PhD in computer science. Rather than have him develop software, they preferred that he attend client presentations, because the Chinese customers were so impressed that the company had a Chinese-speaking foreigner. He eventually quit. But what happened to Fat Paycheck has now become the norm.

"The latest status symbol in Beijing isn't a Mercedes-Benz or a foreign passport. It's having a white person working for you," says Ben. As more and more foreigners become fluent in Mandarin, Chinese companies are hiring them to impress clients. The companies will search—often on the Internet—for Mandarin-speaking foreigners, print up suitable name cards, create a PowerPoint presentation and fly the foreigner to meet a customer in, say, Dalian. For a fee, the foreigner pretends to be an employee of the company and makes the presentation, in Chinese.

As always, Ben and I debate the tension between freedom and control, between chaos and regimentation. My friend's years of doing business in China have given him unique insight. Ben disputes the received wisdom that the Communist government impedes progress. And indeed, China's gross domestic product is up 10 percent, industrial production is up 14 percent and the country enjoys a trade surplus of $163 billion, a current-account balance of $160 billion and nearly $1 trillion in foreign reserves.

"The Communist Party has been essential for China's development," he says. "It eliminated triads, the mafia, prostitution, the local militia and the armed thugs who stopped all progress at the village level. The Communists created the huge infrastructure that makes China work today—the reservoirs, the irrigation systems, the roads."

Without a dictatorship, Ben suggests, China could not have maintained its incredible growth. Lying in his lounge chair, he points to the nearby airport expressway, where crews are widening the road. "In any other country, it would take six months to a year to finish. Here it will be done in six weeks. The Party can order people to work night and day. There's an endless supply of labor from the provinces. They can move in heavy machinery from all over China." At the moment, China uses half the world's construction cranes. In 2000 it concentrated all available ones in Shanghai, enabling it to eclipse Manhattan in skyscraper count. Now, with the Olympics looming, the government is deploying the cranes in Beijing.

Ben says another reason for China's rapid development is the lack of civic opposition. Before the masses fully wake up to the notion of property rights, the Communist Party is sending SWAT teams into neighborhoods armed with buckets of red paint. They daub a single character on any building destined for destruction: *chai*. It rhymes with "buy," and it means "demolish." The character is so ubiquitous that a British friend in Beijing tells me her little girl recently asked, "Mommy, is that why they call it Chai-na?"

7

Alumni

Six days have passed. Tao Jie hasn't answered my fax. There's no word back from the Chinese Academy of Social Sciences, either. Meanwhile, Long March Wang reports back that the Beijing Library has five former employees called Zhang Hong and is refusing to release any information. I'm reluctant to go to Beijing University because I have little desire to see Fu the Enforcer, but I have few moves left.

On August 7, I decide to return to the scene of my crime. I make Fat Paycheck go with me for moral support. From his point of view, he's coming along to humor the insane. Like our children, he's inured to my ways. Post-9/11, when I decided to test airport security by smuggling box cutters and many other sharp implements onto a couple of transcontinental flights, he shrugged as the taxi pulled out of our driveway heading for the airport. "We'll visit you in jail," he said, waving. I didn't end up in jail, and no fighter jets forced down the planes. But after my story ran, Air Canada was deeply unhappy and made me sign a contrite letter—drafted by the airline's legal department—in which I promised never, ever to do that again on pain of a lifetime ban. The technique reminded me of the Chinese Communists. (I signed the letter and wrote another story, this time about the letter.)

In Toronto, when I told Fat Paycheck I planned to look for Yin, he was deeply skeptical. "I think it's highly unlikely you'll be able to find her," he said. "You had one fleeting contact with this woman thirty-three years ago. You know she was expelled, which certainly wouldn't have been a good thing. You know nothing about her, no idea who she was. Where would you even start to look?"

Fat Paycheck has never condemned me for turning Yin in. As someone who lived in China from the very beginning of the Cultural Revolution, he of course understood the consequences of what I had done. He knew Yin would have been sent back to wherever she came from and would have been left without any prospects, marked as a *huai ren*—literally, a bad person. But he also knew that if I had truly appreciated what would befall Yin, I would never have reported her. In contrast to him, I had lived in China for less than a year. Unlike him, my Chinese was not yet fluent. Most important, where he had made friends with old China hands—Americans and Brits who had lived in China for decades and who helped him understand what was going on—I had only Erica. Worse, she had only me.

As our taxi heads toward the university, he tries to console me. "You weren't much different from Chinese teenagers. They didn't know what they were doing either. They really believed all that stuff," he says. "The older, more experienced people knew. People who had been through earlier movements knew how serious this would be."

It's true that young people in China didn't know their own history then, and still don't today. There had been a continuous series of political purges throughout the 1950s and 1960s. Mao always won, and of course the victor wrote the history. Neither parents nor teachers dared set China's youth straight. That was far too dangerous. And by the time the Cultural Revolution began in 1966, the reign of terror was in full swing. The average Chinese teenager hadn't a clue how serious an accusation could be—and neither had I.

Beijing University is located on the site of a Qing-dynasty estate in the northwest suburbs. With its lake, lotus ponds and traditional imperial-style buildings, it is one of the most beautiful campuses in China. In the 1970s, it would take me an hour to bicycle into downtown Beijing. The route, White Stone Bridge Road, was two lanes wide, flanked by agricultural communes. A bike path shaded by willows and poplars was bucolic enough that peasants took roadside naps there. Now, it seems, a taxi takes as long as a bike used to. Stuck in gridlock, Fat Paycheck and I stare out at a Beijing we no longer know. White Stone Bridge Road has been transformed into an eight-lane expressway. The farm fields have vanished, replaced by a crop of office towers. We recognize nothing.

The taxi drops us at the campus's South Gate. Fat Paycheck used to fill in triplicate forms at the reception office here when we were dating. Well, trying to date. Such bourgeois frivolities were frowned upon during the Cultural Revolution. Mostly, we read *Das Kapital* together. After ten at night, the gatekeeper would padlock the high iron gate and go to sleep. Norman could have scaled the fence, but he needed to get his bike out. So he would wake up the gatekeeper, and then I'd get into trouble with both Fu the Enforcer and the administrator in charge of foreign students, Huang Daolin. Fu the Enforcer would scold me. Cadre Huang, a bony man with an unhealthy pallor, would giggle with embarrassment. During Maoist-style criticism sessions, he'd tell me the Communist Party cared about me, that my paramount duty was to study Mandarin and that he was positive my parents wouldn't approve. (He was right about that last bit, at least for the first twelve years of my marriage.)

I'm always nervous walking through the gates of Beijing University. I've been conditioned by the repression that followed the 1989 Tiananmen Massacre, when the police frequently detained foreign reporters trying to sneak onto the campus. Now I spot a security guard standing outside the old reception office. To draw attention away from myself—foreigners always stick out—I make Fat Paycheck walk behind me. But neither of us gets stopped.

On the right is my old dorm, the prosaically named Building Twenty-Five. For old times' sake, I take a quick look inside. Little has changed. The dormitory doors are still institutional yellow, the bathrooms the same old squat porcelain bowls. And they still stink. I stick my head in an office and explain I'm looking for former classmates. The woman suggests I try the Student Society Office in Building Twenty-Six next door. Unfortunately, like much of Beijing, Building Twenty-Six is under renovation, so the Student Society has temporarily moved.

I head toward the Triangle, an informal meeting spot near the center of the campus. When I ask someone about the current location of the Student Society Office, I get a blank look. I ask someone else, who doesn't know either. It dawns on me that they are tourists. I look around and notice the place is crawling with them. My alma mater has become a must-see attraction, like the Ming tombs.

Impatiently, I head inside the New China Bookstore, where a clerk suggests I try the Alumni Office. What is this? Harvard? There was no alumni office during the Cultural Revolution. Beijing University was about making revolution, not networking. At 11 a.m. the air is stifling. I have to retrace my steps almost back to the South Gate. The Alumni Office is in a new building called the Yingjie Exchange Center. Naturally, it's also under construction. I climb over a pile of sand and find my way in. The Alumni Office has computers and filing cabinets. I am instantly hopeful. They must have records of Scarlet and Future and Wen Liming. Maybe they will even be able to find Yin.

"We have no records for the 1970s," says the clerk behind the counter. "Prior to 1952, we have them, and after 1980. There's nothing in between. Our records are very good for the last two years. It's the Cultural Revolution that is a problem."

I'm shocked. The entire Maoist era is a black hole. Twenty-eight years of the university's history is missing. Who attended, who studied what and earned which degrees, our transcripts, our trespasses, our triumphs, all gone. According to university records, my classmates and I never existed. We have been airbrushed from history, in this country of meticulous record-keepers, in a nation with the longest unbroken historiographical record in the world.

Seeing my expression, the clerk politely suggests, "Why don't you try the Beijing University Foundation?" A foundation to raise money—that didn't exist in Mao's time either. The clerk gives me directions. Sigh. It's on the far side of the campus, which is a hundred and fifty hectares (370 acres) big. As Norman and I trudge through the heat, my mind is still reeling. Who destroyed the data? Or was it fire or flood or some other disaster? I had been so taken aback I forgot to ask the clerk *why* the records are missing. Were we, the alumni of Mao, one big mistake, an embarrassment the authorities would now like to forget? The loss of records is worrisome. The death toll from the Tiananmen Massacre has never been revealed, and I have always assumed it was a state secret. I've believed that the number has to be somewhere in the archives. Now I wonder. It would be terrible if the Tiananmen records have been destroyed, or were never written down in the first place—if the victims did not even matter enough to be counted.

Fifteen sweaty minutes later, we reach the liaison office of the Beijing University Foundation. A dainty mosaic path leads through a bamboo grove and a small orchard of date trees, snow-pear trees, cedars and honey locusts. The courtyard-style building looks like a perfectly preserved Qing-dynasty pavilion, with painted beams and a gray-tiled roof with curved eaves. I can't believe I missed it when I lived here before. The shiny red lacquered gate is locked. A handwritten sign says everyone is on vacation. I pound on the door anyway, and a young man eventually answers. He tells me everyone is on vacation. When I remark on the immaculate condition of the pavilion, he shrugs. "The building is only two years old." Like the "restored" Ming wall, it's a fake. Still, it looks great. And I suppose you have to look good to hit the alumni up for donations.

I give up trying to find Scarlet or my other classmates here. I have only one more stratagem left: Cadre Huang. He must have retired by now. I don't have especially fond memories of him criticizing me for reading *Newsweek,* but he might know something about Yin. Perhaps the Foreign Students Office will help me find him, and he in turn will help me find Fu the Enforcer. She'll remember because she's the one to whom I snitched on Yin.

I know the Foreign Students Office has relocated to a collection of nine buildings called Shao Yuan . . . all the way over on the west side of the campus. I helped build Shao Yuan during our regular stints of hard labor. (My romance with Fat Paycheck began in earnest when I broke my toe dropping a brick on it during one afternoon of labor. He began fetching me take-out Chinese from the Long March Restaurant, but that's another story.)

It's nearly noon by the time we reach the Foreign Students Office. Naturally, it shut down moments ago for lunch. "I don't think they'll be back today," a janitor tells me. "They've taken two busloads of foreign students to lunch far away." I feel like bursting into tears. Norman takes over, scribbling a note in Chinese that explains I was one of the first foreign students at Beijing University. The note asks the office to contact Cadre Huang and my old teacher, Fu the Enforcer. The janitor, a neatly dressed middle-aged woman, kindly agrees to pass it on.

I don't know what makes me think I can find Yin. No one, for instance, has ever found the Tank Man. An Associated Press photographer, Jeff Widener, took the iconic photo of the lone protester halting a column of tanks on June 5, 1989. Jeff was on a balcony at the Beijing Hotel. I was watching from another balcony, still shell-shocked from the massacre a day earlier at Tiananmen Square.

"You'd better get out here," Norman had shouted. I ran out, my heart in my throat. I watched as the tank twisted left, then right, trying to maneuver around the man instead of crushing him. Finally the tank switched off its engine. Unbelievably, the man clambered onto the turret. Then he climbed back down. Eventually, bystanders pulled him away.

The tanks revved their engines and proceeded down the Avenue of Eternal Peace.

Ever since, people have wondered who he was. Some think those who pulled him away were plainclothes police. I think not. When Chinese cops grab you, they manhandle you. They twist your arms, knuckle you in the head, punch you in the kidneys. The bystanders who pulled the man away did so almost protectively. He might even have known them. He certainly did not resist. He ran with them to the side of the road and melted into the crowd. Who was the Tank Man? He wore the garb of Everyman, a white shirt and dark trousers. He carried a small bag. His hair was medium length. He was probably in his twenties, given how easily he clambered up the tank.

Three weeks later, an Australian journalist named Alfred Lee flew into Beijing. He wrote an amazing story, which was published in a British newspaper. According to Lee, the Tank Man was a nineteen-year-old named Wang Wei Lin, the son of Beijing factory workers. Lee attributed the information to the young man's friends, who said they had spotted him, his head shaved like a criminal, being paraded on state television. Prime Minister Margaret Thatcher congratulated Lee on his world exclusive. Our editors screamed at us to match the story. The resident foreign correspondents, who spoke Chinese and had excellent sources, tried hard to duplicate the story. No one could. A journalistic scoop starts to look suspicious if no one can ever match it, like a lab experiment that has produced astonishing but one-time-only results.

In 2006, a British filmmaker, Antony Thomas, wrote and produced a documentary called *Tank Man*. He talked to Alfred Lee, who said he had had three sources who told him the man's name was Wang Wei Lin. "I knew that once his name had come into the public domain, the Chinese authorities wouldn't be able to do anything to him," Lee told Thomas. "They couldn't execute him. It would have brought outrage from the world."

Five days after Lee's "scoop," the London *Evening Standard* published an article by its Beijing correspondent, John Passmore, stating that Wang Wei Lin was now dead. In the article, Passmore attributes the information to American intelligence reports. Thomas interviewed Passmore as well, asking if the journalist recalled that article. He did not. "And now you tell me that it was American intelligence sources. I know it couldn't have been me writing it because I didn't have any American intelligence sources," Passmore said.

Thomas: "So you don't have any evidence that he was executed."

Passmore: "No. I never knew who he was or what happened to him."

Thomas: "And is that usual? Because it's your name there. Is that usual that reports are attributed to a journalist that actually [weren't] written by him?"

Passmore: "Oh, absolutely."

The last official word on the Tank Man came in 1990. Barbara Walters, the American television personality, was interviewing Jiang Zemin, who would soon become the president of China. Jiang said he could not confirm whether the Tank Man had been arrested. Asked if the young man was dead or alive, Jiang became uncharacteristically coy.

"I think," was all he would say.

It was up to Walters to interpret what Jiang meant by "I think." She thought he meant that the Tank Man had not been executed.

No one has ever found him.

8

The Decade of Disaster

With Beijing University a washout, I'm thoroughly demoralized. Norman tactfully refrains from pointing out the obvious—that this is a hopeless quest. Instead he suggests lunch, which always cheers me up. He reminds me that his former boss lives nearby. At least Xu Kongshi did three years ago. We're hoping he hasn't moved or changed his phone number in the meantime. We're also hoping he and his wife are free for lunch.

Hallelujah, we win the trifecta. They tell us to meet them outside their apartment and we'll go to lunch nearby. We jump in a taxi—and promptly get lost. Even though they're just a few minutes away, the taxi driver takes us too far south. Like so many taxi drivers in Beijing these days, he's a migrant who doesn't know the city. By the time we turn around, Xu and his wife, Yao Yuexiu, are waiting impatiently for us on the street. He was the director of the Software Institute of the Chinese Academy of Sciences. When the Cultural Revolution ended, he was daring enough to hire Fat Paycheck, a foreigner, which at the time was not a status symbol but a political risk. A brilliant computer scientist, Xu retired several years ago and now lives up to his name, Kongshi, which means "Time of Confucius." He spends his day savoring fine tea, studying calligraphy and visiting old friends. He uses an old-fashioned fan. He refuses to set up an email address or a fax machine. "I hate spam and junk faxes," he says.

He and his wife want to show us a new restaurant in a Mies van der Rohe–style office tower built on the site of the old Institute of Computing Technology. The restaurant, Jade Garden, is as stunning as the Four Seasons Restaurant at the Seagram Building in New York. It has soaring walls of glass, high ceilings and an aquarium of billowy-tailed goldfish. Dark lacquered tables and chairs are spaced far apart. A glass wall zigzags through the dining room, displaying hundreds of bottles of dry California red and Shanghai Cabernet Sauvignon. Each table is decorated with a bowl of long-stemmed artichokes tinged with purple, which, upon close inspection, turn out to be fake. Of course they are. I've never seen an artichoke for sale in Beijing.

In Mao's time, most restaurants stopped taking orders by 6 p.m. and aggressively swept up while customers were still eating. Fat Paycheck and I found only one place that served food after eight at night, a tiny wonton shop down by Yongdingmen (the Gate of Eternal Stability). It was marvelous—a few pennies for a steaming bowl of tiny dumplings, the broth flavored with microscopic dried shrimp and squares of nori seaweed. But it was still just a bowl of wonton.

The Cultural Revolution was, it is now clear, an aberration. China, like France, takes eating seriously. Both cultures revolve around agriculture and cuisine. The everyday greeting here is *ni chi le mei you*—"Have you eaten?" As an experiment a couple of years ago, I decided to see if I could find a single street in Beijing without a restaurant. I ignored any blocks that were entirely construction sites. During a half-hour taxi ride across town, I spotted at least one restaurant on every single street, often two or three. I asked a friend, James Miles, Beijing correspondent for *The Economist,* if he could think of any street without a restaurant. He thought for a moment, and said, "Tiananmen Square."

Jade Garden specializes in one of China's greatest cuisines, Suzhou-Zhejiang-Huai, a southern region famous for delicate dishes of ultra-fresh fish, bean curd and bamboo shoots. As a whippet-thin hostess in a silk gown leads us to our table, I whisper to my husband that we must make sure to grab the check. This place looks terribly expensive. We open the celadon-green menus, bound in silk, as big as an atlas and nearly as thick. Yao is a petite woman, prone to daintily shielding her mouth with her hand when she laughs. "This place is very, very cheap," she laughs without bothering to cover her mouth. As the waitress hovers, Yao happily orders too much food: steamer baskets of dim sum, various bowls of soup noodles, lima beans poached in rice wine, green-tea pastries.

We are old friends, too. Now retired, Yao was a Portuguese translator at Radio Beijing. In 1988 she kindly accompanied me on my first reporting trip to Zhejiang, her native province. We spent several days in a village where the pitch-black, window-less latrines oozed with maggots and slime. In our dingy hotel in Shaoxing, the nearest city, a millipede as big as a hot dog sent me screaming out of the bathroom.

So when I excuse myself to rinse the sweat off my face and arms after trekking through Beijing University, I'm wary. But the ladies' room at Jade Garden is as sleek as the dining room. Behind a giant door of brushed aluminum, the walls, stalls, counters and sinks are covered in more brushed aluminum. The place is spotless. It doesn't smell. And there is something I've never seen before in China: a dispenser for paper toilet-seat covers. The washroom feels like a sleek spaceship, a millennium away from the maggoty latrine in Zhejiang. I'm sorry if I'm obsessed with bathrooms, but years of horror have warped me. As I'm using the facilities, I notice another piece of the ingenuity gap. So that you don't have to touch anything, everything from the taps to the liquid soap to the paper towels to the flush is motion-activated—everything except the toilet-paper dispenser, and I'm sure some Chinese entrepreneur somewhere is working on that. But just like at the automated teller machine, a human being is stationed here too, a white-jacketed attendant who squeegees the sink after each use.

I return to find the table loaded with food, and the waitress bringing more. A hostess in a silk gown stops by to ask if everything is to our satisfaction. Confusingly, she starts spouting percentages. "She's trying to sell us 'favored customer cards,'" Yao explains. Buy a one-thousand-yuan card, and get an extra two-hundred yuan in purchasing power. Buy a four-thousand yuan card, and get an extra thousand. At restaurants in Toronto, if you buy a hundred-dollar gift certificate, you get a hundred dollars. At Barnes & Noble, an annual twenty-five-dollar fee gets you a 20 percent discount on hardcover books and 10 percent on paperbacks, but there's no volume incentive and no requirement to hand over cash up front.

"The more you pay in advance, the bigger the discount," says Yao, adding that hair salons, spas and massage parlors all sell them—any business that tries to attract a regular clientele. I'm for buying a coupon right away, but there's a catch. The hostess says we can't use it at this meal. When we decline, she doesn't stop. Relentlessly, in a polite, sweet way, she returns twice more to ask if we want to become "favored customers," as if our earlier refusal never happened. She drops by three times more to urge us to order more food. When we don't, she conducts a charm offensive, sending over a platter of sliced melon and tiny bowls of iced tapioca in coconut milk, compliments of the house. And when we ask to wrap up the abundant leftovers, the hostess packages the dumplings and green-tea cakes in reusable Tupperware-like containers and stacks them in an elegant gift bag. This all makes Yao very happy—and convinced this is a place where she'd like to become a favored customer.

During Mao's rule, the love of the deal went dormant, but it was never extinguished. A half-century of communist rule, after all, is a mere blip on the consciousness of a civilization that first expressed its mercantile instinct in the Silk Road. Any year now, China will become the world's biggest exporter, according to forecasts by the Organisation for Economic Co-operation and Development.

Beijing has become the city of the hard sell. Myles Morin, a vice-president at Manulife Investments in Toronto, recalls a street vendor trying to sell him a fake Rolex watch as he got out of a taxi in Beijing. "I said, 'I don't need a watch,'" he said, showing her the one on his wrist. Even as he shook his head, the peddler kept lowering her price. He kept saying no. She kept cutting her price. Enchanted by her persistence, Morin bought a watch. "And then she tried to sell me two," he told me, laughing.

Everything is a sales opportunity. At Beautiful Lodging, flat-screen monitors in the elevator lobby grab that unproductive moment while you wait. They advertise Fords and BMWs, energy drinks, even immigration consulting for Canada. At the

Silk Market, I've noticed that the gimlet-eyed vendors are expert psychologists. If your eyes linger for a second on, say, a pashmina, they leap up. In English, Chinese, Russian, French, they shout, "Pashmina! You like? Many colors! Good price!" They watch to see what language works, and from that they extrapolate your nationality. Americans pay the most, Russians the least, and the French are very emotional. At Red Bridge, a huge indoor bazaar, I once loaded up on scarves and shawls from one vendor. As I staggered away with my purchases, the vendor at the next stall didn't feel envious; she tried to sell me more. "Pashmina? Good price! Buy mine!" she said.

Vendors who don't want to rent stalls lurk outside the Silk Market. At the intersection in front, a tiny woman waves a few pairs of socks. Most pedestrians brush by as if she's invisible. I stop because Ben and Sam need socks, although I fret that the Playboy logo won't pass muster with the school uniform police. Gray is the obligatory sock color at their school, which, being French, has strict sock-color rules. When I hesitate, the peddler reaches in her bag and thrusts more socks at me, including some plain gray ones. She, of course, assumes I'm Chinese. Her price, five pairs for 15 yuan ($2), is dirt cheap. But precisely because she assumes I'm Chinese, I'm now obliged by my ancestors' mercantile traditions to bargain hard. Before you know it, I've bought twenty pairs at some ridiculously low price. Clearly, though, I haven't bargained hard enough. Two other sock vendors eagerly approach.

Selling is in Beijing's blood. When I buy ripe local peaches from a sidewalk peddler near Beautiful Lodging, he persuades me to buy twice as many as I intended. Then he cajoles me into buying two giant mangoes. When I finally pay for my purchases and hold out my hand for my change, he says, "Take another peach instead!" Without waiting for agreement, he thrusts another piece of fruit into my bag.

After our lunch, Yao goes home to nap while Xu shows us around the new skyscraper that replaced the software institute. My cellphone beeps. Long March Wang is sending me a text message. Every day the Chinese send billions of text messages, which cost less than two cents each. Using their thumbs and the numerical pad, they input the strokes of each character. The software figures out, from the context, the most likely characters. "We're a nation of thumbs," a young Shanghai woman told me.

Long March has good news. Tao Jie, my contact from the Journalists Federation, is still working on Scarlet, but he has found phone numbers for both Future and Wen Liming. I call Future immediately. He's pleased to hear from me but not surprised. He's long ago gotten used to me dropping in and out of his life. We agree to have dinner together the next night.

My phone rings again. "Guess who I am?" a husky female voice demands in Chinese. I can't guess. I think hard and draw a blank.

"Guess who I am?" she repeats. I feel embarrassed, annoyed. Were I back in Toronto, I would have hung up by now. Instead I say as calmly as I can that I don't know who she is.

"I'll give you a hint," she says, laughing. "All my brothers and sisters have the same name."

Fu the Enforcer. It's been more than three decades, but she still has a magical ability to embarrass and annoy me. Her father, a military commander-in-chief in Henan province, named all six of his children Fu Min, using different characters for Min. (He's like George Foreman, who named five sons and two daughters George.) A hard-line Marxist who always toed the Party line, Fu analyzed everything through the prism of class struggle. To her, I was politically suspect because I came from the wicked West. In her view my restaurateur dad was a blood-sucking capitalist who exploited the proletariat by making them cook chicken chow mein.

Fu had studied Chinese language at Beijing University and was hired as faculty directly upon graduation. In 1966, when the Cultural Revolution engulfed the campus, she joined the most radical, most violent Red Guard faction. At the time, Deng Xiaoping's eldest son, Pufang, was a student in the physics department. In 1968, after Deng was labeled Mao's "Number Two Enemy," Red Guards tortured his son. He later fell, or was pushed, from a fourth-floor window on campus, breaking his back and rendering him a paraplegic. Was Fu's faction responsible? She has never said.

Deng Pufang will not discuss the Cultural Revolution or his defenestration. Now chair of the China Disabled Persons' Federation, he was asked during a 2006 press conference how he became paralyzed. "Thirty-eight years ago?" Deng murmured to the person beside him. The person nodded. Deng turned back to the reporter, a Reuters correspondent. "As I've said many times before," he said carefully, "the Cultural Revolution has brought great disaster not only to me but to the entire Chinese nation. Lots of inhumane acts were committed."

Even for someone as powerful as Deng Xiaoping's eldest son, the Cultural Revolution remains too painful and too risky a subject. An estimated one million Chinese died unnatural deaths between 1966 and 1976. To discuss this history would be to question the Communist Party's very legitimacy. And so the regime resists any debate over China's holocaust, obliquely labeling it The Decade of Disaster. There is no Truth and Reconciliation Committee. Only a handful of top officials were ever punished, including Mao's wife and her so-called Gang of Four. The vast majority of victimizers simply went back to work, beside their victims. To this day, the Cultural Revolution remains taboo.

Millions of ordinary Chinese are complicit. They avoid reflecting on individual responsibility. They withhold blame for the violence and destruction. It is a "peculiar amnesia," notes Judith Shapiro, author of *Mao's War against Nature*. And yet how many members of the Ku Klux Klan have sought out those they persecuted? *Stasiland,* Anna Funder's brilliant account of lives brutally shaped by the Berlin Wall, also describes a history that is being deliberately, consciously suppressed in the former East Germany.

After the violence of 1968, Fu Min and other faculty were packed off for consciousness-raising labor to remote Jiangxi province. At Carp Island Farm, Fu was on evening patrol when she noticed that a young English teacher, Zheng Peidi, was not in her bed. Her suspicions aroused, Fu went out to hunt for Peidi. She found her by the river, chatting to a young male lab assistant. Fu couldn't wait to snitch. After all, Peidi was married. Fu rushed to report the juicy news to the military officer in charge of the farm.

"She called me a *po xie,*" says Peidi, who subsequently became my good friend and introduced me to Fat Paycheck. *Po xie* means "whore," literally a "broken shoe," worn out from so many feet trying it on.

In 1973, when Yin asked me for help, I didn't know about Deng Xiaoping's son. I hadn't yet met Peidi. And no one in China was talking publicly, or even privately, about what was happening during the Cultural Revolution. Deng's son had spinal surgery in Ottawa in 1980, but the operation was kept a secret. When the *Ottawa Citizen* got wind of a "special patient," the Chinese embassy claimed he was a relative of the ambassador. I wouldn't even find out about what Fu had done to Peidi until the 1980s. When I did, it only confirmed my opinion of my former teacher. But by then I had already forgotten all about Yin.

In hindsight, I couldn't have ratted her out to a worse person. But my thoughts are wandering. Fu the Enforcer is talking, fast. I focus. She tells me she retired "ages ago." She and her husband—they never had children—live in campus housing at North Yenching Garden.

"I'm here for a month," I say. "I'd love to visit you." There is silence. I know Fu is squirming.

"Come to my house," she says finally, with false enthusiasm. According to Chinese etiquette, I'm supposed to decline. If the other person is sincere, she'll repeat her invitation three times. Otherwise my ritual refusal is supposed to leave a face-saving way out. But it's payback time.

"Great!" I say. "When?"

Fu the Enforcer starts to cough. "Oh, my house is so messy," she murmurs.

"No problem," I say heartily. "I'll bring my kids and my husband."

"Is he an ethnic Chinese or a white person?" she asks.

That's vintage Fu. Just for yuks, I'm tempted to say Fat Paycheck is black.

"He's white," I say, caving. Then I pause. "Is that a problem?"

"Oh, no," says Fu, matching me on the hearty-o-meter.

We agree that I'll go to her apartment for lunch in four days, with my white husband and my half-breed kids.

9

Forbidden City

Right after Fu the Enforcer hangs up, my cellphone rings again. It's Cadre Huang. "So you've come back!" he says, giggling nervously. I tell him I'm back for a month, with my family. I don't tell him Fu the Enforcer and I have just made a date. And I don't tell him that I'm looking for Yin.

"We'll have a lunch for you at Beijing University," he says. "How about August 14? I'll invite everyone I can find, Teacher Fu, Erica's teacher."

I agree on the spot.

The next morning I hurry to buy tickets to an upcoming cello concert. I'm afraid it will sell out. How little I understand the local arts scene. The Chinese are willing to pay for name-brand artists such as Yo-Yo Ma, but not for—in this case—a recital by two dozen Chinese and Swiss student cellists. However, local authorities consider large swaths of empty seats a loss of face when foreign groups are involved. So state-owned companies are typically forced to purchase blocks of tickets. They in turn hand the tickets out free to employees, many of whom promptly sell them to scalpers, or, rather, reverse-scalpers. On the night of the cello concert, the reverse-scalpers stand outside the theater, hawking tickets on the cheap, the price plummeting drastically as curtain time approaches. But I don't know this.

The concierge at Beautiful Lodging informs me that the closest ticket kiosk is at nearby Sci-Tech. In addition to being a hotel and health club, Sci-Tech is also an office tower, department store and the site of Beijing's only Bentley Motors dealership. Luxury cars are big in Beijing. China is Rolls-Royce's third-biggest market, after the United States and Britain. I've already seen Ferraris, Porsches, even Hummers on the roads. Inside the department store, the clerk at the Sci-Tech ticket kiosk apologetically explains that we have to wait while she dials up a connection for her modem. As one of Beijing's earliest luxury complexes, Sci-Tech is so last decade. All the newer buildings, including Beautiful Lodging, are on high-speed wireless Internet. While I wait, I idly watch a young woman training another young woman how to be a store greeter.

"You can't wag your shoulders," the veteran tells the rookie. Sashaying like a supermodel, she demonstrates, her legs swinging from the hips, back and neck ramrod straight. The rookie self-consciously imitates her. "Not bad. Not bad," the veteran says, encouragingly. "The first time, everyone is nervous." Both women are slender and pretty, silken hair twisted into beribboned chignons. They're identically dressed in high heels, black skirts, white ruffled blouses and fuchsia vests. Their job is no different from that of a Wal-Mart greeter, except they have to wear heels. Even as the rich buy Bentleys and Porsches, China overflows with cheap labor. At supermarkets, restaurants, hotels, shopping malls and museums, young women in pastel dresses or Mandarin-collared gowns stand at entrances, a decorative echo of the traditional Chinese gatekeeper. They chirp the same greeting as the 7-Eleven clerks: "Welcome your approaching luminous presence!"

The kiosk clerk still hasn't managed to connect to the Internet. Bored, I notice a free electric shoe-polishing machine at the main entrance. I don't remember seeing any a year ago, but now that I think about it, there's one in the lobby of Beautiful Lodging too. My friend Kathy Wilhelm, the lawyer, confirms that they are everywhere. "People ruin their shoes walking through the construction dirt," she says.

Change often happens overnight in Beijing. In the 1990s, when the authorities decided the masses should start taking taxis, tiny yellow minibuses flooded the streets. A few years later, they vanished just as fast when authorities decided the minibuses were an eyesore. The same has now happened to the cheap, red Xia Li taxis. A year ago, they were all over the city. Now not a single one remains, replaced by fleets of slightly roomier sedans, also painted red.

You can get whiplash, swiveling your head to see that "Ming" city wall as your taxi speeds by. It's so huge, so imposing, so *old*-looking that you think, *How could I have missed that?* You'd have to have been there before the new millennium and have kept a steady grip on your memory to realize the wall is a 2002 creation.

To me, the shoe-polishing machines symbolize China's economic progress. Beijingers are no longer shod in the cheap cloth shoes of the Mao era, but now the world's largest construction site is sullying people's expensive leather shoes. An entrepreneur pinpoints a brand-new need and starts manufacturing the machines. Building managers, hungry for a competitive edge, snap them up.

The damned modem still isn't connected. I notice international symbols posted at the Sci-Tech entrance. You can't smoke. Dogs aren't allowed. Inline skating, photography and firecrackers are banned too. Beijing is, and always was, the Forbidden City. When one of my predecessors, John Burns, took that train ride, he reported that the announcer spent some time describing the rules of behavior:

> Those travelling on business should take good care of their papers. Those with children should take them to the toilet regularly and keep them from sticking their heads out the windows. Everybody should try to keep the train clean . . . Passengers travelling with quantities of gasoline, dynamite and nitroglycerine, or any other substances that are explosive, inflammable or radioactive, should hand them over to the crew members in carriage No. 7 for safekeeping.

China's fixation on rules stems from Confucian times, when the great sage decreed that everything and everyone had a correct place. Virtue derived from obedience to hierarchy. It all feels quite French. In *Paris to the Moon,* Adam Gopnik notes that "the French taste for order reach[es] even into the rich man's locker room." He quotes, in translation, the prohibitions posted at the Paris Ritz steambaths, known as *hammam:*

> 1. The shower is obligatory before using the installations.
> 2. It is forbidden to shave in the sauna.
> 3. Reading of newspapers is strongly discouraged in the hammam and sauna.

4. Children of less than twelve years are not
   authorized to use the installations.

At parks, Gopnik writes, the French think "encyclopedically" about all the things you can't do. Ben and Sam learned that when we took them to Paris. After too many museums, the boys, then six and nine, made a beeline for the park at the Jardin des Tuileries. A stern *policier* pounced. "No walking on the grass," he said, ordering them out.

Or perhaps the French got their obsession with rules from China. "Chinoiserie," after all, is a French word. At their own parks, the Chinese impose myriad regulations. In Beijing, at a strip of grass beside the "restored" Ming city wall, an imposing stainless-steel sign displays fully twelve icons indicating that it is forbidden to bicycle, drive, pick flowers, climb fences, litter, sound horns (or maybe play trumpet—it's hard to tell from the icon). It is also forbidden to skateboard, play ball, deliver anything by pedicab, walk a dog, light a bonfire or set off those firecrackers. Oddly, the sign doesn't actually rule out walking on the grass. But everyone already knows that is not allowed.

A few days later, at the cello concert at the Forbidden City Concert Hall, an announcer reads out nine rules: "In order to maintain an elegant environment, don't chew gum. In case of an emergency, don't panic. Don't applaud between movements. Don't bring in plastic bags. No drinks. No children under 1.2 meters allowed. Put pagers and cellphones on silent mode. Don't smoke. Those who are unsuitably dressed will not be permitted to enter the auditorium."

There are rules, and rules. As in Paris, Beijing's pervasive no-smoking rule is more honored in the breach. At the Sci-Tech Health Club one afternoon, I'm reading a Chinese real estate magazine while Ben and Sam shoot some pool. At the next table, two men light up. I check the sign on the wall. Sure enough, it says "No Smoking." Now, I'm a bad enough mother to allow my boys to waste an afternoon in a pool hall, but I draw the line at second-hand smoke. I jump up and splutter, pointing to the sign.

"Where are *you* from?" one man asks belligerently, exhaling a plume of smoke. It's not a geographic query. It's a status question. He really means, *Who the hell are you?* Being Canadian and naturally resentful of elitism, I give him a literal answer. "Canada," I say.

That's a mistake.

"This is China," he says, taking another drag.

"This is a Chinese sign," I retort.

His friend tries to mollify me by stubbing out his cigarette. Ben and Sam, mortified, assure me they're fine with cancer. Mr. Smokers' Rights flicks his ash into an ashtray. "If there's no smoking," he says triumphantly, "why are there ashtrays here?"

I stomp over to the bar where a scared young attendant is pretending he's deaf and invisible. When I press him, he says that, the sign notwithstanding, smoking is permitted. I ask him to get the manager on the phone. He does. Before he hands the receiver over to me, he asks his boss, "You can smoke here, right?" I have no idea what the boss tells the attendant, but the manager tells me that smoking is indeed prohibited. However, in a thoroughly Chinese solution, he declines to enforce the rule by actually showing up. Meanwhile, Mr. Smokers' Rights has finished his cigarette.

At Sci-Tech, the dial-up connection is finally complete. The clerk asks which seats I want. The counter lights up with an embedded computer screen, another example of the ingenuity gap. In Toronto, unless I schlep in person to the theater or the baseball stadium, I buy seats blind. I'll know I'm in, say, row KK, seats 36 through 40, but I won't know exactly where those seats are until the concert or the game. I pick four seats in the front-row balcony. Unsold seats are in green. The moment I pay, the seats go red. The price includes courier delivery the next day to Beautiful Lodging.

Beijing movie theaters offer the same service. It's brilliant not just for moviegoers, but for mall owners. In Toronto, if a movie is a hit, friends have to go early to get seats together. Then they sit there in the dark, stoically ignoring the commercials. In Beijing, customers buy reserved seats then wander off to shop, dine or otherwise spend money. Theater owners could probably negotiate reduced rent for all the extra spending they bring in.

That evening, both Fat Paycheck and Sam are too tired to go out after dinner. I haven't had a chance to explore the neighborhood around Beautiful Lodging and want to look around. Ben, bless him, agrees to accompany me. We both don sturdy shoes. I can't fathom how some women navigate the torn-up streets in strappy high-heeled sandals.

There are other risks to wandering the streets of Beijing. The *China Daily* says crime is on the increase. The *People's Daily* reports that fifty Beijing police precincts have excessively high crime rates, including ours. No hard statistics are provided, but the types of crimes indicate a certain desperation. Besides car theft, burglaries, rapes and muggings, people are stealing utility covers. The metal is worth 35 yuan ($4.50) on the black market. And you'd need at least two people and some kind of cart to schlep the covers away. But 35 yuan is about a day and a half's pay for a migrant worker.

Like the families heading to California in John Steinbeck's novel *The Grapes of Wrath,* migrants have flooded into Beijing and other cities from the hinterland. Between 1982 and 2000, about 200 million peasants left the countryside, the largest demographic shift in the history of the world. An additional 180 million will migrate to the cities by 2010. In Beijing alone, the municipal government says, one in four residents is a migrant, or 4 million out of 16 million.

Migrants are the foot soldiers of China's Industrial Revolution. They work at all the dangerous, dirty, exhausting jobs that legal residents shun, and they face discrimination on every front. They are blamed for the crime rate. Unscrupulous employers fail to pay them their first and last months' wages. Their lives are literally cheaper. If a driver hits and kills one, he pays up to 80 percent less in compensation than for a legal Beijing resident. Yet the migrants keep Beijing's economy humming. They are indispensable as maids, construction workers, dishwashers, road crews, delivery men, movers, masseurs and prostitutes. Middle-class Beijingers employ them, even while blaming them for the rising crime rate. According to a recent survey, one in three Beijingers hires migrants as maids, one in four hires them for home renovations and nearly half buy fruit and vegetables from them.

Migrant workers earn an average of 20 yuan ($2.60) a day, compared with 128 yuan a day for the average Beijinger. But migrants aren't interested in mere survival. They burn with ambition. In their view, a day off is a lost financial opportunity. Many work seven days a week, year round, saving as much as they can so they can return home to start a business. Walk around Beijing and you will see mysterious numbers scrawled in red or black on sidewalks, walls and concrete barriers. These are cellphone numbers for "consultants" peddling counterfeit identities. For a few weeks' pay, you can buy everything you need to reinvent yourself for the new millennium: ID cards, residence permits, passports, bank statements, high school diplomas, advanced university degrees.

These consultants target migrant workers, who lack *hukou,* legal residence permits. The best they can hope for is a temporary *hukou,* issued by the police, but that can be revoked at any time. Without one, a migrant can be forcibly expelled from Beijing. And without a permanent *hukou,* a migrant also has limited access to medical care, decent housing, pensions and education.

Banned from public schools, migrant children enroll in unlicensed, substandard private schools. A day earlier, I read in the *China Daily* that authorities are closing 136 migrant schools—without finding corresponding places for the children in public schools. Some migrants tell reporters they believe this a deliberate move to reduce Beijing's "floating population" before the Olympics. But even if there were spaces, a survey found, migrants are afraid to send their children to public schools. They fear that the teachers will ignore their children and that local students will refuse to play with them. Zhang Yue, twelve, told the *China Daily* she wouldn't go to a public school even though her own private migrant school had now closed.

"I'm afraid that I might be looked down upon by others in a public school even if my parents can afford the higher fee there," she said.

• • •

As the evening air cools, it is possible to wander without swooning from the heat. Ben and I walk out of the well-lit entrance of Beautiful Lodging and head south. The crescent moon is a pale orange nail clipping. The evening sky glows flamingo pink from smog, dust and the exhaust produced by 16 million people. Two weathered fluorescent-orange traffic cones mark the abrupt end of Constructing China Road South. Beyond it is rubble and a high mound of dirt.

That can't be. I know the city extends far to the south. Ben and I clamber over the dirt and keep walking. A few minutes later we see the strangest sight—a half-finished elevated expressway stopping abruptly in midair. A young man, his legs tucked under him, perches fearlessly on the brink of the abyss. It must be an eighty-foot drop to the ground, yet he sits there, right where the expressway-to-be ends, gazing at the pink haze, as unmoving as Rodin's *Thinker*. It isn't just where he has chosen to sit that seems so strange. It's also odd to see *one* person, a solitary person, in this city of millions. The thinker has chosen a spot where no one else can pass. His aloneness reminds me of the Tank Man.

The street ends, I see now, because of expressway construction. Just beyond is the Tonghui Canal, which, in the Yuan dynasty, circumscribed the city wall. Barges of tax grain floated on it, heading for the emperor's storehouses. When water levels dropped during the Ming dynasty, the barges were offloaded here and the grain was transported overland the last few kilometers. Modern maps call it the Tonghui River, but it is now just a concrete-lined storm channel.

Ben and I turn down a narrow lane, and suddenly I'm back in the Beijing of the 1970s. Dreary four-story apartment buildings line the alley. Shoddily built of cheap red brick, they were once coveted as a step up from the overcrowded, crumbling courtyard homes. Further on, we pass a tiny lean-to with a rumpled bed, a television, a small electric fan and a two-burner stovetop. The roof is made of scraps of corrugated tin, weighted down by loose bricks. The dusty *hutong* is also home to a hole-in-the-wall tailor shop and a two-seater barbershop. We spot another barbershop, and then another. I count half a dozen in one short lane. They must be brothels—the barbers are all young women in tight jeans and high heels. I've interviewed such "hairdressers" before. They usually sit on display in the windows, a grimy bed tucked behind a curtain at the back.

China, which has the world's largest standing army, reportedly has more sex-trade workers than soldiers. The lowest-paid prostitutes service migrant workers at construction sites. Next are the "hairdressers." Then there are the dancers who work in nightclubs and the prostitutes who make random phone calls up to hotel rooms. At the top of the hierarchy are concubines and mistresses, the *er nai,* "second breasts." I am explaining all this to Ben—I do want my children to have a well-rounded education—when I suddenly realize hair *is* being cut. But why are so many men having their hair trimmed at night in this one alley?

The answer lies around the corner: a night market is in full swing. One merchant has laid out pairs of worn-out shoes on a tarp, lovingly polished, the way a jeweler would display ruby and emerald rings. A man with black cloth shoes in tatters is negotiating for a pair of old shoes. Someone else is selling second-hand cellphones. Other peddlers offer used paperback books and pop-music tapes, new keychains, flashlights and sets of soft-porn playing cards of buxom blondes.

These are the desperate dealing with the desperate. A

middle-aged man picks through a mound of second-hand clothes. He tries on a pair of trousers over his shorts, and starts to bargain, hard. The vendor shakes his head. The man is insistent. He presses money into the hand of the vendor, who still refuses, pushing the crumpled bills back. Each side tenses. They are one yuan—fourteen cents—apart, and the difference matters to both. Finally the vendor caves. I notice someone selling new clothes—underwear, T-shirts . . . and gray socks. The asking price: six yuan for two pair. In the interests of research, I bargain, guiltily. The vendor briskly agrees to sell me two pair for four and a half yuan.

The buyers, sellers and lookers-on are all male. Some wear flip-flops and shorts. A few are bare-chested. Their hair is gray with dust. They're all young and strong, with hardened faces, mahogany skin and rough hands. And then I understand. They are the construction workers who are building the expressway. After working twelve-hour days, this is their leisure time, the only part of the day they can call their own. That is why the barbershops are filled with young men getting haircuts and shaves.

Behind us, the half-finished elevated expressway looms. Ben and I walk alongside a ramp until it is low enough for us to hop onto. Dozens of people are strolling along the elevated asphalt, as if it were the Champs-Elysées. In the glow of the pink sky, it feels post-apocalyptic. The survivors walk aimlessly at night, the only sound the slap, slap, slap of plastic flip-flops. One young man in ragged pants squats by the edge of the road, silently sending a text message on his cellphone, the cheapest way of communicating. How strange that an eight-lane expressway-to-be is the most peaceful place we've found in Beijing, the only spot we can walk without risking being run over, or tripping over debris, or falling into an uncovered manhole.

On the road beneath, a convoy of trucks roars past, shattering the silence. From our elevated height, we have a panoramic view of some new high-rise towers beside the expressway, a chic condo development of stark white, minimalist towers. It takes me a moment to figure out why they look so arresting. And then I realize the towers are set on an angled checkerboard pattern. It's the most dramatic rejection I've seen in Beijing of the Yuan-dynasty meridian, in which all construction faces due south. The white buildings are the Jianwai SOHO development, one of the most famous condo projects in Beijing. I spot a small gated garden with a brand-new playground of swings and climbing bars. Staring into one apartment, I can see a chandelier, fresh flowers, and a huge, red abstract painting on the living-room wall.

The road-construction crew is living, literally, in the shadow of Jianwai SOHO. At the foot of the towers are rows of shacks made of discarded, stained drywall. This is by nature a temporary neighborhood, existing only until the migrants move on to build the next expressway, the next office tower, the next airport. Just as the Mongol rulers forced the subjugated Han Chinese to live apart, economic imperatives now segregate the new coolies of Beijing. This is the Chinese City of the twenty-first century, a Chinatown within China. But unlike under the Mongols, this migrant settlement is just one of hundreds throughout Beijing.

Ben and I walk down a ramp to get a closer look. Some of the shanties are windowless. A few have old window frames crudely nailed into the drywall. Peeking into a gap in the wall, we see that the men sleep five or six to a room, on bunkbeds draped in soiled mosquito netting. Ragged laundry dries on improvised clotheslines. The toilets are a row of battered, filthy portables, plastic doors hanging askew. At a makeshift trough, two men fill plastic buckets to take back to their shanties. They are young, but their bodies are already worn out, their spines curved. One man is showering in his underpants on the street, straight from a hose, the icy artesian well water streaming down his back.

Not surprisingly, migrants account for a disproportionate number of China's infectious diseases. The U.S.-based *Journal of Infectious Diseases* estimates that they contract measles at nearly eight times the rate of permanent residents. With no access to public medicine, migrants rely on unlicensed clinics, which rarely report statistics to the government. The World Health Organization figures that one-third of tuberculosis and measles cases are never reported. Meanwhile, China still requires citizens to pay for routine childhood immunizations.

We come across more shanties, this time under the elevated highway, their residents wisely taking advantage of the shade and shelter. The hovels are evocative of George Orwell's 1933 classic *Down and Out in Paris and London*. The migrants work and save, and work and save, and some sleep literally under a bridge. Their dream is to return home as soon as they can, to the Yangtze River delta, the mountains of Jiangxi, the Loess Plateau of Gansu, the plains of Sichuan. With their nest eggs, they will open their own factory, restaurant or road-construction company.

So much for Chairman Mao. So much for decades of propaganda. In this self-described proletarian nation, everyone wants to be a blood-sucking capitalist. Yin was way ahead of her time.

10

Building Beijing

"I need to cancel," says Fu the Enforcer. She coughs loudly over the phone. "I have a fever. I have a terrible cold. You shouldn't come to my home. I don't want to get your two little treasures sick."

So there it is. I feel no surprise, only a mild letdown. This is vintage Fu. During the Cultural Revolution, the Communist Party had to approve any visit by a foreign student to a Chinese home. Scarlet went to the trouble to obtain permission for me and Erica to have dinner at her house. So did Erica's roommate. But even while Fu spent the year paying lip service to international friendship, she never once invited me, her one and only student, home. She always said her campus apartment was too small, too plain. That rejection resonated when I was a foreign correspondent and Tibet denied me a travel permit. Authorities sent back a telex explaining that Lhasa didn't have enough oxygen. (Fat Paycheck says that's actually true in the winter.)

"I will see you on Monday anyway," Fu continues. "Cadre Huang has invited me to your banquet."

"Okay, see you then," I say with false cheeriness.

Damn, damn, damn, I mutter after hanging up. Now I have to figure a way to get Fu alone so I can ask about Yin. But I'll worry about that later. Tonight, I'm meeting Future. Maybe he'll remember something about Yin.

Mao believed that everyone needed to do hard physical labor. Bad people needed to do it to become good people. Good people needed to do it to avoid becoming bad people. Half the time, I had the dorm room to myself because Scarlet was away with her class at an agricultural commune, a factory, a seaport or a military base. During the Cultural Revolution, Beijing University was one of Mao's ideological strongholds. After Red Guards like Fu the Enforcer nearly destroyed the university with factional fighting, Mao sent in a "Workers Propaganda Team." They came from the Beijing Number One Machine Tool Factory, one of six model work units intensely loyal to Mao. The Workers Propaganda Team effectively became the university's administration. It was still in charge when Erica and I arrived at Beijing University, so it was natural for them to send us to their own factory for a little thought reform.

In the spring of 1973, Fu the Enforcer accompanied me to the Number One Machine Tool Factory. Erica and her teacher, Dai Guiying, went too. For fifty days we operated lathes and pneumatic drills, counted screws and lived in dingy workers' dorms. Erica and I loved it. Well, we didn't like getting up at 6 a.m., and we hated counting the number of screws in a box, but we enjoyed substituting pneumatic drills for tonal ones. Originally a munitions factory, the Number One Machine Tool Factory was a sprawling collection of low-lying brick workshops on the remote east side of Beijing. In 1973 it was the industrial hinterland. In 2006 it is the heart of Beijing's up-and-coming Central Business District. The forest of angled white towers I saw from the half-completed elevated expressway *is* my old factory, or at least stands where it once stood.

"The Beijing Number One Machine Tool Factory is now Jianwai SOHO," says Qiu Hai, my cousin's cousin, who works in the SOHO complex. He knows where my factory's last surviving workshops are and has agreed to show me them during his lunch hour. "There's just a bit left of the factory," he warns.

SOHO is run by a power couple, Zhang Xin and her husband, Pan Shiyi. They're Beijing's answer to Donald Trump. Pan nearly agreed to a Chinese reality-television show that would have been produced by Mark Burnett, the *Apprentice* producer, but backed out after his wife, a former Wall Street investment banker, objected. The publicity-conscious couple look more like art dealers than condo developers. Zhang, who once worked in a Hong Kong sweatshop, admires left-wing British intellectuals. She wears Christian Lacroix and dyes an ash-blond streak in her short-cropped hair. She speaks English. He doesn't. Pan, a peasant's kid, grew up poor in Gansu province, the Chinese equivalent of growing up poor in the South Bronx. He believes in Taoism and wears avant-garde glasses and Prada suits—the genuine stuff, not Silk Market knock-offs. Like Trump, Zhang and Pan drive their sales force relentlessly. Every three months, they fire the bottom 10 percent of performers. To counter criticism, Pan has published a book, *Game of Survivor,* filled with their employees' inspirational rags-to-riches tales.

SOHO is an acronym for "small office, home office." With unerring instincts, Zhang and Pan have tapped into a post-Mao demand for functional design. The Jianwai condos are aimed straight at Beijing's affluent, hip cosmopolitans, many of whom own start-up companies. Three-fourths of the buyers are Chinese, mostly under thirty-five years old and often educated abroad. The condos have small bedrooms and large living rooms with sliding walls that allow easy conversion to a home office. At 70 to 200 square meters (about 750 to 2,150 square feet), they sell from $140,000 to $400,000. While most new condos are sold as concrete shells, SOHO's have fine wood finishes. Traditional boxy Beijing apartments are darkened by an enclosed balcony for storing junk. These condos have stunning floor-to-ceiling windows that flout an old Beijing regulation requiring them to start at least one yard above the floor. Initially some buyers complained of vertigo.

The couple own SOHO outright and are joint chief executives. He's the construction guy. She is the designer. To keep profit margins up, she vetoes granite, marble and stainless steel. "We used to buy so many things for buildings that were imported," she told *BusinessWeek* magazine. "Windows, toilets, air conditioners, flooring. Today less than 5 per cent of our materials are imported. All of these factories that used to be in Germany and in America are today in China. China is the factory of the world."

Pan was a nobody from a province so arid that the local peasants set rocks on the fields to retain moisture. His mother was an invalid, his father a political "rightist." Two of his sisters were given away at birth. Pan got his start speculating in real estate in Hainan, the chaotic, go-go island province euphemistically called "China's Hawaii." In the 1990s, he registered one of Beijing's first shareholding companies, Vantone Industry Ltd. It made a splash developing New World Plaza; the complex sold out—before construction began—at a record $7,800 a square meter.

Zhang's parents were overseas Chinese who fled Burma in the 1950s during the anti-Chinese riots. In Beijing they joined the Foreign Languages Bureau, where Fat Paycheck would later work. Zhang's parents joined rival factions during the Cultural Revolution and ended up divorcing. In 1980 she and her mother left for Hong Kong, where they found jobs in a garment factory. At fourteen, Zhang worked the day shift and went to school at night. Her teachers encouraged her to go to England after graduation. She got a secretarial job, and eventually earned a master's degree in economics from Cambridge. She ended up on Wall Street working for Goldman Sachs.

In 1994, on a flight back to Beijing, a homesick Zhang read a Vantone prospectus sent by a Cambridge classmate. Intrigued, she arranged a meeting. Pan proposed four days later. In 1995, he left Vantone and founded SOHO with Zhang. Now in their forties, they have two sons, born in 1999 and 2001. Perversely for the offspring of developers, the boys' names, Rang and Shao, mean "Concede" and "Less."

In 1999, their company got a tremendous boost when the Chinese government enacted the country's first mortgage law. Spurred by the Asian financial crisis, authorities wanted to stimulate domestic consumption. SOHO New Town, the company's first major project, was nearing completion. After the mortgage law passed, Beijingers lined up through the night and snapped up all two thousand residential units. In an industry rife with corruption, bribery and fraud, the image-conscious couple have managed to keep their reputations clean. In recent years, SOHO has either ranked first in sales or has paid more taxes than any other Chinese real estate company, and has accounted for more than half the real estate sales, by revenue, in the Central Business District.

Zhang and Pan's projects are typically huge in scope and ambitious in design. SOHO Shangdu, designed by maverick Australian architect Peter Davidson, is an office and shopping complex of two fractal-geometric towers. Rising like icebergs in the Central Business District, it will have 450 shops, 5 sunken gardens and 270 furnished offices. Another SOHO project won a prize at the 2002 Venice Biennale. The development, Commune by the Great Wall, is as much an icon for Beijing as the Guggenheim Museum is for New York. The couple gave carte blanche and one million dollars each to a dozen Asian architects. The result: twelve fanciful villas on a wooded slope with priceless views of the Great Wall. One is built of laminated bamboo, another of rammed earth. Originally intended as weekend homes for Beijing's new rich, they have become part of a complex that includes a boutique hotel, a convention center and a tourist attraction.

Jianwai SOHO is their most ambitious project. Designed by Japanese architect Riken Yamamoto, it consists of three hundred shops and twenty towers, each with a rooftop garden. Like other SOHO projects, it sold out before completion. At the opening gala, Zhang and Pan threw a dinner in a huge white tent for five hundred guests. The entertainment included dancers from South America performing a steamy tango. That was followed by a fashion show—make that a fashion *xiu*—of models dressed in Valentino and draped in Bulgari jewels.

As Qiu Hai and I walk through the SOHO development, he points out that deliveries are made through the network of underground garages. I duck inside to check one out. The garage is staffed by uniformed attendants and full-time cleaners.

There are free, immaculate public washrooms. It seems so civilized and feels so un-Beijing. The angled towers are connected by a dazzling white plaza humanized by curved footpaths and newly planted trees. It is shockingly pleasant to walk upon smooth, clean concrete without risking death by speeding car.

"The guy who owns this is the richest man in Beijing," says Qiu Hai without rancor or envy. Looking up, I notice another example of the ingenuity gap. The buildings are all numbered—in a huge font—at the *top*. Pedestrians can figure out which tower they want to go to without studying a schematic map or walking up to each front door.

Qiu Hai is part of China's baby-boom generation, born just after the Communist victory. The Cultural Revolution disrupted his schooling. Like millions of youths, he joined the Red Guards and was subsequently sent among the peasants to do hard labor. Eventually he attended university and even went to England to study packaging technology. In the early 1990s, eager to escape his state-owned factory, he asked me if I knew of any joint ventures that might hire someone like him. About the same time, my friend Ben Mok asked if I knew of any reliable, educated Chinese technicians. It was a match. Ben hired Qiu Hai as a manager in Coca-Cola's Hangzhou bottling plant. Qiu worked there fifteen years before taking early retirement to move closer to his elderly parents. Now he works in Beijing for a Chinese beverage company.

Suddenly the clean white concrete ends and we hit a dusty alley bordered by temporary brick walls, slapped together with leaking mortar. "There it is," says Qiu Hai, pointing to the remnants of two vast red brick factory workshops. "The factory has been split up in many parts. Some divisions have relocated to

Tongzhou and Shunyi counties. This area will eventually be made into green space, but the city hasn't paid for it yet. That's why these workshops haven't been torn down."

The workshops look as though they have survived a bombing raid. The windows are dusty and cracked. The roof on one side is falling in. A young man is sitting outside the entrance at a small table, doing absolutely nothing. Behind him, pasted to the door, is a sign in Chinese: "No visitors allowed after July 15, 2006." A Canadian would just sigh and walk away. A Chinese assumes the rules are made for others. That is how citizens carry on in a nation of rules. That is how they survived years of Communist dictatorship.

"Master, we just want to take a quick look," says Qiu Hai, invoking the respectful honorific apprentices use to address their mentors. He points to me. "She worked here at this factory many years ago. We won't be long." At fifty-five, Qiu Hai is old enough to be the guard's father, so the young man is quite pleased by his deference.

"Sure, go ahead," he says, waving us in.

The workshop is strewn with rubble, rotting garbage, dirty foam lunch boxes, plastic bags and a torn brown vinyl chair. Memories flood back. I can see the lithe, beautiful young women of the Iron Women's Team who taught me to use a pneumatic drill. I can see anxious-looking Master Liu who taught me how to operate a lathe. I can almost hear the workers at lunchtime in the canteen. They helped my Mandarin take a great leap forward. By eavesdropping on the guys in front of me in line, I picked up vocabulary that Fu the Enforcer had neglected to teach me: (a) *wangba dan*, "bastard," literally a turtle's egg; (b) *ta ma de*, literally "his mother's," which become fighting words if you dare to say *ni ma de*, "*your* mother's," the exact meaning of which becomes clear with; (c) *cao ni ma de bi*—"fuck your mother's cunt."

If I look hard, I can see traces of the old factory. There are the metal tracks in the floor for the carts that transported the cast-iron machine cases we drilled. There is the cement trough where we washed the brown grease off our hands with coarse yellow soap and bits of rags when the lunch bell rang. I can still make out a few fading slogans high on the walls, something about safety and quality. Only one is still legible, and it's not even from the Mao era. It says, "Establish a marketplace mentality. Earnestly strive to produce quality exports."

Suddenly I see curious faces peering at me through holes in the grimy drywall. One end of the workshop has been boarded up for housing. "Migrant workers live here," Qiu Hai says. "But only until it gets torn down." Perhaps they are the migrants building the SOHO condos. Or perhaps they are part of the road-construction crew. I can't decide which is better—sleeping under a bridge or in a decaying workshop. As I part ways with Qiu Hai and head back to my apartment, I think how strange it is that Beautiful Lodging is just two blocks away from my proletarian past.

I'm having dinner tonight with Future. My classmate changed his phone number, but at least he didn't move. I'd been to his apartment seven years earlier, when I'd gone to Beijing with Robin Benger, the documentary filmmaker. But the city has changed so much that if Future hadn't given me precise directions, I would never have found it again.

"I live in CBD," he says, in Chinese.

"Where?" I ask.

"*CBD.* You don't know CBD?"

It takes me a moment to figure out that Future, who doesn't speak English, is referring to the Central Business District by its trendy English initials. To my surprise, he lives a couple of blocks from Jianwai SOHO, and about six long blocks from Beautiful Lodging. If it weren't so hot and polluted, I would walk to his home. Instead I take a taxi, which, of course, just worsens the pollution.

When he first moved here, this was still the hinterland. But Future stayed put, and the future caught up to him. The old Beijing never had a business district because there was no business. Now it needs all kinds of financial services to accompany China's entry into the World Trade Organization. Future is waiting for me in the *hutong* outside his apartment. When I ask why he has a new phone number, he says the volume of residential lines increased so rapidly that the city had to create new exchanges. Then, a few years ago, Beijing went to eight-digit phone numbers. "The whole neighborhood had to change phone numbers."

To test my theory about Chinese phone books, I ask if he is listed. He shakes his head. "I'm not in there. There's no point." His hair, always cropped in a brush cut, is flecked with gray. His thick glasses are as unfashionable as ever. But he's never lost his joie de vivre, his curiosity, his enthusiasm for new things. Before we go inside his compound, he stops and points northward. "Soon there will be three hundred skyscrapers built there. It's going to be like Manhattan," he says.

The CBD will have seven huge malls, including a Wal-Mart. City forecasters say the CBD will eventually be home to 70 percent of foreign offices, 65 percent of white-collar workers, 90 percent of foreign banks and eight of Beijing's ten largest hotels. "That's the new Central Chinese Television tower," he says, pointing to a worksite in the distance. The CCTV tower, rising on the site of a military motorcycle factory, is one of Beijing's most controversial projects. When completed, it will house ten thousand employees and be second in area only to the Pentagon, the world's largest office building. Designed by OMA, the Dutch firm founded by architect Rem Koolhaas, it will consist of two vertiginous skyscrapers, bridged at top and bottom into a gravity-defying trapezoid. The top link will be Beijing's own aerial Arc de Triomphe, a ten-story L-shaped acrobatic overhang more than forty storeys above ground.

The lead architect, Ole Scheeren, is a thirty-something German best known for designing Prada stores in New York, Los Angeles and San Francisco. Some critics fear that he may lack the chops for building in an earthquake zone—in defiance of all existing building codes. "It's the safest big building in China, if not the world," Scheeren has told Chinese reporters. He noted that Chinese engineers have reviewed the plans. He also acknowledged that such a structure could not have been attempted anywhere except Beijing.

I count fourteen building cranes on the site. The CCTV headquarters is one of a dozen megaprojects, any one of which would sap the resources of a city in the West. Beijing is building them all simultaneously, along with new expressways, subways, light rail lines and the airport. All cities pledge new venues, of course, when they win an Olympic bid. But no other city has ever completely remade itself the way Beijing is doing for the 2008 Summer Olympics. Such a transformation could be rammed through only by a government that does not fear being punished by voters. The megaprojects, all symbols of the regime's might, are timed for Beijing's international debut. In 1949, Mao proclaimed, "The Chinese people have stood up."

Now they are strutting the world stage, in the architectural equivalent of diamonds and furs.

"My apartment building will be torn down in two or three years," Future says, as we walk into his brick apartment building. He doesn't sound unhappy. He expects his work unit, the Chinese Academy of Social Sciences, to provide him with new, better housing elsewhere, presumably funded by the sale of this now extremely valuable piece of CBD real estate.

He lives at the top, on the sixth floor, and the building has no elevator. We climb the stairs, stamping our feet to turn on the stairwell lights. (To conserve energy, there are no switches, only sound-activated timed lights.) Amid our stomping, I hear someone practicing scales. Like Chinese overseas, many Beijingers want their children to play the piano, now that classical music is no longer condemned as bourgeois. Future says piano sales are booming. The *New York Times* estimates there are 30 million piano students and 10 million violin students in China, which now dominates world production of pianos, violins and guitars.

Future's previous home was in a traditional Beijing courtyard. He, his wife and their daughter squeezed into a single room with no privacy and no room for his books. His wife developed insomnia. The kitchen was a lean-to. Water had to be fetched from a tap they shared with more than fifty neighbors. So this, their current apartment, was a dream come true. It has three rooms—a real bedroom, a tandem study and a kitchen with a countertop. The hallway doubled as their daughter's bedroom, but for the first time, the family had a sink and toilet of their own. Future was so happy he spent thousands of yuan installing bookshelves.

Six flights is exhausting in the heat. When we finally reach Future's apartment, I am shocked. His apartment, which seemed so grand eleven years ago, looks ancient. The kitchen is dingy and cramped. The treasured bathroom reeks, oddly, of cabbage. "We use dirty kitchen water to flush," Future explains. "Beijing is very short of water."

I'm mystified how it could have deteriorated so fast. Then I realize the apartment didn't change—Beijing changed. Nowadays, no one thinks a great apartment is one where you use the hallway as a spare bedroom. A great apartment has floor-to-ceiling windows and a pristine underground garage.

Like my cousin's cousin, Future joined the Red Guards when he was in high school. Every single teenager did in those days, unless they were the offspring of the village landlord or of a Kuomintang general. When the education system collapsed, Future was sent to the countryside to work. Later he was accepted at Beijing University, where I met him during my second stint. (After a year studying Mandarin with Fu the Enforcer, I returned to Canada for my final year at McGill. After graduating in 1974, I abandoned my Maoist ambition to take over the Chinese Students Society with Ben Mok, and went back to China on a Canadian government scholarship.)

Future and I enrolled in the same three-year degree program, majoring in Chinese history. In 1975, I voluntarily joined my classmates for eight months of hard labor at a farm south of Beijing. We planted rice, wheat, peanuts, eggplant and tomatoes. We built our own brick dormitories, mixing cement by hand and pounding the dirt floors with an old tree stump. Future, one of the few kids in my new class willing to risk contact with me, became one of my closest friends. He often asked me about the West. But, unlike Yin, he never expressed any desire to leave China. He was merely curious about the outside world—a curiosity that led him to collect stamps.

Naturally, I gave Future the stamps from my mother's letters. I did not realize this was dangerous. A classmate snitched on Future to Pan Qingde, a junior faculty member only a couple of years older than we were. Pan didn't actually teach us. He was a Marxist watchdog whose full-time job was monitoring our ideological purity. He was priggish, humorless and strict. His name, Qingde, meant "Celebrating Virtue." My classmates so disliked him that, behind his back, they called him Quede, a Confucian curse that meant "Lacking Virtue."

"It's reactionary to put a queen on a stamp," Lacking Virtue Pan berated Future. "Reactionary" was not a word anyone used lightly. Reactionaries could be shot. *Well, Canada can't exactly use Chairman Mao on its stamps*, Future wanted to retort, but he kept that thought to himself. Reasoning that he was going to get an undesirable assignment to punish him for collecting stamps, Future boldly volunteered for a hardship post in Tibet. No one else in our class did. Taking advantage of this moral high ground, he applied for Party membership and was accepted.

Future wasn't insincere or opportunistic. He believed in the moral code of a Communist Party member—selflessness, an end to exploitation, equality of the sexes. He was also genuinely curious about Tibet. He was assigned a job as a high school teacher in Lhasa, where he stayed eight years. After his Tibetan adventure, he was transferred to the Modern History Institute in Beijing, where he is now a researcher and archivist.

While we wait for his wife to arrive home from work, I ask Future if he knew Yin. "I heard about her," he says. "I never knew her. She was expelled before I arrived at Beijing University."

He reminds me that expulsion wasn't unusual. "Lots of people were kicked out," he says. "You could get expelled for all kinds of reasons." He mentions a student in another department who masqueraded as the son of a senior Communist Party official. The ruse got him girlfriends, loans, chauffeured cars and free meals—until he was caught. Future notes that our own class president, a soldier, was expelled for seducing a classmate. The cad had promised to get her accepted into the Communist Party if she had sex with him. When he failed to fulfill his end of the bargain, she ratted him out.

I tell Future what I did to Yin.

"So you feel *nei jiu*," he says kindly. I don't understand the term. He grabs a dictionary and flips to the right spot. "Guilty conscience," the entry reads.

I nod. "I want to find her to apologize. But I don't think I'll ever find her."

He considers the situation. "I guess there are many possibilities as to what happened to her," he says slowly. "She might have returned to her village or factory. If she had no other big problems, this would not have been a matter of life or death. And after 1976 she would have been all right," he says, referring to the year of Mao's death and the official end of the Cultural Revolution.

After 1976 she would have been all right. Perhaps Future is right. Or perhaps he's just trying to make me feel better. People in China understand there is no easy solution to all the wrongs of the Cultural Revolution. Some things just aren't reversible. But his words do not comfort me at all. He doesn't know for sure what happened—he's merely providing a plausible scenario. I was hoping Future would know something more specific. He thinks for a moment.

"After 1977, she could have applied again to university," he says. "There were lots of thirty-year-olds who went to school at that time. Lots of university students had children. And later there was no restriction on going abroad. Anything is possible."

When I sigh, he tries to reassure me. "This was merely a contradiction among the people," he reminds me, using the Maoist terminology we're both so familiar with. "If it wasn't, they would have shot her." He pretends his hand is a gun, and pulls the trigger. Seeing my downcast face, he says, "I'll ask around the office, see if anyone there knows what happened to her." Then he frowns. He forgot he'll be working at home for the next few days. His building, naturally, is under construction.

"No one is going to the office these days. We're changing all the windows. We're renovating the whole building."

11

Neither of Us Can Handle
the Twenty-First Century

Tao Jie at the All-China Journalists Federation has tracked down Scarlet and asked her to call me.

"Bright Precious!" she screams. (I missed out on the revolutionary names. Being three generations in Canada, my parents gave me a traditional, girly one, which I never used until I arrived in China.)

"Scarlet!" I scream back.

"Bright Precious! Where are you?"

"Where are *you*?" I can't help retorting.

Since we last met, it turns out she has moved five times and changed her phone number even more often.

"You would never have found me," she says, laughing. She sounds wonderful, happier and more confident than when we were at university together. We make a date to meet in four days. But I don't want to wait until then to ask about Yin. I remind Scarlet about her, and ask if she knows anything.

"I think she was from Dongbei," she says hesitantly, using Manchuria's unpoetic name, the Northeast. Well, that narrows it down to just three provinces with a combined population of

100 million. Scarlet is calling from her new home number. When I ask for her cellphone number, too, she confesses she has changed it so often, she can't remember it. She says she'll call me right back on it, and then I'll know. We hang up. My phone rings again.

"So what's my number?" she says. I look blankly at my Chinese cellphone, which Ben keeps trying to teach me how to use.

"I can't tell," I admit.

Scarlet sighs. "Neither of us can handle the twenty-first century."

"Why does every street look the same in Beijing?" Sam asks. He's right. Everything looks homogeneous. It's one reason I keep getting lost. When I ponder his question, I realize the entire city is being rebuilt at the same time. Yuan-dynasty visitors probably had the same problem after Kublai Khan redid the capital. On one half-hour taxi ride through the city, I tally each building crane, which some wag has called the national bird of China. I count thirty on sixteen sites, and that's only from my side of the taxi.

Normal cities evolve over time. They have old districts and new ones, landmark heritage buildings and modern plazas. But Beijing's high-rise condos and office towers are clones, cookie-cutter designs all constructed at the same time. They are as homogeneous as Toronto's soulless suburbs, where it helps to remember the color of your garage door in order to make it home. Confusion abounds, too, because Beijing's skyscrapers tend to have similar names. "Can we come up with some new names for buildings?" complains Kathy Wilhelm, the American lawyer. "Everything is 'Trade Center,' 'Finance Center,' 'International' this and 'World' that."

Paradoxically, in the midst of this mind-numbing sameness, Beijing is commissioning some of the world's flashiest architecture. Ancient Rome had the Coliseum, and modern Beijing has a gigantic Swiss-designed Olympic Stadium. Besides Koolhaas's radically vertiginous CCTV headquarters, there's the National Aquatics Center by global design firm Arup and, just west of Tiananmen Square, the National Grand Theater by French architect Paul Andreu. Critics say the theater's gigantic titanium dome resembles the mounded tomb of the great Qin Emperor. That's a bad omen, considering the Qin dynasty barely outlasted him. In the *Records of the Historian,* written between 109 BC and 91 BC, the imperial grand historian Sima Qian recorded the construction of the Qin Emperor's tomb: "They dug through three subterranean streams and poured molten copper for models of palaces, pavilions and officials . . . Artisans were ordered to affix crossbows so that any thief breaking in would be shot. All the country's streams, the Yellow River and the Yangtze, were reproduced in quicksilver and by some mechanical means made to flow."

Qin Shihuang's tomb held 8,000 life-sized terra-cotta warriors and horses. The opera house will seat 6,500. Like the emperor's tomb (and the Opéra Garnier in Paris, made famous in the musical *Phantom of the Opera*), Beijing's new opera house is set on an artificial lake. Concert-goers must enter and exit through a subterranean hallway. Mockingly dubbed "The Egg," "The Blob" or "The Tomb," it has been criticized as unsafe in an earthquake zone. (The criticism grew louder after the roof on an Andreu-designed airport terminal in Paris collapsed in 2004, killing four. An inquiry blamed a variety of technical causes and the lack of margins of safety in the design. Andreu blamed poor execution by the builders.)

For all its rules and repression, Beijing attracts its fair share of eccentrics. Alfred Peng is a mercurial Chinese Canadian. He's the one who offered to meet us at the airport and never showed. In the 1980s, he quit his Toronto architectural practice and moved to Beijing, where he founded Great Earth Architects and Engineers International. He also got a professorship teaching architecture at Qinghua University, China's premier science school. A flamboyant man, Alfred used to cruise around Beijing in an ancient Mercedes-Benz limo that once belonged to his dad, a Kuomintang general who fled to Taiwan with Chiang Kai-shek. When Alfred's students joined the hunger strikers in 1989, he donned a white lab coat favored by Chinese doctors and dashed down to Tiananmen Square. Waving a Red Cross flag, he theatrically rescued students as they fainted, and even when they didn't. He also came to my rescue in the days following the massacre, lending me his limo after the police stole my car and I needed to slip onto the Qinghua campus. The guards, recognizing Alfred's Benz, waved me through.

Alfred has offered us an architectural tour of Beijing. I accepted, partly because I'm curious to see what he makes of the international invasion of swashbuckling celebrity "starchitects." I know he won't be shy about expressing his opinions. He never is. He's the kind of source who'd call me at two in the morning to continue an earlier conversation, even if I was obviously half asleep. We're meeting at the Panda Circle, a roundabout north of the Drum Tower, exactly on the meridian that slices through the heart of Beijing. Alfred has given me his license-plate number and told me to look for a black Mercedes-Benz. On the way there, we pass one of his 1990s buildings, the China Travel Service Hotel. Like Future's home, it hasn't stood the test of time. It is clad in unfortunate white bathroom tiles, which were an upscale material at the time. The building's corners, which Alfred designed to look like traditional pagodas, now seem kitschy next to all the modern skyscrapers.

When we arrive at Panda Circle, there is, alas, no sign of Alfred. The boys are wilting in the heat. We stand in the shade of a scholar tree to wait, the only entertainment the low-priced civic help. At bus stops all over the city, middle-aged citizens are hired to flag down buses, keep orderly queues and hustle passengers aboard as fast as possible. At intersections, even ones with traffic lights, they are paid to act as crossing guards.

At this roundabout, I watch the cyclists and pedestrians accumulate. Suddenly the crossing guard flaps his little red flag, blows his whistle and edges gingerly out into the road. Six lanes of traffic ignore him. He waves his flag more frantically. Another crossing guard on the other side does the same. Ours inches out until he finally reaches the middle of a lane. Only then do the cars screech to a halt, and the pedestrians and cyclists race across.

The traffic wardens wear blue caps and khaki shirts emblazoned with red characters: "Traffic Cooperation Administrator." When ours is safely back on the sidewalk, I take advantage of the brief lull to ask him what he did before. He tells me his name is Zhang Yang and he's in his fifties. He was a steelworker until authorities forced his company, Capital Steel, out of Beijing to reduce pollution. The traffic job supplements his monthly pension of 900 yuan ($115).

"What can you do if cars don't stop?" I ask.

"When I put the flag down, cars have to stop," he says, as if trying to convince himself. "If they don't, I report the license plate to the police. It's the same for cyclists. They have to listen to me."

To demonstrate his incredible power, he flaps his little red flag at a lone female cyclist. "Go ahead," he tells her. "Cross." She hesitates because it is apparent he has no intention of stopping traffic for one person.

"C'mon. Hurry up," he barks, conscious that I'm watching. "Move it."

The cyclist looks dubious. He yells at her again. "Go!" Reluctantly, she hops on her bike. When there's a momentary gap, she darts like a dragonfly across six lanes of traffic.

I hear Alfred before I see him. A disembodied voice booms in English, "Jan Wong! Jan Wong!" A sleek Mercedes-Benz swoops into view. Alfred appears to be shouting at me over a public-address system built into his car. It's the same kind of loud-hailer Chinese traffic cops use to berate the populace. Alfred isn't driving his dad's old Mercedes. He's in a new, black S-Class 320, worth about $100,000. The crossing guard is suitably impressed, even though Alfred has stopped illegally in the middle of Panda Circle. The guard smiles and flaps his flag in a friendly manner.

Always dapper, Alfred is wearing a straw fedora, a white button-down shirt, aviator sunglasses and Dockers khaki pants. He's forty minutes late but doesn't apologize. As for his no-show at the airport, he says airily, "I forgot. You have to remind me." We glide off and Alfred starts barking in Mandarin into his microphone. "Cyclist! Get out of my way." He pushes a button, and a police siren sounds, *Oooh, oooh, ooh*. Alfred beams. Ben and Sam are thrilled.

"The Traffic Administration Committee gave the siren and loudspeaker to me," he says. "They hired me as a consultant. I said that should cost 200,000 Canadian dollars. They said they couldn't afford it, so they gave me this device instead." Each year, Alfred tells me he invites the Traffic Administration Committee to a lavish banquet. "Then they give me the secret code so I can hack into their computer and delete all my outstanding traffic violations," he says, cackling.

He pulls up across from an unsightly mall. Behind it are kitschy reproductions of Burmese and Thai temples. Alfred jumps out to take a photograph. "It's built by the son of Municipal Party Secretary Bai," he says angrily. "This is prime real estate, right near the Olympic site. The land was supposed to be zoned for green space, not commercial."

When he was virtually the only foreign architect in Beijing, the authorities listened to him. They appreciated that Alfred had thrown in his lot with China. But now that the country has money to burn, it's giving the showiest, richest commissions to the biggest names in architecture, all foreigners. The new Great Leap leaves Alfred struggling to be heard. He has urged Beijing, for instance, to move its municipal government out of the ancient city core. Within the Second Ring Road, Beijing's density—its plot ratio—is nearly double that of historic European cities. "It's a disaster in the event of biological warfare, or a SARS epidemic," Alfred says.

A short man, powerfully built, at sixty-three he has an endless reservoir of energy. He has organized petitions against the architectural madness descending on the city. He makes public speeches and writes letters to the *New York Times* (which they don't publish). In his view, foreign architects are seducing China with wasteful, egomaniacal buildings that would never pass muster in their own countries. The new opera house, he sputters, is an inexcusable extravagance. "China's per capita GDP is less than one-fifth that of the U.S., yet the theater is costing four times as much as Lincoln Center."

Ask Alfred about the CCTV building, and he erupts. "*Zhao si* [courting death]," he snorts. "Beijing is in an eighth-degree seismic zone. A cantilevered building with a seventy-meter overhang—Europe won't do it." He glances at my notebook. "Write that down," he orders.

Under Mao, China was xenophobic; now it worships the West. "The foreign moon is rounder than the Chinese moon," says Alfred contemptuously, reciting an aphorism that sums up China's national inferiority complex. He likens the boom in out-there architecture to haute couture shows in Paris. "Nobody actually wears the stuff. That's what these buildings are like. They're not practical. They're just show-off buildings. They're very pretentious, ostentatious. They cater to the instant-rich mentality. In Boston, the Big Dig is trying to cover up the expressway. Here they light them up like Christmas trees." Alfred is right, literally. As a latecomer to the Auto Age, China is so enamored of its roads that it festoons new expressways with mauve, blue, red or white lights. At night the city looks like a giant video game.

He wants to pick up a colleague, a Chinese American structural engineer who is working with him on a museum in Shandong province. Michael Liao, who is seventy, has built many big stadiums in North America, including the Carrier Dome in Syracuse, New York; the Pontiac Silverdome Stadium in Pontiac, Michigan; BC Place Stadium in Vancouver, Canada;

and the Hoosier Dome (now the RCA Dome) in Indianapolis, Indiana. With Michael sitting in front and Norman crammed in the back seat with Ben, Sam and me, Alfred heads for the Olympic Stadium. Nicknamed the "Bird's Nest" for its twiglike latticework, Beijing's Olympic Stadium is one of the most dramatic sports venues in the world.

"We call it the Instant Noodle Stadium," says Alfred sarcastically. "Write that down."

It is the creation of Swiss architects Jacques Herzog and Pierre de Meuron, the 2001 Pritzker Architecture Prize laureates famous for converting a London power plant into the Tate Modern. The Olympic Stadium, which seats 100,000, was originally projected to cost 3.5 billion yuan (450 million U.S.). That price was halved after the Politburo, finally concerned about costs, scrapped plans for a retractable roof. The Olympic site is due north of the Forbidden City, but the Swiss architects have pushed the stadium off to the east. Alfred is deeply offended that it defiles the meridian laid out by Yuan-dynasty planners nine centuries ago. "The central axis has been violated," he declares angrily. "Write that down."

The Olympic Stadium site is closed to visitors. At the gate, Alfred flicks on his siren and haughtily points to the pass on his windshield. It's apparently issued by China's State Council, equivalent to the U.S. Cabinet. I'm impressed. The guard actually salutes as we glide by.

"I forged it," says Alfred, chortling. "It's counterfeit." In the back seat, the boys exchange glances.

Alfred parks his gleaming car beside a pit of brackish water filled with rotting fruit and leftover take-out food. The workers must use it as the garbage dump. Sam holds his nose. Alfred hands his digital camera to Michael and orders him to take a photo of us. He does. "Take our picture again," Alfred orders.

We watch eight cranes hoisting steel bars up to a small army of welders. They cling, like ants on a melon, to the curved exterior of the stadium. Michael says that the Bird's Nest should have required additional steel. "When I first saw the design, I thought they would have to use 100 percent extra steel. But they glued it together. Welding is like glue," he says, frowning. "You don't glue a structure like this together. It's not the right way to save money."

Alfred agrees. "They were going to use 136,000 tons of steel, but there were too many protests. I signed the petition. Now they are down to 80,000 tons." He glances at my notebook. "Write that down," he orders.

Next he wants to show us the construction site of the National Aquatics Center, the largest Olympic swimming venue ever built. Again he flicks on his siren, points to his forged pass and zooms past the guard. Nicknamed "the Water Cube," the Aquatics Center will look like a giant box of blue bubbles when it's finished. The transparent cladding, a tough, recyclable membrane known as ETFE, or ethylene-tetrafluoroethylene, weighs only 1 percent what an equivalent-sized piece of glass would. The bubbles will turn the building—the first of its kind in the world—into a greenhouse. Twenty percent of the trapped solar energy will heat its five pools, including one the size of six Olympic pools.

"This architecturally is fine," says Michael.

"It looks like you're in an architectural supplies junkyard," Alfred sniffs. He takes a few photos and then orders Michael to take more pictures of us. Back in the car, Alfred flicks on his siren and zooms through the construction site. "This is how I keep myself young," he says, laughing. As he pulls onto the Third Ring Road, he berates some cyclists struggling in the heat. They're blocking his way. Ahead, a compact car is hogging the passing lane. Perhaps it's the driver's first day on the road; he is oblivious when Alfred starts tailgating him. "If you're not driving fast, get out of the fast lane," Alfred shouts through the loudspeaker. The man meanders along. Alfred shouts some more. The man glances back and, visibly startled, switches lanes. Alfred whizzes past.

At the parking lot to Alfred's office, a guard in a red beret salutes and lifts the barrier. Then he obsequiously and rather comically jogs alongside us to point out an obvious parking space. Alfred ignores him. Great Earth is organized into semi-independent design studios employing nearly seven hundred people. Alfred says he tolerates a moderate amount of corruption as a fact of doing business in Beijing. "If water is too clean, there are no fish," he explains, quoting another Chinese proverb. As chairman of the board and chief architect, his job is quality control and trawling for commissions. The walls of his private office display photos of him with top Chinese leaders, which is as good as money in the bank. It means you have connections and clout.

By Alfred's decree, the entire office is smoke-free, unusual for China. Once he caught someone smoking in a cubicle. "I threw the ashtrays out the seventh-floor window," he says proudly. Ben and Sam are goggle-eyed. Seeing how impressed they are, he adds, "I once grabbed a guy in the elevator who was trying to smoke." He demonstrates his throttling technique. The boys giggle nervously. I make a mental note to bring Alfred the next time we shoot pool at Sci-Tech.

"Feel my muscles," he demands, proffering a forearm. We all dutifully poke. "Feel my calf," he says. Only Ben touches his leg, sheepishly. "I play basketball twice a week at Qinghua University," Alfred boasts. "I can jump so high I can stuff the baskets."

On our way out, he spots the parking attendant. Without so much as a "May I?" Alfred adjusts the red beret on the young man's head. "You should tilt it like this," he advises. The boys are exhausted by this outsized personality. But the day is young, and Alfred has more architectural follies on his guided tour. He pops a Johnny Rogers country music cassette into the tape deck and drives up the road to what pundits call the Great Mall of China. At 5.8 million square feet, the New Yansha Mall claims to be the world's biggest, eclipsing Canada's West Edmonton Mall, which held the record for two decades at 5.3 million square feet. It takes Fat Paycheck and me a moment to realize the mall is on the former site of the Evergreen People's Agricultural Commune, one of the farms we used to bike past on our way from Beijing University into the city.

Alfred pulls into the parking garage, which has four levels, holds ten thousand cars and is utterly empty. Inside the mall, clerks outnumber shoppers. "Why would anyone build a mall like this?" I ask Michael.

"They don't do a feasibility study or a marketing analysis," he says. "They got a lot of money and they don't know what to do with it, so they build a mall. I heard of a former policeman who started an express-parcel service and sold it to FedEx for 4.1 billion yuan [about $530 million U.S.]. What kind of investment decision do you think he'll make?"

"But who are the developers?" I persist.

Alfred says one was Huang Rulin, a real estate mogul from coastal Fujian province. The other was Jia Qinglin, the former Communist Party secretary of Beijing, a former head of Fujian province and currently the fourth most powerful official in China. Alfred says that they obtained the prime land in a sweetheart deal. Despite widespread allegations of corruption, Jia remains in power. He's a member of the ruling Politburo standing committee and chairman of the Chinese People's Political Consultative Conference. I later find out that his protector is Jiang Zemin, the former Party chief, who considers him like a son. A few years back, Jia's wife, a powerful trade official in Fujian province, fell under suspicion in a multi-billion-dollar smuggling case involving Lai Changxing, the most wanted man in China (who took refuge in Vancouver). Jia divorced his wife—until the furor died down. She has always protested her innocence, and no charges were ever brought. The divorce has since been "annulled."

Alfred tells us he recently had dinner at this mall. After, when he went to his car, he found the parking-garage doors locked. "I got mad," he says, spinning around to snap a picture of the empty garage. "One kick. I broke the door."

A security guard in a fluorescent orange safety vest glides by on a bicycle. He is startled to see us there, taking photographs and gabbing loudly. From his slack-jawed stare, I assume he's a migrant worker. Alfred opens the car door and grabs his microphone. "What are you looking at?" he shouts angrily through the mike. The disembodied voice confuses the guard, who freezes.

"Get out of here!" Alfred says dismissively.

We all pile back in the car. Alfred drives to the Fourth Ring Road. This time a black Audi with military plates blocks the passing lane. Enraged, Alfred flicks on his microphone. "Hey! You don't know how to drive an army car! Get off to the side!" he yells.

"He'll get out a machine gun," Michael says mildly.

"I have an Uzi in the glove compartment," says Alfred.

I laugh, but Sam's eyes are like saucers. He nudges me and shows me something he's found in the seat pocket in front of him. It's a knife, six inches long, with a serrated blade.

Now Alfred is flashing his high beams. He's turned on his caution lights. The red emergency light on his dashboard is revolving. The siren is wailing. "Army car! Army car! Get out of the way," he shouts into his loudspeaker. The Audi finally notices us. Insolently, it slows down. I wait for a gun battle to erupt. Michael falls silent. Sam ducks in the back seat. Norman lifts an eyebrow. Suddenly the army vehicle finds an opening in the traffic ahead and roars off.

A few minutes later, we pull into Qinghua. Like Beijing University, Qinghua is plagued by tourists. It tried banning them, but after a public outcry, it now resorts to keeping crowds down by charging twelve yuan per person for tour buses. Alfred feels personally affronted by the rubbernecking tourists. When a driver stops to consult a map, blocking the road, Alfred grabs his mike. "This car from Henan province," he shouts, reading the license plate. "Get out of here! You're on university property. Obey the rules. Hurry up!"

He points to the side of the road. "See those signs?" he says proudly. "They're my doing. It means no one can park along this street." He resumes hectoring the car in front of us. "Get moving! What are you doing!? Silver car!" he shouts, like a Maoist Red Guard. "If you want to stop, go to a parking lot."

We're supposed to have dinner with Alfred, but Ben and Sam have reached their limit. I pretend to be maternal so I can escape too, and take the boys home. Fat Paycheck, who has been exceedingly patient, looks relieved when I suggest a raincheck. We part ways with Alfred and Michael. After a whole afternoon with the crazy Canuck architect, I want to go rest up—tomorrow is the banquet at Beijing University.

Besides, I'm ready for a drink. Actually, Ben and Sam are. For all its rules, all the restrictions, all the nasty totalitarianism, China has *no drinking age.* After we arrive home, the boys rush into the 7-Eleven to buy coolers. While they watch a pirated Disney DVD, *The Wild,* Sam knocks back a Bacardi Breeze rum cooler. Ben drinks a peach-flavored vodka cooler. I'm a bad mom. All I say is, "Can I have a sip?"

12

Seeing Flowers from
a Galloping Horse

At 11 a.m. I cut the boys' Mandarin lesson short. I hustle them and Fat Paycheck out the door and into a red taxi. I'm a bundle of nerves. It's August 14, and we have to be at Beijing University at noon. We can't be late, both for reasons of protocol and because this meeting will be crucial. Future's suggestion that Yin is probably okay hasn't reassured me at all. I think he's just trying to make me feel better.

All my old adversaries—Cadre Huang, Fu the Enforcer and whoever else they can muster—will be at the banquet. There will be no better chance to discover what befell Yin and where she is now. After two weeks of getting nowhere, I'm impatient. And yet I'm dreading the meeting too. Maybe ignorance *is* bliss. Maybe the truth will be terrible.

We hit a wall of traffic on the Third Ring Road. The delay gives me time to calm down. I know if we're late, I have the habitual Beijing excuse: traffic was terrible. As we crawl along, it occurs to me that were it not for the risk of dying, I could probably get to Beijing University faster on a bike. Average rush-hour speed on major arteries between the Second and

Third Ring Roads—exactly where we are now—fell to less than 10 kilometers (six miles) an hour in 2005, one-fourth the average speed when I last lived here, in 1994.

Until the 1990s, rush-hour traffic consisted of rivers of bicycles. Now, with 3 million cars on the road, many driven by rookies, biking in Beijing has become perilous. Every year, about 1,600 people die in traffic accidents, nearly five times the rate in New York City. Nationwide, traffic fatalities exceed 100,000 a year, with seven times that number injured. Even the president of China's bicycle industry association stopped cycling in Beijing, after he was hit by a car. Beijingers report that they now use bicycles for 20 percent of trips, down from 60 percent a decade earlier. As cars literally squeeze out bikes, bike paths are shrinking and, in some cases, vanishing entirely.

"Seeing flowers from a galloping horse." That's an ancient Chinese saying about the drawbacks of the fast-paced life. Sitting in the slow-moving taxi, I have lots of time to check out the flowers. Beds of orange roses, pink begonias and hot pink petunias, bordered by neatly trimmed shrubs, edge the expressway. For lack of better reading material, I study the billboards. Many promote real estate developments with names like "Versailles," "Chateau Edinburgh," "Rancho Santa Fe" and "Palm Springs." One double billboard advertises Toto bidets. On the left it shows a close-up of a model's face, looking grim. The right side shows her smiling, with the caption "She's washing now."

It has taken me two weeks to realize that a nation of a billion ex-Maoists is obsessed with square footage and bidets. Every time I get together with someone here, they want to talk about real estate. And for a country that recently had some of the world's worst plumbing, bidets have suddenly become the new must-have bathroom accessory. Qiu Hai's mother, my eighty-year-old Aunt

Yuying, recently installed one. She's actually the mother of my cousin's cousin, but in the sprawling web of Chinese kinship she is considered my aunt. She recently purchased a luxury condo in Tianjin, and I made a daytrip there to visit her.

Aunt Yuying showed me her kitchen's granite counters, her light switches with blue light-emitting diodes that glow in the dark and her huge tilt-and-turn windows with clever retractable screens. Like some of those SOHO condo buyers, the expanse of glass frightened her so much that she installed safety bars. Aunt's pride and joy, however, was her made-in-China Toto bidet. Instead of a separate porcelain fixture, the bidet was a space-saving seat attachment that sprayed a jet of pressurized, temperature-controlled water, followed by a cozy blast of warm air. Aunt claimed her bidet solved years of constipation and other digestive-tract problems. At first she hadn't been sure she needed or wanted one. Then the salesman dropped the names of all her friends who'd installed one, and she succumbed to that age-old sales ploy: keeping up with the Zhangs.

Her three-bedroom, two-bath residence is as sleek as any upscale condo in Toronto. She got the insider's price—600,000 yuan ($78,000)—from her former employer, Tianjin University. Her husband, who is eighty-six, initially thought it was too risky to sink all their savings into the condo. Aunt Yuying overruled him, and six months later, the price has doubled. She confided that he also objected because his male pride was bruised. Her status, not his, got them the apartment. That surprised me. When they retired, he was a full professor, and she was merely an associate.

Somewhat sheepishly, Aunt Yuying told me about her secret past. "Old Qiu graduated in 1945, four years before the Communist victory," she said, referring to her husband. "So he was considered part of the old regime. I graduated in June 1949 and was classified as New China's first graduating class."The authorities immediately ordered Aunt Yuying to report to Qinghua University for political indoctrination. On the advice of her professor and mentor, she obeyed without protest. After the indoctrination, she was assigned a technician's job at a factory in Manchuria, the industrialized belt in northeast China. She didn't want to go; she had a faculty job waiting for her at Nankai University, another prestigious university in Tianjin.

Again, her mentor cautioned her. "My teacher told me I must look like an activist or I would suffer later on." So Aunt Yuying "volunteered" for the job in Manchuria. After only one month, however, Nankai University countermanded the order. "I was a fake activist, and now I benefit from that. My dossier says I was a 'revolutionary cadre,'" Aunt Yuying said, laughing self-consciously.

"What happened to your teacher?"

"It wasn't good," she said, sighing. Her mentor had married a Russian. No one foresaw that the two socialist countries would become bitter enemies. "People accused her of being a Soviet agent because she married a Russian. She committed suicide during the Cultural Revolution."

Ironically, Aunt Yuying always shunned politics. She had suffered herself during the Cultural Revolution because she had a foreign connection: a brother who had emigrated to Canada (and married my aunt). Now, after a lifetime of keeping her head down, Aunt Yuying was the university's highest-ranking "revolutionary cadre." After the university president, she got first choice of the units. She declined to pick the most expensive one, a four-bedroom duplex penthouse with a rooftop terrace. She disliked the internal staircase and the summer sun beating down on the roof. Also, she sometimes uses a wheelchair, and worried about being evacuated in an emergency. Instead she chose a condo on a lower floor, facing southeast, the most desirable angle for sunlight.

"If it was up to Lao Qiu's rank," said Aunt Yuying, "we would only qualify for a northeast-facing unit. Everything comes down to rank and money now. Every year of teaching counts as a point. And then there is your contribution to the revolution."

Fifty-eight minutes later, our taxi arrives at Beijing University. It's about the same time it would have taken me by bike, before the city got so modern. We're meeting Cadre Huang at Shao Yuan Building Eight. Like everywhere we go, it's under renovation. He arrives exactly on time. He's not as scrawny as before and his hair is gray. But at sixty-eight, he is as high-strung and energetic as ever, his cheekbones as prominent and round as the table-tennis balls he once delighted in smashing at my face. "You came at just the right time. I've just returned from a vacation in Moscow," he says.

The right side of his face is bruised, purple and chartreuse. There are two angry red scabs at his temple. "What happened?" I ask, over the crash of sledgehammers and the buzz of pneumatic drills. "I fell down in Moscow and hit the side of my head," he says, giggling the way he always did, inappropriately and unnervingly.

Just then Fu the Enforcer arrives with Dai Guiying, Erica's Chinese instructor. It's been thirty-three years since I last saw my teacher, now sixty-eight. We do not hug. We stand awkwardly grinning at each other. "You're aging!" she says in her untactful way.

"How is your cold?" I ask.

She coughs self-consciously. "Much better. I was terribly sick," she says, sounding not at all sick. During the Cultural Revolution, Fu wore thick glasses with clear plastic rims. Her hair was her pride—her braids fell to her waist. She hated her skin because it was naturally dark; she thought it made her look like a peasant. Now, the long braids are gone, replaced by a salt-and-pepper pixie cut. She's wearing a cream blouse, loose-cut gray pants and flat shoes. Unfashionably large glasses, tinted ocher, cover her face like a protective shield. Her lone concessions to China's consumer age are a small black purse and a thin gold wedding band engraved, incongruously for a Marxist, with the characters for prosperity and long life. Teacher Dai, always a chic dresser even when she could wear only gray Mao suits, is attired in a gauzy blouse accessorized with a carved white-bead necklace. Her hair is permed. She carries a white handbag over her wrist.

Like me, Fu and Dai cluck over Cadre Huang's wounds. "I'm better off than another professor," he says, giggling. "She was visiting Lenin's tomb last year. She tripped and fell and died. Just like that."

"Just like that?" Fu the Enforcer shouts, over the din of pneumatic drills.

"Just like that," he says.

Fu and Dai both shake their heads as if to say: Such bad luck to die outside Lenin's tomb.

Cadre Huang confides to me that his daughter, his only child, now lives in Canada, not far from Toronto, after earning a Ph.D. in Chinese history overseas. He wants to show us around Building Seven, a new foreign-student dormitory. A two-bedroom suite with a living room and bathroom looks so much nicer than the white-washed cell Scarlet and I shared. "Your children can come and study here," he suggests. I translate that for Ben and Sam. They look stricken.

"Just smile and say, *xie xie,*" I tell them, using the Chinese word for "thank you."

"*Xie xie,*" they say, shooting me dagger looks.

In 1972, Erica and I were the only Westerners on campus. We were later joined by nine North Koreans, one Palestinian and two Laotians. Now there are five thousand foreign students. "Seventeen foreign students became ambassadors," Cadre Huang says proudly. He doesn't say how many became reporters.

We head to a quieter building for lunch. Cadre Huang explains that he invited Lacking Virtue Pan, the Communist Party cadre in charge of my history class. "Unfortunately, he had to go out of town on business. So I had to invite someone you don't know from the Foreign Students Office. We're all retired. We needed someone with an expense account," he says, with another giggle.

At the university canteen, a multi-story building offering everything from Peking duck to spicy noodles, we take the elevator up to the faculty dining room. Outside a private room, a slim young woman waits. She's the very picture of a modern Communist cadre. Her smile is cold, her handshake limp. She's wearing a navy skirt, a lacy blouse and high-heeled sandals.

"This is Teacher Zhou. She is a department head," says Cadre Huang, formally introducing us and giving her rank. Teacher Zhou never reveals her full name, a means of keeping her distance and of letting us know who's in charge. Like Lacking Virtue Pan in my day, she doesn't actually teach. She is a Communist Party functionary. My heart sinks. With this cold, prim stranger presiding, how will I ever bring up a sensitive topic like Yin? Teacher Zhou will shut down the conversation before it starts.

Our private room is furnished with a large round table and beige slip-covered dining chairs. As is the custom at banquets, the waitress proffers a tray with a dozen different beverages. Fu, Dai and Cadre Huang order thin, sweetened yogurt, the latest Beijing trend in drinks. It's a bizarre custom, I think, because dairy clashes with Chinese food. Knowing I'm too distracted to intervene, Ben and Sam choose Red Bull, the caffeine-spiked energy drink that is just as pricey and popular in China as it is in America. I have smoky sour plum juice, a traditional Beijing specialty. Fat Paycheck, the only discerning one among us, chooses green tea.

The meal is pre-ordered and lavish. There is thinly sliced five-spice beef; braised fresh bamboo; cold poached duck in rice wine; steamed fluffy white buns stuffed with minced pork and water chestnuts; prawns with fresh peas; sliced boneless sea bass with Chinese water spinach; fresh crabmeat sauced with oil-poached egg whites and served over blanched asparagus; sweet-and-sour pork garnished with fresh Beijing peaches; emerald-green Chinese broccoli; a whole steamed Mandarin fish.

Fu watches me struggle to pick up a slippery morsel. "You still don't know how to use chopsticks," she announces with a huge smile. My boys chortle. Indeed, I have never learned to use chopsticks properly. I glare at Fu, who is oblivious. It's as if we're back in 1972; I can't think of a single retort.

Out of politeness, I try to make small talk with Teacher Zhou even though I couldn't care less about making the acquaintance of one more apparatchik. I find out she is thirty, which means that she wasn't even born when I was studying here. She says she was hired directly after graduating from Beijing University eight years ago.

"What did you study?" Fu asks, also politely.

"Politics," she says.

"Oh," says Fu. Everyone at the table, except Ben and Sam, knows that's code for Marxism. In China, there's no other kind of "politics." The table falls silent. None of us is interested any more in talking to a Marxist. "*Duo chi,*" Teacher Zhou says, formally urging us to "eat more." She doesn't crack a smile. She never thaws. It's obvious she can hardly wait for the meal to end. We're all a burden to her—me, Fat Paycheck, Fu the Enforcer, Cadre Huang—all Maoist remnants that must be banqueted according to protocol. Well, she's a burden to us too. We ignore her. We chat about the bad old days while taking advantage of the university's largesse and gorging ourselves on shrimp and crab and wine-poached duck.

"We were so left. Ultra-left," says Fu, with a giggle.

"We filled you full of ultra-left thinking," says Cadre Huang, sipping his yogurt drink.

"Ultra-left" was once a serious counterrevolutionary label. Chairman Mao used it to attack his enemies. Now people fling it around the way we use "liberal" in the West. "Left" and "right" have become meaningless in the new Beijing. I remember that Dai, like Scarlet, was always trying to get accepted into the Party. "Are you a Party member now?" I ask her. She laughs delicately and shakes her head.

Fu jumps in. "Now young people are different. They don't want to enter the Party. They just care about money." She sighs and thoughtfully chews a piece of five-spice beef. "In the old days, we had a *zhandou mubiao* [a battle objective]," she says.

"'Serve the people.' 'Everything for the revolution.' Now there is a spiritual crisis. People have no goal except to get rich."

We keep eating. The food is delicious. Nervously, I can see my opportunity to grill Fu slipping away. Suddenly she and Teacher Dai excuse themselves to use the washroom. I run after them. As we wash our hands, I remind Fu the Enforcer about the young student named Yin. "She asked me to help her go to the United States. Do you remember I reported her to you?" I say.

Fu looks blank.

"She was in the history department," I persist. "I told you, and you told the Foreign Students Office."

Fu shakes her head. "I don't remember," she says slowly, her expression cautious. Seeing I'm crushed, she quickly adds, "I guarantee you she left the country. For sure."

Teacher Dai chimes in. "Absolutely. Anyone who was like that in those years would be gone now. She would have left."

I search Fu's face to see if she's lying. It seems she really doesn't remember. To be fair, I didn't remember Yin either until I reread my diary. But the difference is that Fu the Enforcer doesn't care. She's not the slightest bit upset. Perhaps the landscape of her memory is littered with bodies. One more victim means nothing. She probably doesn't remember my friend Peidi, either, whom she accused of being a "broken shoe." Snitching in Chairman Mao's China was routine and was easily forgotten, like the number of times it rained in a year.

In East Germany, the Stasi had 91,000 staff and 174,000 unofficial collaborators, a ratio of 1 spy for every 62 inhabitants. It kept files on many people who weren't even aware they were being monitored, because the Stasi didn't always act on the information. It merely stored facts away in case it needed to use them. After the fall of the Berlin Wall, records in the Stasi archives, if stacked, would have reached 180 kilometers. It boggles the mind to consider the thickness of the dossiers China maintains on its 1.3 billion citizens. In translation, both Stasi and KGB mean "Ministry of State Security," the same name China still uses. Unlike in East Germany, no one knows how many ordinary Chinese were collaborators. It's safe to say during the Cultural Revolution millions were, because snitching was perceived as a civic, moral duty, the way an American might report child abuse. For years, Mao had the enthusiastic support of ordinary citizens like Fu the Enforcer. Fu did not work for the Chinese Stasi. She was an ordinary Party member, a Mandarin teacher at Beijing University. I vaguely recall that when I told Fu about Yin, her reaction was mildly approving. She did not hint to me that I was in fact reporting a serious crime. I told her the information, she accepted it and we simply carried on with my Chinese lesson.

Years later, I keep trying to understand why I did what I did. I had come from a sheltered, middle-class Montreal family. I had never left home, except for one year in a university dorm. At home, we never discussed politics. In fact, I don't remember any conversations of any significance at the dinner table. Mainly, after chanting in Cantonese, "Mother, eat rice," I focused on getting enough to eat before my two brothers scarfed down all the food. We attended church because my parents thought it was something an assimilated Canadian family should do. I chose my churches by proximity or piano teachers—first the Rosedale United Church (near our first house), then the First Baptist Church (my piano teacher was the minister's wife) and finally the Montreal West Presbyterian Church (near our second house). For years I wondered why Baptists donned hip waders for baptism and Presbyterians sprinkled water on your fore-head. No one explained that these were rival denominations.

Like most teenagers in the West in the late 1960s and early 1970s, I was desperate to conform. Cher was hot, so I grew my hair to my waist. Admiring Twiggy, I got my first set of contact lenses. My university friend Patti Wolfe and I custom-ordered a rubber stamp that said "This Exploits Women." Then we ran around the streets stamping pantyhose and movie ads we found offensive, without realizing we were pretty offensive ourselves.

At university, I joined sit-ins and tried hard to be rude to my professors, except that I liked them too much. I saved my honor at one sit-in by whacking a leather-jacketed cop on the shoulder. When he whirled around, I was such a coward that I smiled sweetly and pretended it was all an accident. I never burned my bra. I didn't get into sexual promiscuity. And I not only didn't inhale, my one attempt at hash failed miserably. A friend instructed me to use a drinking straw to suck in the smoke. I did, and the glowing fragment zipped up the straw, scorching my tongue. That was the end of my career as a druggie.

When I arrived in China in 1972 at the age of nineteen, I was a middle-class Montreal Maoist. Teenage rebellion was in full swing in Beijing too, and I yearned to be part of the in crowd there. Instead of looking to Gloria Steinem, kids there were taking their cues from Chairman Mao. Like adolescents everywhere, though, I could turn on a dime. All the cool kids were denouncing capitalism and complaining about authority figures. I joined in. Sure, it was a sacrifice when Cadre Huang scolded me for listening to the Rolling Stones. The trendy music there was "The East is Red" (which I can still sing). I didn't really want to dig ditches on a Saturday afternoon, but I volunteered because I desperately wanted to fit in. I had grown up an out-sider in Montreal, always perceived as "Chinese." Here, for the first time in my life, I physically resembled everyone around me. I cut my hair and wore dorky pigtails because that's what every other girl did. I dumped my Western wardrobe of embroidered hippie caftans and tight jeans faster than you could say "A revolution is not a dinner party."

In 1972, the adolescent experience in China was to be a Maoist. Scarlet and Future and virtually everyone else their age became Red Guards and attacked adults because adults had power and authority. I was an outsider—not eligible to join a Red Guard faction—and I was only just beginning to learn the language, but like adolescents anywhere, I was adept at picking up behavioral clues. I may not have understood *why* I was doing something, but I knew what I had to do to be accepted.

Fu the Enforcer, Teacher Dai and I walk back to the private dining room in silence. Teacher Zhou is impatient to end the banquet. She stands up, the signal that the banquet is over. In the corner she has stashed some gift bags. She gives university key chains to Ben and Sam, who try to look thrilled. Fat Paycheck gets a university tie, and doesn't look thrilled. For me there's a pen holder made of finely grained wood, embossed with the university seal. I actually like it. On the side, carved into the wood, is a brief history in Chinese and English: "The university's traditional values of patriotism, progress, democracy and sci-ence, together with the educational style of diligence, exacti-tude, truthfulness and innovation, have been passed down from generation to generation."

Truthfulness? No longer caring what Teacher Zhou thinks, I ask Cadre Huang if he remembers anything about Yin. Fu would have reported her to the Foreign Students Office, which means him. He looks startled. After a moment, he says he remembers nothing. But, unlike Fu, he promises to ask around.

"Do you think Yin was in the class that entered in 1971?" I ask.

"There was no class in 1971," he says. "There was only a class in 1970. That was the first class." In other words, the Cultural Revolution had shut down schools across China. Beijing University, one of the first institutions to resume accepting students, took in its first class in 1970. But in 1971, China—and Beijing University—were still in disarray and no new students were enrolled that year.

It's a crucial piece of information. Scarlet entered Beijing University in 1972, the same year I did. But Scarlet has always said Yin was in a more senior class. That means Yin had to be in the class of 1970. That also means she was in the same class year as Lacking Virtue Pan. At the time, there were only two possible history majors: world history and Chinese history. And each section was intimate, with only about thirty-five students. It seems that Pan would have known Yin very well.

13

Made in China

On the way home from Beijing University, I feel exhausted and depressed. Neither Fu the Enforcer nor Cadre Huang nor Teacher Dai remembered anything about Yin. And I found it hard to see them all again, just as I'm sure it was hard for them to see me. They brought back all my locked-away memories of Maoism.

When we pass IKEA on the Fourth Ring Road, the boys are raring to go. For them a two-hour banquet with a bunch of aging Maoists in a language they can't understand wasn't much fun. IKEA they can understand. The seven-story store is the size of ten soccer fields, the biggest IKEA in the world outside Sweden.

"Let's check it out," says Sam. And why not? This, after all, is the new Beijing that I want them to see. China is fertile new ground for big-box stores. In the past two decades, home ownership has skyrocketed from zero to 70 percent of all housing today. The $50-billion market for home improvement and furnishings is growing at 12 percent a year, in part because new apartments are sold as concrete shells—without doors, plumbing, wiring, flooring, kitchens or bathrooms.

IKEA's first Beijing store, which opened in 1999, grossly miscalculated how fast the middle class would grow. Located closer to the center of Beijing, it was small and had inadequate parking. IKEA assumed most customers would take the bus. No one foresaw that a thousand new cars were about to hit the road every day. I went there with Ben Mok, the Coca-Cola executive, in 2003. The line to get into the parking lot was an hour long. Entire families flocked there for the sheer novelty of sitting on upholstered furniture, as opposed to the wooden chairs they had at home. Some took naps on the real box-spring mattresses. The company must have had smart country managers—they never shooed people away. IKEA lived up to its Chinese name, Yi Jia, which means "Delightful Home."

In Beijing, it's so crowded on the streets that I've noticed when people bump into you, they often don't apologize because, well, isn't it obvious there isn't enough space? Or perhaps they don't apologize because the only way to survive is to tune everyone else out. IKEA is its own cultural revolution, with abundant shopping carts and extra-wide aisles. Shoppers must be mesmerized by the displays because the public-address system constantly pleads for delinquent parents to pick up their only children; the playroom limits free babysitting to sixty minutes.

IKEA's Scandinavian aesthetic is changing Beijing's style, promoting Western ideals of domestic space and decor. And yet the stuff of this ideal is actually manufactured in China. Chinese consumers are buying Chinese-made goods, through the intermediary of a foreign-owned company. Practically overnight, Beijingers have shifted away from Stalinist dowdy to blond-wood modern. Yet the Swedish company doesn't otherwise impose blond standards. The large black and white photographs on the wall feature Asians, not Caucasians, which is more than you can say about the ads in Chinese department stores.

We take the extra-long escalators up to the first floor, where sofas and mattresses are displayed. I notice no one is napping, even though one bed has a clear plastic sheet printed with these characters: "Lie down and try this." How nice, compared with all the things you *can't* do in a Chinese park. In a model bathroom, however, the toilet bowl is covered with a plexiglass sheet helpfully stencilled, "Customer washroom is in the dining room."

The products are virtually the same as at any IKEA store. I see the same computer desk I have at home, and the same swivel stool that Sam sits on to practice cello. There are the same water glasses and navy-blue plastic spatulas, at the same prices. This is globalization. The only unique-to-China items seem to be some of the plush animals. Stuffed bats and rats probably wouldn't sell well in Toronto, but here bats are a pun for wealth, and rats are part of the Chinese zodiac. Ben decides a stuffed rat is just the thing for Tash, his girlfriend back in Toronto.

As I've said, Fat Paycheck isn't thrilled about shopping. He heads to the restaurant for coffee. After we walk through the entire store, we join him. The cafeteria looks just like the one at the Toronto IKEA, right down to the gray-striped melamine trays, except this one seats seven hundred. Like that bad joke about Chinese food, an hour after the Beijing University banquet Ben and Sam are hungry. They could have stir-fried pork or chicken curry and rice, but they pile up their trays with plates of Swedish meatballs and cheesecake.

A pretty young woman is selling Absolut vodka cocktails for fifteen yuan, about two dollars. None of the other shoppers are interested, but I can't resist a bargain. (Fat Paycheck says I'd order strychnine for dessert if it were on promotion.) The young woman suggests a Sunrise Cocktail, made with a jigger of Absolut Mandarin, crushed ice, raspberry cordial and orange juice. She mixes it altogether and, after a perfunctory shake, pours it into a tall glass and adds a slice of lemon and a straw. It's delicious.

I notice a customer perched on a stool eating spaghetti and salad with chopsticks. A band—two electric guitars, a keyboard and drums—is singing, in English, "As Time Goes By." Ben notices that IKEA charges only five yuan for a half liter of Beijing-brand draft beer. "Can I get it?" he asks. "I just want to know how much I can drink." What the hell? I'm drinking vodka in the middle of the afternoon. Ben and I both get red in the face before we're halfway through our drinks.

On the way home, we get stuck in rush-hour traffic. Suddenly I see a young man dashing between lanes on the Fourth Ring Road, tossing little cards through cars windows, tucking them under the windshield wipers if the car is stopped. At first I think he must be a lunatic. Then I see a second young man doing the same. "What are they doing?" I ask the taxi driver.

"Advertising," he grunts.

It's direct marketing. In Beijing, everything is a sales opportunity, even a traffic jam.

That evening, Cadre Huang phones me with Lacking Virtue Pan's cellphone number. Pan falls into the same category as Fu the Enforcer: people who were nastily dogmatic before and who I don't really feel like seeing again. I remember that he was willing to ruin Future's future over a postage stamp. He certainly couldn't have thought much of me, the foreigner who supplied the stamp. I'm sure Pan will know about Yin. But if I spook him, I'll break one of the few threads that might lead back to her. Unsure of what to do, I do nothing.

The next morning, Future phones me very early, waking me up. He's on his way to the Institute of Modern History, and will make inquiries about Yin. "What have you found out?" he says.

"Not much," I say sleepily. "But I've figured out what class year she was in." I tell him that she must have been in the same year as Lacking Virtue Pan.

"I have his cellphone number," I say, "but I'm afraid to call him."

"Be careful," Future cautions. "Don't tell him what happened or your role in it. If you do, he will tell you nothing."

"What do I say?" I ask helplessly.

"Say it this way: 'There's a classmate. A long time ago, we had a *lai wang* [relationship]. I've been thinking about her a lot and would like to see her again, but I don't know where she is. I think she left the university in 1973. I'm so sorry I can't pay you a visit in person—this trip my time is really tight. But can you help me out here?'" I scribble down, word for word, what Future is saying. It's a masterpiece of vagueness and etiquette. When I ask him if he'd like Teacher Pan's phone number, I can almost hear him recoiling.

"No, no, no," he shouts. He still hasn't gotten over what Lacking Virtue Pan did to him. This is not encouraging. No one is eager for contact with their Cultural Revolution persecutors.

I hang up and call Lacking Virtue Pan's cellphone. He's very friendly. "I'm so sorry I missed your banquet yesterday," he says. "I had to go Datong with a delegation of visitors."

Too many years of Maoist China have scarred me. I'm sure his warmth is fake. After we exchange a few pleasantries, I read from my notes, exactly what Future instructed me to say. It works beautifully.

"Her name is Yan Luyi," Teacher Pan says instantly. I'm confused. If her name is Yan, not Yin, then I've had the wrong surname. "Is she *hai zai* [still around]?" I ask carefully. The phrase is as ambiguous in Chinese as it is in English. Without setting off alarm bells, I need to know whether Yin/Yan survived. But Pan is still filling me on her past.

"She majored in Chinese history. She left the university in 1973. She returned to Jilin province, a place called Baicheng." For the first time, I have a province and an actual place name. I feel a chill go down my spine. I've never heard of Baicheng, so it must be a small town. Maybe I can find her after all.

"She owned a business and was rather successful." My heart leaps. I feel immense relief. That means she's probably alive.

"Then she went abroad," he continues. Abroad? I was right, and so indeed was Fu the Enforcer. Yin/Yan *did* leave. I envision myself chasing her around the world, to Australia, perhaps, or San Francisco.

"Where?" I press.

"I forget," says Teacher Pan.

My disappointment is almost palpable. The trail has gone cold. Then he drops a bombshell.

"She came back. She's in Beijing now. We often see each other."

"What's her phone number?" I practically shout.

"I don't have it," he says. "She recently changed her cell-phone number."

My heart sinks. Cellphone penetration in Beijing is approaching 100 percent. Nationwide, the two main cellular carriers in China have 450 million customers, with 5 million more signing up each month. Without Yin/Yan's cellphone number, I am stuck.

"I'll ask around," he promises. "I'll try to get you the phone number."

I thank him profusely. In my mind, Lacking Virtue Pan has just morphed back into Celebrating Virtue Pan.

14

Stand a Head above Others

Alfred Peng phones. "About that pass," he says, without so much as a how-are-you. "I was only kidding. I didn't forge it." He hangs up.

When I tell Ben, he scoffs. "I've looked at other passes," he says. "There's always printing on the back, too. His was blank. He forged it."

A few hours later, my cellphone beeps. Alfred is sending me a text message. It's a joke. I have to keep hitting buttons to finish reading it. I wish I hadn't.

> An American boasts to a Chinese: "When we finish our gum, we don't spit it out wherever we want. We recycle it, and make it into condoms we export to China." The Chinese replies, "That's nothing. When we finish our condoms, we don't just throw them out. We turn them into gum, and export it to the U.S."

We decide to experience the Great Mall of China without

Alfred. The 5.8-million-square-foot New Yansha has six floors, a thousand stores, a hundred restaurants, 20,000 employees, 230 escalators, a climbing wall and an ice rink. People stroll up and down the air-conditioned halls, but most don't even glance at the $500 cashmere sweaters or $10,000 golf clubs. Some people even bring their own snacks. No one is making money, including at the climbing wall. Ben is the only customer of the morning. When he attracts a crowd of gawkers, I spot a money-making opportunity, but I suppress my ancestral entrepreneurial urge to sell tickets.

We head up to the top floor to choose from among the hundred restaurants—Brazilian barbecue or Korean barbecue, pizza, spaghetti, Japanese, dim sum, all-you-can-eat buffets and every kind of Chinese provincial cuisine. Ben and Sam, naturally, want McDonald's, which they spotted on the main floor. I waver. If I'm not going to yank vodka coolers out of their fists, then how can I get all moralistic about junk food? But Fat Paycheck and I want Chinese. We agree to let the boys go downstairs on their own provided they wait until we pick a restaurant. Fat Paycheck and I choose a classic Beijing dumpling house. Like those barbershop prostitutes, we take a table right by the window. I point to the red and gold sign above—which the boys can't read—and tell them we'll wait there, at the table in the window under the red and gold sign.

Our waitress hovers like a sommelier while I flip through the extensive illustrated menu—which goes on for twenty pages. I order chilled tofu dressed in light soy, vinegar and chopped cilantro; flash-fried thinly sliced pork liver with garlic; dumplings of napa cabbage and pork; spicy dan dan noodles. At the next table an elderly couple feed their chubby granddaughter snacks while they wait for their dumplings. The toddler scarfs a container of fruit-flavored yogurt, washed down with a sweetened yogurt drink. Next she gobbles a bag of candies, a paper cup of vanilla ice cream and half a canister of Lay's potato chips. The grandparents urge her to eat more. Millennia of famine have left love and food intertwined in this culture (which must be why I've just caved on McDonald's). But now, for the first time in Chinese history, prosperity is expressed through Western-style sweets. Obesity is on the rise. Not surprisingly, when the dumplings arrive, the little girl is full.

Norman excuses himself to use the washroom. He reports back that there are ad-sponsored Chinese jokes in the toilet stalls. A sample:

> Man calls the police station. His wife has disap-
> peared.
> MAN: Can you help me find her?
> POLICE: What does she look like?
> MAN: She's short, a little on the heavy side, slightly
> balding, with a big nose.
> COP: Why are you looking for her?

I ought to text-message that to Alfred.

The restaurant gradually empties. When the boys do not return, I grow concerned. I forgot to have a Plan B. Fat Paycheck waits by the plate-glass window while I start hunting for the boys. The food floor is the size of six football fields. At the top of an escalator, I hesitate. What if they come up another of the 230 escalators while I'm going down? I start to panic. Then I see them, two specks in the distance, running up and down the food floor. I shout and wave.

"We couldn't find the restaurant!" Sam says, breathlessly.

"We just kept looking for restaurants with red signs, which turned out not to be too effective because they *all* had red signs," Ben adds.

After misplacing my children in the world's biggest mall, I realize I'm crazy to think I can find Yin/Yan in this sprawling, ever-changing metropolis of 16 million people—if she is even here. My initial euphoria at the news from Celebrating Virtue Pan is fading fast. How do I know he's telling me the truth, and not merely fabricating some happy-ending story about Yin/Yan?

Pan is not someone I can trust. Not only did he persecute Future over the postage stamps, he also betrayed *me*. In 1976, when Fat Paycheck and I were planning to get married, I asked Pan, the class Communist Party secretary and thus the teacher in charge of us, to pass on a wedding invitation to all my class-mates. As a foreign student, I felt obliged by protocol to invite them through the formal Party structure. But Pan never passed on my invitation. On my wedding day, no one showed up, not even Future. I felt terribly hurt until I realized that none of them had received my invitation.

But if Pan is indeed telling the truth about Yin/Yan, I still have to rely on him to come through with her phone number. He simply may not be able to find it. Or now that he's had a moment to consider my request, he may remember that I reported her, and then he might well be skittish about provid-ing the information. Of course, he would never actually say that. He would just not call me back. And like everyone else here, he'd just get a new cellphone number, and I'd never find him again.

I need to calm down. I need to get my hair cut. I tell Norman and the boys I'll meet them in an hour at the skating rink, then I hunt for a hair salon. The mall has dozens of them, all offering big discounts for big cash advances. If I pay 3,000 yuan ($390) up front, all services are half price. But to get my money's worth, I'd have to squeeze in two hundred hair cuts before I leave. The full price is 30 yuan, which includes two shampoos, a cut and a blow-dry. That's right: here they wash your hair twice—after the cut too—so you don't walk around for the rest of the day shedding bits of hair.

China has too many people and not enough work. A tout stands outside the salon, luring me in. A receptionist takes my order. A third person hands me a pink L'Oréal smock. A fourth person shampoos my hair. A fifth person sweeps up. A sixth person actually cuts my hair. Wang Lin, my stylist, is wearing tight jeans and a turquoise Al Capone T-shirt. Like the peach vendor and the sock ladies, he tries to sell me more. He suggests a dye job or a perm.

"I only have one hour," I say.

"What about a hot-oil treatment? It will make your hair shine."

"No thanks."

"Eyebrow waxing?"

"No thanks."

"Special conditioner?"

"No thanks. Just a haircut."

He's twenty-five and has been cutting hair for seven years, ever since he dropped out of high school in Anshan, an iron, steel and coal-mining city in Manchuria. Like Yin, his dream is to leave China. He once got as far as South Korea, but came back half a month later. Life there was too tough. Now he works at the mall eleven hours a day, six days a week. "It's exhausting," he sighs. He snips the hair around my ears and asks me where I'm from.

"I want to emigrate to Canada," he says. "Canada is next to the U.S., right?"

"Right."

"And on the other side is France, right?"

"Not exactly," I say.

Wang Lin says he's trying to learn English but is making no progress. He is thinking of applying to Canada as a skilled immigrant. I tell him as gently as I can that hairdressing skills aren't in demand.

"Relatives of Canadian citizens can get in easier, right? Can I be a godson? Or could I be adopted? How can they prove you're not?"

I can see where this conversation is going.

"Can you be my guarantor?" he says. "Or could you say you're my relative?"

I don't answer Wang Lin directly. Instead I ask, "Why do you want to leave?"

"There's too many people here," he says. "I can't make any money."

It's August 15, my 54th birthday. I'm just past the mid-point of my trip, with two weeks left before we board a plane back to America. Maybe Pan is wrong. Maybe she's not in Beijing anymore. With so little time left, I'm losing hope.

But I'm looking forward to seeing my old roommate. Like Future and virtually every other teenager in China in 1966, Scarlet had joined a Red Guard faction in high school during the Cultural Revolution, enthusiastically attacking her teachers and school administrators until the entire education system shut down. In 1973 when we parted after a year as roommates at

Beijing University, she gave me her red armband as a gift. As a wannabe Red Guard, I was deeply touched.

Scarlet had warned me that the road outside her condo, like everything else in the city, is still under construction. As my taxi pulls up, I see her waiting by the half-finished road. She has just dropped her granddaughter off at nursery school and was afraid I would have trouble finding her building. At fifty-five, Scarlet has gained a little weight. She was the tallest girl in our class and she had excelled at volleyball, her height enabling her to jump high enough to spike the ball at the net. She used to wear her Mao suits a size too big to conceal her figure. Now, she's still hiding her figure with a denim jumper that has—I can't believe this—an American flag embroidered across the chest. She gives me a huge hug, and grabs my hand, just like the old days. As we walk toward her building, I tell her I tried every way to find her.

"I'm no longer at Beijing Library," she says. "I'm semi-retired. Sometimes I do some work at the Ministry of Culture, but you wouldn't have known that. It's a good thing you asked the All-China Journalists Federation to help. Normally, Beijing Library won't give out my phone number."

"I went to Beijing University to look for you."

"Oh, they couldn't find me," she says shaking her head. "I have nothing to do with them." Like many students of the Cultural Revolution era, including me, she doesn't have fond memories of her alma mater. The last time I saw her, seven years ago, her husband had taken early retirement from his state job at the Forestry Ministry and started a wildlife documentary business. As he prospered and expanded into equipment rental, television series and feature films, Scarlet kept trading up homes. "I've moved five times in seven years," she says, laughing.

One house had 3,400 square feet and, like Ben Mok's villa, was near the airport. Her biggest was an 8,600-square-foot monster home north of Beijing. "Then Mao Mao had a baby," she says, referring to her only child. "I'm a granny now. So we moved back to the city." She and her husband live with their daughter, son-in-law and granddaughter. Mao Mao, a graduate in film editing, works in the family business. Scarlet's son-in-law is a battalion-level officer in the People's Liberation Army. "I didn't tell you that last time—because the army shot at people. I thought you wouldn't approve."

In past visits, Scarlet and I have discussed the Tiananmen massacre only briefly. It's too sensitive. Most Chinese I know agree that it's safer to avoid the topic altogether. In 1999, she treated me to a dinner of Mongolian Hot Pot. Her husband's friend drove me home, while Scarlet sat in the back seat. It was the eve of the fiftieth anniversary of the founding of the People's Republic—and the tenth anniversary of the massacre. As we crossed Tiananmen Square, Scarlet reminded me that the wheels of cars used to buzz as they ran over the tank-roughened surface. Now they didn't. The friend explained, "It's freshly paved. You can't feel the ruts any more." I had asked Scarlet if the government would be successful in suppressing memories of the massacre. "Of course, people will remember, Bright Precious," she said quietly. "I myself will never forget what happened. But we remember in our hearts. Violence isn't the way to change China. We will *heping yanbian* [evolve peacefully]."

Scarlet had been prescient. There had been no turmoil, no riots since 1989. And in the meantime China had prospered. We take the elevator up to her eleventh floor condo, which she's renting until her next home is ready. "We're moving again. We bought another villa. Construction starts in October."

"Isn't it exhausting to move so often?"

"You get a moving company," she says, shrugging. "You don't have to lift a finger."

Scarlet told her maid not to come in this morning so we could talk in peace. A maid! I remember when she competed with me to be the first to mop the concrete floor in our dorm room every morning before dawn. Now we sit, side by side, on her soft black leather sofa. Her living room is expensively furnished with carved mahogany bookcases and curio cabinets. She apologizes saying that most of her stuff is in storage. She remembers I like green tea, and prepares a pot from a stand-alone dispenser that provides instant hot, boiling filtered water. As she pours me a cup, she reminds me her name is no longer Scarlet. She changed the *Hong* character to one that sounds the same but means limpid pool of water. "I didn't like such a revolutionary name," she says.

Scarlet, Limpid Pool of Water. Addresses, phone numbers, roads, buildings, even people's names—nothing is the same. But after going through the Cultural Revolution with my roommate, I just can't think of her as "Limpid Pool of Water." To me, she'll always be Scarlet. It reminds me that I still don't even know the full name of the young woman I turned in.

"I think her personal name was Luyi," says Scarlet.

Now I'm really confused. I thought Scarlet originally told me it was Luoyi. And since then, Pan has told me her full name is actually Yan Luyi.

Scarlet takes my notebook and writes down what she thinks are the Chinese characters: *Yin Luyi.* I stare at them. *Luyi* means "Road of Friendship." The surname, *Yin,* is the character that means "silver."

"I'm trying to find her," I explain. "Lacking Virtue Pan tells me she is in Beijing. I want to apologize to her."

"No one does that," Scarlet says, raising an eyebrow. "No one even talks about the Cultural Revolution." But after rooming with me for a year, she's used to my strange ways. In 1994, when I first asked Scarlet about Yin, she provided only the sketchiest details. Now when I ask how Yin came to approach me, she furrows her brow, the way she always did when she was unsure what to say. "She met you through me. Yin and I were on the varsity volleyball team. She had entered Beijing University ahead of us. We were the only two history majors on the team, so we became friendly. She was very pretty, very vivacious."

I didn't know Scarlet had been the conduit. In my memory, Yin had approached Erica and me out of the blue. This now means that, in the context of the times, Yin endangered Scarlet by involving her in the quest to leave China. Scarlet suddenly looks upset. "In hindsight, I was so gullible," she says, sounding resentful. "I hardly knew her. She used me. She deliberately befriended me to get to you."

As she absentmindedly refills my teacup, I sense that she's reliving our student days. We all had tried so hard to live up to Maoist standards of behavior. Now she is the wife of a rich man, living in a city that worships wealth. From that new perspective, Scarlet reconsiders Yin's request. "Actually, she didn't ask for much," she muses. "She just wanted to go the United States. It was no big deal. Except that she was very much ahead of her time. We just didn't understand."

I press for details of what happened next. At the time, China was a nation of secrets. Scarlet naturally would have been forbidden to breathe a word to me, a foreigner. "I remember in 1994 you told me that Yin had been denounced," I prompt.

Scarlet shakes her head. "It wasn't a *pipan dahui* [a denunciation rally]. It was a *piping hui* [a criticism session]," she says, drawing a crucial Maoist distinction. Fu the Enforcer and Cadre Huang had frequently subjected Erica and me to criticism sessions. It was like being summoned to the principal's office in high school—not pleasant, but not devastating either. A denunciation rally, on the other hand, was brutal and vicious. I was relieved to hear that it had been merely a criticism session.

"She had a lot of *sixiang*," Scarlet continues. *Sixiang,* a loaded word, is hard to translate. It means ideology, thinking, big ideas, second thoughts. Indeed, Yin had boldly declared her dreams, and suffered terribly for it. But if she had only been criticized, not denounced, then why had she been expelled? Before I can ask, my roommate says, almost dreamily, "They wanted me to repudiate her. I refused. I had no idea what to say. So someone else wrote my speech for me."

That's not what Scarlet said in 1994 when I sought her out after reading my diary. Back then she implied that she had remained silent. I don't challenge this new revelation. I don't think she even remembers what she told me twelve years ago. Perhaps, like me, she is only just beginning to come to terms with what she did in the past. Perhaps in the ensuing time she has, well, peacefully evolved.

"Remember Hu Guocheng?" she says, interrupting my thoughts.

I did. He was a male classmate, smart as a whip, articulate and attractive, with ambitions to join the Communist Party.

"He wrote the denunciation. I had to read it aloud. I didn't dare refuse. Others spoke, too," says Scarlet.

Scarlet looks discomfited. I don't condemn my roommate. In a political culture as repressive as China's, how much choice did individuals really have? I had a choice. If I had never tattled on Yin, nothing of consequence would have happened to me.

I was a foreigner, an outsider, a person with a passport. I would not have been punished. In contrast it would have been suicidal at that time for Scarlet or any other Chinese person to take a principled stand. She had to obey the order to denounce Yin unless she wanted to risk being punished herself. My roommate was complicit in Yin's disgrace, but she was also under immense pressure to cooperate. In light of what I did, how could I ever judge her?

I knew the criticism meeting had been held in Building Thirty-Six, Yin's own dormitory, but I had few details. "Did she cry?" I now ask.

"No, she didn't. She didn't say a word. She just stood there."

"Then why was she expelled?" I ask.

"She wasn't expelled. They didn't call it *kaichu* [expulsion]. She just didn't receive her diploma. They sent her home."

That sounds like an expulsion to me. But China has always been a culture rooted in the written word. *Kaichu,* expulsion, was a precise, legalistic term. We sit in silence for a moment. Then Scarlet says, "You should try to find Wang Chunmei. Do you remember her?"

Spring Plum Wang was slender, energetic and tough as iron. She looked good in a Mao suit, like one of the fanatical Red Guards in the propaganda posters waving Mao's Little Red Book. As I recall, she was the Party representative for the class ahead of Scarlet's.

"Spring Plum Wang was hired on as faculty after graduation," Scarlet says. "She's now Communist Party secretary of the entire history department. Maybe she'll know about Yin."

I hear a door opening. Scarlet's husband, Zhang Congmi, walks into the living room. He has come home mid-morning especially to see me. (Yes, he has the same surname as Scarlet, as does their son-in-law. That's what happens when there are a hundred million Zhangs in one country.)

Scarlet abruptly stops talking about Yin. She had told her maid not to come, so we could talk without being overheard. Now it seems she doesn't want her husband to hear us, either. Everyone in China compartmentalizes the Cultural Revolution, storing the nightmare away in the far recesses of their minds. Spouses hide what they did from each other. They don't tell their children or friends. It's not a topic anyone seems eager to revisit.

Zhang has a round face and all his hair, which is dyed coal black. He wears blindingly white trousers and a crisp white shirt, a subliminal signal that he does no manual labor. Scarlet dutifully fetches his slippers, placing them at his feet. Then she gets him a chilled can of Coke from her huge refrigerator, pops it open and puts it on the coffee table in front of him. Somehow her behavior bothers me. One of Mao's most famous quotations was "Women hold up half of heaven." Yet Scarlet has morphed into a dutiful wife.

Zhang fills me in on how his company has expanded in recent years. In addition to his equipment-leasing and film businesses, he has a television series starring Dr. Henry Lee, a Chinese American forensic scientist who has worked on the JonBenet Ramsey murder, the O. J. Simpson trial, the Laci Peterson murder case, the post-9/11 investigation, the sniper shootings in Washington, DC, and the suicide death of deputy White House counsel Vincent Foster. Zhang tells me he's leaving that afternoon for a month-long shoot in Henan province for a movie about a 1940s Chinese war hero.

At sixty-three, he is a rich man. His company employs fifty people and has revenues of several million dollars U.S. a year. "My husband always wanted to *chu ren tou di,*" Scarlet says proudly, using an aphorism that means "stand a head above others."

Even though Scarlet doesn't raise the topic of Yin, I want to know what Zhang thinks about my quest. He shakes his head ruefully. "In Mao Zedong's era, we worked so hard and we were always hungry," he says, swallowing a mouthful of Coke. "Now, as long as we don't speak about politics, our economic development is fast. We say in five years the world market will be ours. Let them discuss politics at the very top of the government. We'd rather not ourselves."

Zhang tells me his family fled a famine in Shandong province in the 1930s. They ended up in Manchuria, where they opened a business and prospered. Wartime inflation wiped them out on the eve of the Communist takeover. That turned out to be a fabulous stroke of luck because it meant they escaped persecution during the Cultural Revolution. Zhang's capitalist-class background, however, disqualified him for university. He was working as a photographer in the propaganda department at the Beijing Petrochemical General Factory when Scarlet showed up. (History degrees weren't much use for anything but propaganda work.) She was leggy, curvaceous and a graduate of the best university in the country. He was eight years older, a go-getter, handsome and charismatic. Despite a problematic family background, he had successfully made it into the Chinese Communist Party. That was Scarlet's goal, too. They married, and immediately had a daughter, Mao Mao.

I ask him why they keep moving. He laughs. "To get a parking space," he says. When I laugh, too, at his wittiness, he says, "It's true. In 1999, when I'd get home late at our apartment near the Science Center, there were no parking spaces left. In 2003, at our second home, there was no space either. We moved to Rose Garden because it had a double garage."

I have heard of Rose Garden, on the outskirts of Beijing. It was renowned as the most expensive, over-the-top housing development in the city. Their villa had five bedrooms, six bathrooms, his-and-hers saunas, a table-tennis room, a pool-table room, a library and a swimming pool. He eventually realized it was too big and too much trouble. "When you don't have something, you really want it. When you get it, you realize how much work it is to have so much. It was so tiring to barbecue all the time. We had to clean the pool every two days. I had to sit with guests in the sauna. We had to buy lightbulbs by the case."

Now he wants to rent. "Places are getting more and more luxurious every year. I want to keep upgrading. If you rent, you can leave any time."

Scarlet interrupts. "I want to own a house," she says. "I also want a million-yuan Mercedes-Benz. I want something from the SEL 300 series. They're starting to manufacture them here. There's already a waiting list."

I'm speechless. I never dreamed my Maoist roommate would covet a $130,000 car. When she sees my shocked expression, she quickly points to her husband. "I want him to have a safe car." Scarlet reminds me of that song. Like Janis Joplin, she is waiting for her Mercedes-Benz. The Zhangs currently have two cars, including a Nissan luxury sedan with leather seats, darkened windows and burled-wood trim. I have no doubt the next time I visit, Scarlet will have her Mercedes.

"In the 1980s, if we had twenty thousand yuan, we felt rich. In the 1990s, if we had a hundred thousand yuan, we felt rich. Now we have millions of yuan. Five million is nothing. Now one hundred million yuan [$13 million] is something." Despite their wealth, adjusting to all the changes in Beijing hasn't been easy. Scarlet doesn't know how to drive and she no longer rides her bike because of the traffic and pollution. Every weekend the family goes for an outing to the countryside to relax. "My husband has a license, but he's afraid to drive now. Mao Mao drives, or our son-in-law. Sometimes we use a chauffeur."

Zhang finishes his Coke and gets up to leave. After, Scarlet confides that last spring she ignored his wishes to rent a house. Taking Mao Mao with her, she checked out a new development seventeen kilometers north of Beijing. In deference to his aversion to monster homes, she bought a 3,900-square-foot villa for 2.7 million yuan ($350,000 U.S.). The developer is a subsidiary of Poly Technologies, a military conglomerate founded by Deng Zhifang, the younger son of Deng Xiaoping. I interviewed Zhifang in 1981 for the *New York Times Sunday Magazine,* cornering him in a library carrel at the University of Rochester. He was then a doctoral student in quantum optics. After graduating he went on to use his father's connections to control a multi-million-dollar stake in real estate, shipping and construction in Shanghai and Hong Kong. In recent years, Zhifang has fallen into disrepute following several business scandals and, crucially, Deng Xiaoping's death.

When I remark on how little gray hair she has, Scarlet looks at me like I'm an idiot. "I dye my hair," she says. And then she informs me she has had her eyelids surgically redone, too. "You didn't notice," she says, reproachfully. She tells me she didn't like her single-fold eyelids, which predominate among Asians. A few years back she had a surgeon slit her eyelids horizontally and stitch them up to give her double folds. As far back as the tenth century, Chinese prized the rarity of a double-fold lid, which they thought made a man or woman—but especially a woman—look more attractive. I can hardly believe this is my old roommate, the one who never glanced at herself in the mirror, who was shy about changing in front of me. She always refused to go out without her Mao jacket. A sweater alone was far too revealing or, as she put it back then, *nan kan,* "hard to look at."

Scarlet tried so hard to enter the Communist Party. It never happened. Always she was rejected as not quite good enough. "I gave up," she says now. "I didn't care anymore." Her husband is the new Beijing oxymoron, a rich capitalist card-carrying Communist Party member. She says he's supposed to attend Party meetings for retirees but never goes. "He hasn't gone in ten years. They phone him. He tells them, 'I'm tied up.' He still has to pay his Party dues every month, so he sends our son-in-law with the money. The Party officials tell him, 'You're not allowed to send someone else with your dues.' They assign him internal Party documents to study. He sends our son-in-law to pick them up, but he doesn't bother to read them."

She laughs. "Sometimes there are surplus monies in the Party coffers, so they distribute goods."

"Like what?"

"Recently they gave out a bottle of soy sauce. He sent our son-in-law to pick it up."

15

It's Like Looking for
Her in a Vast Ocean

M y meeting with Scarlet has failed to provide new leads, and Pan has yet to call me with Yin's cellphone number. I now am convinced my initial excitement at his information was premature. I have a sinking feeling he isn't going to help me further. It isn't enough for me to know that Yin has survived, if indeed she has. I need to know what happened to her. And I want to apologize. I can't just sit around hoping Pan will come through—I have to keep hunting for Yin on my own.

Oliver August, a journalist with *The Times,* suggests I hire a private detective. I'm surprised. There were none when I was here in the 1990s, but upon making inquiries I discover that about three hundred detective agencies have opened in Beijing. That's another advantage of a police state gone bourgeois: you can hire an ex-cop to do what Beijing cops have always done— filch records, spy on people, tap phones, open mail, tail someone, pry into the government's confidential databases.

Long March Wang, the boys' teacher, has called ahead to check the fee at one called the Beijing Ming Hao Private Detective Agency (literally, Smart and Meticulous). To find a missing person, they offer a quote of 3,000 yuan, about $400. The Smart and Meticulous Private Detective Agency is located in a luxury residential condo development called Fu Li Cheng, which means "Rich and Powerful City." If I'm to have any chance of finding Yin, I'm glad to have as reinforcements a smart and meticulous detective agency successful enough to locate in a rich and powerful city.

The grounds are lavishly landscaped with an Italian theme. I walk through shaded porticoes reminiscent of Bologna, past fountains with cement cherubs and, strangely, a miniature amphitheater that might seat, oh, five max. The agency is on the thirtieth floor of Tower A2. As at Beautiful Lodging, the elevator is laden with the accoutrements of conspicuous consumption: dark wood paneling, granite flooring and outsized gilded mirrors, one of them cracked.

I knock on the door of Apartment 3012. A man in his thirties answers. He's expecting me. He's dressed in khaki trousers, leather shoes and an orange polo shirt and has a military-style brush cut. With both hands, he presents his business card. (To use just one hand would be offensively casual.) I politely extend both hands to receive it. The card is embossed with a silhouette of Dick Tracy in a fedora. I flip it over. On the back is a list of the agency's services. It's a neat although inadvertent summary of Beijing's social headaches in the twenty-first century.

Smart and Meticulous handles:

> extramarital affairs
> tracking of debtors
> theft of trademark
> property searches
> tracing phone calls and content of text messages

    assisting school transfers for Beijing children
    helping out-of-town children enroll in Beijing schools
    spying on sons and daughters who are away from
      home
    intellectual property rights inspection
    providing proof of industrial espionage
    searching for missing persons

The last item on the card is what I want. Yin isn't missing, of course. I'm sure her family and friends know exactly where she is. *I* just can't find her. According to the card, the detective's name is Han Cheng, which means Honest Han. He tells me he's thirty-two. He has what the Chinese would call an "open" face—good-natured, well-meaning. But he also has the insolent slouch of a Beijing cop, and I sense he's wilier than he looks.

Honest Han ushers me into his office, which is furnished with two desks, two computers and several telephones. Behind his desk is some framed calligraphy. Someone has tucked two small photographs of Chairman Mao into the frame. I ask what the calligraphy means. "*Ming Cha Qiu Hao,*" he reads aloud, explaining it is an aphorism which gives the agency its name. The four characters mean "Smartly Detect Tiny Changes."

Chinese detective agencies are a brilliant merger of communism and capitalism. Like any other business, they must register with the government, but they operate in a legal gray zone. At Smart and Meticulous, a cabinet displays, like a collection of fine porcelain, the paraphernalia of the trade: army helmets, police badges, walkie talkies, binoculars, a webcam, a VoIP phone and a couple of computer motherboards.

"What are your credentials?" I ask Honest Han.

"I was originally in the army. After that I joined the Ministry of Public Security," he says. "Four years ago I quit the police to start Smart and Meticulous. We have more than forty detectives and operate twenty-four hours a day. There is always someone available to answer the telephone."

On cue, the phone rings. Honest Han picks it up. "Yes, yes, I just received a call. . . . I'll get the police there to stop them." He hangs up and turns back to me. "Our main business is looking for people, people who owe money," he says. "But recently we've been very busy with marital problems. We check out cheating husbands, follow them around, take photos. We mainly work for the wives." He grins at me in a way that makes me squirm. "We protect women."

I remember when it was impossible to get a divorce in Beijing. Fat Paycheck worked at the Foreign Languages Bureau in Beijing with a senior editor, a Communist Party member, whose husband was convicted of bigamy. Yet even after he went to prison, the Party refused to grant her a divorce. Now the divorce rate in China rivals that in the United States. Extramarital affairs are big business, not just for detective agencies, but also for filmmakers and writers. A Chinese author, Qian Fuchang, is transmitting a novel about an extramarital affair via text-messaging, one seventy-word chapter at a time. I should make sure Alfred's on the list.

"We also trace phone calls, check text messages," Honest Han says. "We have someone in the phone company who provides records for us."

"That's fabulous," I tell him, and I mean it. Obtaining phone records without a court's permission is the dream of every investigative, or just plain nosy, journalist. Unfortunately, it's also terribly illegal at home.

I tell Honest Han I'm searching for someone I met briefly at Beijing University in 1973. It occurs to me that, like Teacher Zhou, he wasn't even born at the time. I add that I'm unsure of her precise name, and that she studied history. "Some people think she ended up in Manchuria," I add, "but one person has told me she's in Beijing." It all sounds pathetically vague.

Honest Han takes notes, a good sign. He doesn't ask why I'm looking for her, and I don't offer any reason. After a moment, he shakes his head. "It's hard to find someone after such a long time," he says. "There are very few clues. We find 90 percent of people, but this one is difficult." He sighs. "Nineteen seventy-three was the Cultural Revolution. It's very difficult, the decade of the seventies. It was very chaotic. I think the records won't be there."

Essentially, he is confirming what the Beijing University alumni office already told me. "Those were the years of *dong dang*," he says, using the pejorative word for turbulence, upheaval, chaos. "It's like looking for her in a vast ocean," he concludes glumly.

I lean forward. I tell Honest Han that I am anxious to find this person, and am willing to spend what it takes. At that he brightens. His tone turns optimistic. "The person is a female," he says, nodding. "Our medical care is pretty good now. She should be still alive."

I think to myself: *if the biggest plus Honest Han can think of is that Yin is a female, then my search is doomed.*

He keeps talking. "We'd have to start from Beijing University. We have to find an inside source there so we can take a peek at the files. And then we'll need to go through the police to officially request her records. We have someone in the police who can check the Ministry of State Security *Hukou* Records

Database. We'll get a photo from them and show you. See if you recognize her. If she's the right one, and she's in Beijing, it's easy. Otherwise, we'll have to go to Manchuria."

When I ask how much this will all cost, the price magically quintuples to fifteen thousand yuan—nearly two thousand dollars. I don't blink. Two can be inscrutable. "If we can't find her, we'll give you some money back," Honest Han quickly adds. He coughs. "Less receipts for gas, food, taxis, a car to Manchuria, of course, and some bribes and pay-offs." I suspect the "bribes and pay-offs" will round off the bill to, oh, fifteen thousand yuan.

"How about a bit cheaper?" I suggest, knowing he expects me to haggle. Hiring a detective in Beijing is no different from buying twenty pairs of gray socks on the street.

"I really haven't asked for very much," he says reluctantly. "I can't guarantee anything." We both fall quiet. Honest Han breaks the silence. "If we put our energies into it, we should be able to find her. You have come from so far away, we'll try our best."

"How long do you think this will take?" I ask, adding that I'll be leaving Beijing in less than two weeks.

"In the best-case scenario, if things happen fast, maybe one week. If things go slowly, maybe one month. By then, if we are getting nowhere, we'll give up."

I don't really trust Honest Han. I tuck his card in my bag and tell him I'll get back to him.

16

This Is the Big Boss Culture!

I forgot. I do have one more lead. Scarlet suggested I look up Spring Plum Wang. Cadre Huang will know how to reach her.

On August 17, just as I'm about to phone him, he calls me. "I've found her name," he says excitedly. "You're right. It's Yin Luoyi. She entered Beijing University in 1970. It's true she left the school, but it wasn't because of you. It had nothing to do with you."

I don't believe him. Cadre Huang has lied to me before, blandly, smoothly and ever so convincingly. He's half the reason I was initially so naive in 1972. Fu the Enforcer was the other half. For instance, they told me that everyone in China had enough to eat. They told me everyone was happy and content. They assured me that Chairman Mao was infallible. For my part, I accepted everything they said—until my near-expulsion. At that point I began to think critically, to compare what they were saying—"Everyone has enough to eat thanks to the wise leadership of Chairman Mao"—with the reality: food rationing.

Now I assume Cadre Huang is lying to discourage me from picking over old wounds. He probably thinks my quest for Yin will lose face for the university. Anyway, why would he want to help me now?

He interrupts my thoughts. "Do you know Spring Plum Wang?" he asks.

"Yes," I stammer in surprise. "She's the Party secretary of the history department."

"I think she can help you," he says. "She lives in my compound. We're neighbors." He gives me Spring Plum's office number and suggests I give her a call.

I hang up. Why are both Scarlet and Cadre Huang pointing me to Spring Plum Wang? I call her office at Beijing University right away. A woman answers. "Spring Plum Wang is out," she says. I explain that I was one of the first foreign students in the early seventies, and ask if she'll take a message for me. "I think I remember you," the woman says, turning quite friendly. "I was also a student at Beijing University in 1973."

She gives me Spring Plum's home number. I call there too, but no one answers. No answering machine kicks in, either. Beijingers don't use them, possibly because they don't like talking to a machine. And, of course, because everyone carries a cellphone. I know Spring Plum will get the message I leave at her office. I'm sure she remembers me. I hope she'll call me back. I'm not sure why, but I sense I'm on the verge of finding Yin.

To celebrate this tiny bit of progress, I suggest to Fat Paycheck that we get massages. He's dubious, but I convince him a massage parlor might be fun. And—here's the clincher—at fancy ones, there's free food. Leaving the boys at home with a cache of illegal DVDs, we head for the Oriental Taipan Spa. From none when we lived here in the early 1990s, Beijing now has hundreds, possibly thousands, of massage parlors. Some are brothels, of course, but most are legitimate spas. I chose Oriental Taipan for sentimental reasons. It's at the entrance to Pagoda Garden, the gray concrete diplomatic compound where we lived when I was the *Globe*'s Beijing correspondent. Now the spa lights up our drab old entrance with a huge, blinking neon sign.

The building is as flashy as a seafood restaurant but quiet as a Taoist temple. We walk across a little wooden bridge over a fake brook and down a granite staircase. (What *is* it with all this granite?)

Taipan is Cantonese for "Big Boss." And that is how they treat you here. At the reception desk, a young woman in a pink uniform explains the menu of treatments. It includes lymphatic-system therapy "for ladies only" and scary options like "ear candling" and "scraping." The last involves oiling your back then scraping it along the spine and "body meridian." Fat Paycheck thinks it sounds gruesome. I suggest a classic Chinese foot massage, which I've had before. You soak your feet in a tub of scalding water scented with herbs and rose petals; after a while someone comes and pummels your feet, gouges your arches and nearly yanks your toes out of their sockets. It last about forty minutes and is incredibly relaxing—once the pain stops.

"Sorry, all the foot-massage rooms are booked," the young woman says. We settle on hour-long massages. A slippered attendant leads us across slate floors lit by votive candles. We walk past pools of tropical fish, through a maze with doors leading to private rooms. "Private" does not mean individual. It means private for your group. Most rooms hold four to six people—in Beijing you go out for dinner, karaoke or a massage with friends. Beijingers like to do things in groups, perhaps one reason collectivism survived so long. The attendant takes us into a room for three. Before she snaps a privacy curtain across the middle of the room, I glimpse a man lying prone on a massage table on the other side, with two other men, fully clothed, sitting beside him.

"We don't have any more private rooms," she says, apologizing. Our side of the room is furnished with a small cabinet, two white leatherette massage beds and soft pillows wrapped in clean white towels. We each get disposable slippers and freshly laundered red pajamas sealed in clear plastic bags. (Chinese apparently prefer to remain modestly clothed throughout a massage.)

"What would you like to eat?" the attendant says, handing us a snack menu. We order a platter of fresh fruit, toast with peanut butter (the latest in trendy Western foods to hit Beijing) and glasses of iced lemon water. Next we order the therapist. "Would you like a male or a female?" According to the Chinese principle of yin and yang, women should have masseurs and males should have masseuses, but we both decide on males. In less than five minutes, the attendant returns with our snacks. We hoist ourselves up on the beds and eat stretched out, Roman-style.

Meanwhile, I eavesdrop on our neighbor. The two other men must be his underlings, because they grunt assent to whatever drivel he says. Also, they're only having ice water; only those having massages get free food. It seems strange that a boss would bring his staff to his massage, but then, Louis XIV included the court in his toilet sessions. In *Catch-22,* Colonel Cathcart defecates in front of Chaplain Tappman. And President Lyndon Johnson also had a habit of talking to aides while sitting on the toilet. I once had a meeting with a senior editor who pumped breast milk while talking to me about an investigative piece. I think breastfeeding in public is fine, but *that* felt weird.

A cellphone rings. "Hello, Boss," says the guy having the massage. (I can tell because his voice quavers in sync with the pounding on his back.) "I'm having a massage. No problem." Sharing a massage room with someone who brings an entourage and chats on his cellphone would irritate many people. As a reporter, I find it quite diverting. The man sprinkles his conversation with English words—"investor center," "Columbia MBA," "Intel"—and is apparently talking about someone who just got nailed by the tax bureau.

"He set up a fake Chinese-foreign joint venture," he says. "He was trying to evade taxes. He needed at least eight million U.S. dollars for capital. He only had five million dollars." He hangs up and phones his chauffeur to pick him up.

Before we can finish our snacks, our masseurs arrive, dressed in white uniforms. One is from Hebei province, the other from Jiangsu province. Mine starts with my neck and shoulders. It hurts so much that to keep from yelping, I pretend I'm being tortured in Afghanistan to reveal my sources. He works his way down my back. By the time he reaches my calves, I'm sucking in my breath to avoid screaming. He finishes by rubbing the back of my legs so hard and fast that the friction creates heat.

The therapists are surprised by Fat Paycheck's fluent, unaccented Chinese. He tells them he arrived in 1966, at the start of the Cultural Revolution. "I lived here for twenty years," he says.

"But he's never had a massage," I add.

"Then you haven't been here in twenty years," says the one working on me. "We didn't have massages then."

"Only Mao Zedong had massages then," says the one working on Norman. The masseur is right. Chairman Mao never took baths or showers. Instead, someone rubbed him down nightly with hot towels. And while we're on the subject of sensuous pleasures, Mao also had bevies of young women entertain him with song and dance—and perhaps more. When I studied history at Beijing University, two of my prettier classmates—both professional performers, a contralto and a zither player—would disappear regularly. Where they went was all top secret at the time. Years later, Future told me the two had been summoned to perform for Mao in Zhongnanhai.

In the old days, people always referred to Mao as "Chairman Mao," "the Great Helmsman," "the Red, Red Sun in Our Hearts." Although the cult of Mao has never been dismantled, the post-Mao generation has no time for veneration. I notice that the young masseur uses Mao's whole name, Mao Zedong, as if he had been just another guy. It's the lèse-majesté equivalent of calling the queen of England "Liz," which is probably how Cockney masseurs in London talk about Her Majesty.

Big Boss charges 138 yuan ($18) for a ninety-minute massage. The masseurs work seven days a week, eleven to thirteen hours a day. For this they are paid about 75 yuan a day. Hands-on service jobs like these are considered menial. The only Beijingers who deign to do this are the blind. Oriental Big Boss Spa recruits its therapists—none of them blind—from impoverished rural areas, right after high school. It gives these migrants six months' training, temporary residence permits and a bed in a company dormitory. The therapists normally eat and rest only when there are no clients.

It's nearly midnight when we leave. At the reception desk, a manager is berating a young masseuse who looks limp with exhaustion. "You always want to quit working at this time," the manager shrieks.

"That's not true," says the masseuse, looking frightened. "This is the first time. I'm not feeling well."

As we leave, I take a brochure. In addition to describing the spa services, there is a Q&A section:

> Q: In what way is Big Boss unique as a spa and massage chain?
>
> A: Big Boss presently employs a great number of people who are mainly underprivileged and provides them with a home, brings back their self-confidence and creates for them a career path with future prospects. One important element at Big Boss is—happiness brought to you by therapists and staff who are themselves happy in their work! This is the Big Boss culture!

Sam has been playing road hockey with some expat Canadians and Americans. One Sunday, when the game is canceled because of the heat, I propose another massage. Fat Paycheck refuses to go again, but Ben and Sam are lured by the offer of free food. This time we get a deluxe room for three with a shower and a flat-screen television. We change into the red pajamas and lounge on the white leatherette beds. Sam, who has already eaten, orders fresh-squeezed watermelon juice. Ben, who is famished, and who has learned from his mother about getting his money's worth, orders hot lemon tea, iced lemon water, a Coke, fresh-squeezed papaya juice, watermelon juice, toast with peanut butter, Chinese stewed-beef noodle soup, a bowl of rice with scrambled eggs sautéed with fresh tomatoes and a fruit plate of watermelon and sliced snow pear.

The attendant, to her credit, doesn't bat an eye. As the plates pile up, she asks whether we want male or female therapists. I choose a male therapist. The boys choose females, although I'm not sure they're thinking about Chinese principles of yin and yang. "Is it okay if I laugh?" Sam asks, as his masseuse starts on him. He giggles hysterically throughout, to Ben's embarrassment.

My masseur is from rural Manchuria. He works his way down my spine, finding muscles in my buttocks I never knew I had. He slaps my calves, hard, rhythmically and loudly. It kills. He tells me he's twenty-six years old. The two women working on Ben and Sam are nineteen and twenty-three. When my masseur hears we're from Canada, he starts talking geopolitics. "I want China to be strong and powerful," he says. "We hate America, the way it is invading Iraq. Maybe in twenty years, we'll surpass America. Then the world will be stable and peaceful."

"If China replaces America as the next superpower," I say, between gasps, "it will be no different. It, too, will need oil and natural resources."

"Maybe you're right," he says, pounding my shoulders, "but I don't like the way Canada makes immigrants pay lots of money to enter the country. I want China to be powerful. Then when foreigners come here, we'll ask them to pay a lot of money."

I mention that I used to live inside Pagoda Garden. When he asks what I did here, I say I worked as a reporter. "What happened during the Tiananmen Incident?" he asks, using the neutral term. "Is it true that thousands of people were killed?"

"Foreign reporters estimate that one thousand to three thousand were killed," I say. "The lower number was reported by the *New York Times*. The higher number comes from the Chinese Red Cross."

"I was ten years old at the time," he says. "I remember it very clearly. We had a little black and white television in the countryside, and we watched it all night. It was really scary."

"What are you talking about?" says the masseuse working on Sam. She was three years old at the time. The one working on Ben looks up and asks, "What is the Tiananmen Incident?"

I wait to see what my masseur will tell them. He says nothing. I too say nothing. It has been so easy for the regime to airbrush events from history. It is hard enough to teach the next generation much history, even in a country with freedom of speech and a free press. It is impossible in one without. After their massages, Ben and Sam order more bowls of beef noodles. As the boys scarf down the food, I realize that the nation that prides itself on having the longest unbroken historical record in the world can no longer face its own history. The Cultural Revolution is a blank, as is the 1989 massacre by PLA soldiers of unarmed protesters demonstrating for democracy, human rights and an end to government corruption.

When Antony Thomas was making his documentary on the Tank Man, he passed out copies of the iconic photograph to undergraduates at Beijing University, where the protests had begun in 1989. In 2006, students at my alma mater were genuinely mystified. Asked to describe what the picture showed, one said, "I don't know. Maybe it's a parade or something." Another said, politely, "May I ask if this is a piece of your artwork?"

People like Scarlet who lived through Tiananmen will never forget what happened. But even she does not discuss it much. The media in China will not, cannot, touch it either. Yet something is changing. In 1999, when I typed "Tiananmen Square" at

Internet cafés in Beijing, the firewall filters on the Internet allowed through only bland tourist information. When I typed "democracy in China," there was a long pause, and then I got this response: *Internet Explorer cannot open the Internet site. A connection with the server could not be established.* I typed "June 4, 1989." Same response. I typed "human rights in China." Same response.

China's Internet police force is reputed to be thirty thousand strong. They arrest those promoting democracy in blogs. They monitor Internet forums and chat rooms and, within minutes, erase critical comments. But as every victim of spam in the West knows, there are ways to get around filters. During SARS, Beijing tried at first to deny it had viral outbreaks. The news leaked via cellphone text messaging. When I wrote a feature in the *Globe* detailing how the virus had spread in China, and from there to Hong Kong and then Canada, my article—in English—was emailed all over the country. I immediately began receiving comments from Chinese readers.

In 2006, in the privacy of Beautiful Lodging, Ben decides to see if he can do a Google image search. He types in "Tank Man." A page with a dozen photos of the lone figure pops up instantly. The Internet connection is about three times faster than our high-speed connection at home.

A journalist friend in Toronto, Talin Vartanian, is helping me test the great firewall of China. She regularly emails me news reports on human rights abuses in China and on Falun Gong. Everything gets through. I search for "human rights." Google instantly links me to all kinds of websites, including Amnesty International's. I type "Tiananmen Square" into the Apple laptop I've brought from Toronto. Presto! It calls up sites discussing the 1989 massacre, including the BBC, Wikipedia and *Epoch Times*. The latter is especially surprising because it's the newspaper run by Falun Gong, the spiritual exercise group which the Chinese government has denounced as an "evil cult." I bump up against the Chinese censor only when I click on the link to *Epoch Times*. Each time, it takes me instead to a page of ads for Coca-Cola, knapsacks and soccer balls. And when I click on the Falun Gong web address in one article, this message eventually pops up: . . . *could not open the page . . . because the server stopped responding.*

In fact, my colleague in Beijing, Geoff York, tells me that while websites pop up for Wikipedia or Amnesty International, you can't actually access them. Ditto for Voice of America, BBC News, and anything related to Tibet or the Falun Gong. James Miles, *The Economist* correspondent, says that if his Internet searches yield too many sensitive results, the firewall has the annoying ability to shut off Google for a long period. "It could be an innocent question about the development of Buddhist spirituality that produces a lot of FLG [Falun Gong] results," says James. "Even the names of Chinese leaders will produce a shutdown in Google. But the bottom line is there's always a way around."

Sex in Da City

Beijing is being transformed in ways that are erasing its history. It is a metaphor for my search for Yin. How do I come to terms with my past in a place that denies its existence? After class one day, Long March Wang says she'd like to take the boys for a stroll through one of the last intact neighborhoods. Dong Si, or East Four, as it awkwardly translates into English, gets its name from an ornate four-sided wooden archway demolished long ago. Like so much of Beijing, only the name remains.

"They're going to preserve this neighborhood," says Long March, leading us down an alley called Third Lane. Unlike the smelly lane behind Beautiful Lodging, this *hutong* is clean and picturesque. It has century-old gray-brick homes bordered by fragrant locust trees, individually tagged with little metal signs stating they are three hundred years old. We pass a white-tiled public toilet, evidence that the homes still lack plumbing. Sam helpfully runs inside, and reports back that it's clean. The squat toilets have an automatic flush. The soap and taps are automatic too. There is even a ramp and a special toilet for disabled residents.

Farther down we pass a brightly painted set of exercise machines. In 2001, free outdoor rowing machines, elliptical walkers and stationary bikes popped up all over Beijing. Part of a charm offensive during the city's bid for the 2008 Olympics, the subliminal message was: Beijingers are sports enthusiasts. But no matter the motive, the outdoor machines keep people in shape, cut health care costs and, because neighbors get to know one another, reduce crime. If only we installed them next to sandboxes in Toronto, parents could get a workout while watching their kids play.

I notice half a dozen stray cats and dogs. Long March guesses they have been abandoned by fickle owners. "Other people take them in and feed them," she says. Mao banned pets as bourgeois indulgences because food was scarce. He particularly hated dogs because they used to raise the alarm against his guerrilla fighters. Not surprisingly, he labeled his worst two-legged enemies "running dogs of American imperialism." After Mao's death, people began surreptitiously keeping dogs, although they remained illegal until the 1990s. The urban middle class had to content itself with renting them for ten-minute walks in special parks. Special police squads would sweep through *hutongs,* nabbing illicit dogs for rural exile or strangling them outright with steel-wire loops. (I actually interviewed a team of Beijing police who demonstrated how they choked the dogs.)

Halfway down the alley, we spot a blinking sign: "Automated Mahjong Tables. Five yuan. Open 24 Hours a Day. Free Tea." I've never seen a mahjong parlor in Beijing. Like pet dogs and massages, mahjong was considered bourgeois. During the Cultural Revolution, people reluctantly discarded their treasured sets of ivory tiles to avoid persecution by Red Guards like

Scarlet and Future. We peek inside the door. "Come in, come in," says a middle-aged man, with hair dyed coal-black and chalky skin so unnaturally white he looks like Boris Karloff. He tells us his name is Zhang Hanhua (Flourishing China).

Except for four mahjong tables, this den of iniquity looks like an ordinary living room. It has a tan sofa, a coffee table and a white ceramic-tiled floor. Two women nod hospitably. One is Flourishing's wife, Hu Xiaoju (Dawn Chrysanthemum). The other is a friend who has dropped by to chat. "Sit down," Chrysanthemum tells the boys, gesturing to a green-baize-covered table.

"We don't know how to play mahjong," I say.

"It's easy," she says, pushing a button. The table starts to rumble and, after a moment, spits out the dice. The table rumbles again. A trap door opens in the center of it and, like an automated bowling alley setting up pins, the tiles rise up, preset in neat rows, before each player.

Chrysanthemum explains that the game involves skill, strategy, calculation and luck. Each tile is marked with symbols or a Chinese character. The first person who can build sets of three of all their tiles wins. "Let the children play a game," she urges. "No charge." The boys are keen to play. Flourishing deputizes his wife's friend to teach Ben and Sam. Long March is pressed into being the fourth player. Despite her bookish air, she turns out to be pretty sharp at mahjong.

Flourishing presses bottles of orange soda on Ben and Sam. I insist on paying, and he matter-of-factly accepts, an odd combination of traditional hospitality and modern commerce. He says the house belonged to his late mother. Five months ago, he and Chrysanthemum renovated it, imported automated tables from Japan and opened for business. Their take is twenty yuan per table per game. A poster on the wall says, "Small amounts of money don't constitute gambling, but are a form of entertainment and relaxation."

"Isn't gambling illegal?" I ask Flourishing.

"As long as there are no fights, as long as the police aren't called, we're fine," he says, lighting a cigarette. "You *have* to bet money. Otherwise mahjong isn't interesting. Some gamble just one or two yuan at a time. Others come here with five hundred yuan and don't leave until it's all gone."

He tells me he is forty-nine. Like Scarlet's husband, he used to work at the Forestry Ministry but took early retirement. Their university-bound daughter stays in their nearby apartment. He and his wife sleep here because the mahjong parlor never closes. Most customers arrive in the evening and stay until dawn. Chrysanthemum cooks hot meals to order in the back so clients never have to stop gambling.

A white Siamese cat stalks across the floor. Chrysanthemum picks it up and strokes its long white fur. It is wearing a red leather collar studded with rhinestones. "We never let Precious out of our sight. We're afraid somebody will steal him," she says, kissing it on the mouth. "We paid eight hundred yuan for him as a kitten. Now he's worth two thousand yuan." Cats, like real estate, seem to be a good investment.

Chrysanthemum rips open a purple foil packet and hand-feeds her cat a snack of processed shrimp. "We spend three hundred yuan a month on her food," she says. The old Maoist in me can't help thinking that's two weeks' pay for a migrant worker.

Speaking of food, it's past lunchtime. We should leave, but suddenly it starts to rain, well, cats and dogs. The downpour is so heavy even Beijing's ubiquitous taxis stop trying to navigate the *hutong*. We're trapped. Chrysanthemum goes in the back and makes extra rice. Flourishing opens a little round folding table. They ask us to join them for a simple lunch: half a carp braised in soy sauce, stir-fried cauliflower with ripe tomatoes, and a dish of soft green chili peppers sautéed with a touch of sugar and oyster sauce. Over lunch, they try to sort out who we are. We explain that Fat Paycheck is my husband, Ben and Sam are our children, and Long March is their Chinese teacher.

"You *pay* someone to teach them Chinese?" Flourishing says incredulously, ignoring the fact that Long March is sitting beside him. She doesn't look offended. Flourishing exhales a cloud of tobacco smoke. "Your kids should just hang out with us. They will learn Chinese by chatting with us. We could find you an apartment for three thousand yuan, hire a maid for one thousand yuan. She'd come every day to wash your clothes and cook your meals."

It's a thought, letting the boys laze around a smoke-filled gambling den all summer with a migrant worker at their beck and call. I tell Flourishing we'll think about it. The rain has finally stopped. We thank them for their hospitality and head out into the puddles.

"Look, Mom, people are gambling," says Sam, excitedly. "They're throwing dice on the bar counter."

We're at a bar in Houhai called Sex in Da City. Naturally, I order a cosmopolitan. Norman orders an Erdinger Weissbier dark. I point to Sam. "He'll have a Tsingtao beer." I point to Ben. "He'll have the same." The waiter doesn't bat an eyelash. Mahjong parlors and bars are not good places to take impressionable teens. But Sam understands that I'm always doing research, which is why he's helpfully pointing things out.

Despite a dismal human rights record—or perhaps *because* of it—China doesn't curb drinking rights. Just as there is no age limit on buying alcohol, there's no age limit at bars. Foreign children go a little wild here. Some teenage children of expatriate diplomats and businessmen get so drunk they throw up on the sidewalks and get into knife fights with locals. I hadn't anticipated this when I decided to bring Ben and Sam here for a month. In 1972, the city shut down by dusk. The only place to get a drink was—wait, there *was* no place to get a drink. Sex must have occurred, given the steady increase in population, but it was never apparent. Even stuff like underwear was resolutely utilitarian. The only bras available were cotton camisoles. Women sewed their own luridly printed boxer shorts. Today, Beijing's lingerie shops look like outposts for Frederick's of Hollywood.

Houhai is a happening place. It was once one of the Empress Dowager's favorite pleasure grounds, part of a north–south chain of six ornamental lakes slightly east of the Forbidden City. As a bar district, it didn't exist until SARS. During the 2003 outbreak, when authorities shut down Sanlitun, Beijing's original bar district, a new one opened in Houhai virtually overnight, with bars with names like Buffalo, Bed, Silk Road, Blue Lotus.

Sex in Da City is a two-story, neon-lit boîte. We take a prime seat by the window upstairs, overlooking the lake, until the waiter informs me there's a hefty cover charge to sit at that particular table. We quickly decamp to a less choice table, this time overlooking the bar. The Chinese decorator has mustered every Western bar stereotype: red gauze curtains, stainless-steel bar, cushioned divans, fake-fur wallpaper and a huge painting of Marilyn Monroe, her white dress billowing up over her waist.

The place is packed with twenty-somethings. In one booth the patrons have ordered a bottle of Absolut Citron. A Lucy Liu lookalike is getting plastered. The only person my age in the vicinity, apart from Fat Paycheck, is the bathroom attendant. She stands outside the mirrored door to the unisex toilet. She stares at me. I stare back. I feel I should explain that I'm working too.

Sam starts bopping to the music. "I love bars," he says. "Can we come again?"

"What's the name of this song?" I ask.

"It's 50 Cent. He was singing 'Just a Lil' Bit.' Now it's 'Don't Phunk with My Heart.' By the Black Eyed Peas."

"Can this be classified as rap music?" I ask, pen and notebook in hand.

"Yes, Mom," says Ben, sarcastically.

"Omigod, you're so dumb," says Sam.

"It's okay," Ben tells Sam. "It's only been around fifteen years. Actually, twenty." They both roll their eyes. Sam watches me take notes. "Mom," he says helpfully. "You better write that it wasn't actually 50 Cent in the club. The DJ played it."

Suddenly Sam yelps and points. A white male dancer has leaped onto the bar counter. Grabbing a shiny pole, he starts thrusting his pelvis to Britney Spears's "Toxic" (as Sam informs me). Ben Mok was right; hiring a foreigner is the ultimate Beijing status symbol. Many citizens from the former Soviet bloc countries now work in the Chinese capital. This pole dancer might be Polish, but he's probably Russian. He has a hairy chest, hairy arms and a mane of dark curly hair. Dressed in fringed white leather chaps, a black satin cowboy hat and a black mesh T-shirt, he wiggles and thrusts. When he finishes his routine, there is mild applause. "That's what girls like, Mom," Sam explains.

Next a skinny blonde jumps onto the bar. She's wearing gladiator lace-up spike heels, zebra-striped bikini bottoms and a silver mesh halter top. She shakes her blonde mane. She bumps and grinds. The applause, which includes Sam's enthusiastic clapping, is huge. After she finishes, a Chinese female customer climbs onto the bar and attempts a copycat version of the pole dance. In her pink tulle dress, she looks fairly silly. Two Chinese couples also get up to dance on the bar, at which point the bartender gives up trying to serve drinks. A man and a woman wriggle their respective pelvises, simulating copulation. Sam sits there sipping his beer and looking happy.

Had there been a Sex and Da City thirty years ago, perhaps Yin might have ordered a cosmopolitan and jumped onto the bar too. Or maybe not. In 1979 I attended one of the first dances in Beijing. It was held in secret, in an underground military bunker. I was the only foreigner present, invited to provide expertise on Western dance steps. Unfortunately my repertoire was limited to the Twist, the Monkey and the Mashed Potato, none of which were compatible with the only foreign music they had been able to find: "Red River Valley."

When Sam finally yawns, even I know it's time to leave. The male dancer has reappeared, dancing on top of the bar. He rips off his net T-shirt. The DJ calls for a customer to join him. "Is any pretty Chinese woman willing to dance with a white guy?" he asks in Chinese, adding in English for maximum sophistication, "Okay!"

"Should I go up?" I ask Fat Paycheck.

"Yeah," he says, sarcastically. "Go for it."

Ben gives me a withering glance so we call for the bill and head down the stairs. Just then, the blonde bounds out again. Now she's wearing a frilly white miniskirt and a red halter top.

I'm riveted by the possibility that, like Mr. Cowboy, she'll remove her top. I order everyone to wait.

"Is any brave Chinese man willing to dance with this beautiful white woman?" the DJ asks in Chinese, adding again in English, "Okay!"

No one responds. Suddenly the dancer spies us on the spiral staircase. She beckons to us. Actually, she beckons to Ben. Smiling sweetly, she motions for him to join her atop the bar. "Go ahead," I urge my sixteen-year-old. "It's good for my research."

He glares at me. "I'm so going to quote you," he growls. Oh dear. It seems he is writing a book of his own.

18

Sometimes It Takes a While
to Notice What's Not There

I t's been a day since I left the message for Spring Plum. She hasn't called me back. With less than two weeks remaining, I feel the time slipping away. If I'm to believe Pan, then Yin is okay even though nobody has been able to tell me what happened to her in the years following her expulsion. Everyone simply wants to forget the past. But I need to face my fears about Yin's fate. I need to see her for myself.

The August heat is relentless. The *China Daily* reports the day's high at 31 degrees Celsius (88 degrees Fahrenheit). I'm sure it's hotter. After all, *National Geographic* says temperatures in the northern half of China have been hotter than the average in the 1990s. American satellites show that thousands of lakes have disappeared in North China. In Beijing, the lovely green canopy of trees is gone. In a completely unscientific way (meaning whenever I remember to look), I've been tracking residential air-conditioning. It seems that 90 percent of Beijing residents now have it, as opposed to almost none just a decade ago.

I'm meeting China's most prominent environmentalist for drinks at the Grand Hotel. Dai Qing is what people here call a "red princess." She's Communist Party royalty, the adopted daughter of the late Marshal Ye Jianying, who was a confidant of Mao's and one of China's most powerful men. The twist is that Dai Qing is also a dissident, through her environmental work and her struggle for human rights in China.

I figured the rooftop bar, which has the only sunset view over the Forbidden City, would be a nice place to watch the smog. While I wait in the lobby, I check out the security cameras. Somewhere a grand piano tinkles. With millions learning piano and violin, Chinese musicians are so cheap that every four-star hotel offers live music. Sitting on a leather settee, I eavesdrop on a white man struggling to make a restaurant reservation at the front desk.

"The restaurant will only hold your table until six," a sleekly coiffed female concierge tells him in English.

"But I don't want to go that early," the foreigner protests. "I want a later reservation."

"If you go after six, then you have to wait with everyone else."

"Then what's the point of a reservation?"

"The restaurant will only hold your table until six," she repeats.

A Chinese businessman rushes up to the desk. "What's the fastest way to get to the airport?" he asks briskly, in a tone that expects an answer such as "From the rooftop helipad, sir!" Instead the concierge looks puzzled. "There is no way to get to the airport fast," she says.

It dawns on me that Beijing has no traffic helicopters buzzing overhead. For security reasons, the capital's air space is a no-fly zone. I recall that our flight from Newark didn't circle over Beijing while waiting for a runway—it looped deep into Hebei province. The only time I have ever seen helicopters in

Beijing was when military ones buzzed Tiananmen Square a few days before the massacre.

Sometimes it takes a while to notice what's not there. On this trip, it takes me a week to realize I haven't seen any trucks on the road during the day. My *Globe* colleague Geoff York explained that Beijing bans trucks until late evening to reduce gridlock. Come to think of it, I'm not hearing cicadas, either. The transparent-winged insects once blanketed the city with white noise. During the afternoon siesta, observed at every factory, school and office, the buzz of their vibrating abdominal membranes would lull the entire city to sleep. But their habitat vanished as trees were axed to widen roads, and the siesta is no more as everyone scrambles to get rich.

Dai Qing bursts into the lobby, a diminutive dynamo in a sea-foam green linen dress that falls to her ankles. "I'm sorry I'm late," she says, offering the all-purpose Beijing excuse: "The traffic is terrible." We hug and then take the elevator to the rooftop bar. The early evening sky, metallic orange streaked with pink, glints off the golden-tiled roofs of the Forbidden City. Beyond the palace is the inaccessible compound of Zhongnanhai. The Grand Hotel adjoins a block-long monolith of three hotels, collectively referred to as the Beijing Hotel, formerly the Hotel de Pekin and later the Peking Hotel. In 1979, before the Grand was built, I was the first news assistant at the *New York Times* bureau when it operated out of the Beijing Hotel. I remember lurking around the stairwells trying in vain to peek into Chairman Mao's compound. The paranoia of China's leaders was such that all the hotel windows facing Zhongnanhai were frosted and locked. Now Beijing's thick smog provides a security blanket for the Communist Party's headquarters. (Security isn't what it used to be. Back at Beautiful Lodging,

I click on Google Earth and am absolutely gob-smacked to see—on my laptop—the once-secret layout of every building, pathway and pond inside the Communist Party headquarters.)

Dai Qing, sixty-five, is a journalist and writer. She studied rocket science at university. Later she underwent training for the Chinese KGB, the Ministry of State Security. As we're sitting across from the new hulking Ministry of State Security building, I ask, "Is that really the headquarters?"

She laughs out loud. "State Security is not across the street," she says, shaking her silky bob.

"How do you know for sure?"

"Remember the U.S. bombing of the Chinese embassy in Belgrade? It wasn't a mistake. The U.S. bombed us on purpose," she says without rancor. "You know why? China was supporting Yugoslavia. Those three Chinese killed were not reporters. That was just their cover. All three were staff employees of the Ministry of State Security."

She chuckles again. "Guess who erected a memorial sculpture in their honor?" she says. "Not the All-China Journalists Federation. The Ministry of State Security." She tells me that the sculpture stands just outside the gates of the actual Ministry of State Security, which is near Beijing University. "There's no sign on the gate," she adds.

"Why is there no sign?" I ask.

She sips her lemonade and laughs again. "This is a police state."

Indeed, some of Beijing's most important buildings have no sign. If you don't already know, it's probably none of your business. Zhongnanhai, for instance, lacks a sign. Only the huge slogans on the wall provide a hint: "Long Live the Chinese Communist Party." That and the soldiers with fixed bayonets guarding the entrance.

In the 1980s, Dai Qing quit the spy agency to work as a reporter at *Guangming [Enlightenment] Daily*. She made a name for herself writing about the environment. Her book *Yangtze! Yangtze!* criticized the environmental and social impact of the massive thirty-billion-dollar Three Gorges Dam. After the Tiananmen Square Massacre, authorities blamed her for inciting protesters. Dai Qing was arrested and put in solitary confinement. At one point, she was put on a list of people to be executed, for reasons that remain unclear. She was released less than a year later, for equally mysterious reasons. Her critics accused her of recanting and supporting the military crackdown. Her supporters insist she did not jettison her convictions. In an article Dai Qing wrote after her release, called "My Imprisonment," she said, "What I can fight for is to let others know I am innocent, but have a rebellious spirit."

After her release, Dai Qing became the first person to successfully challenge China's exit restrictions. In 1990, Harvard University granted her a Nieman Fellowship, a prestigious scholarship for mid-career journalists. "I applied for a passport, but they wouldn't give me one. They said there were two small conditions. First, I had to give up my *hukou*. Second, I had to be *zhengzhi zhengque* [politically correct]." Up until then, authorities routinely invoked the latter to prevent dissidents from leaving.

That fall, the semester at Harvard began without Dai Qing. Then the U.S. secretary of State, James Baker, arrived to discuss human rights. "The police arrested me again and locked me in a guest house run by *Enlightenment Daily*," she says. Emily McFarquhar, a veteran correspondent for *US News &World Report*, was in Beijing covering Baker's visit. She was also married to Roderick McFarquhar, a Harvard professor and sinologist. At the press conference, Emily tipped off the other reporters. Several asked, "Where is Dai Qing?" Embarrassed, Baker was forced to raise the same question with the Chinese government.

"They had to give way," Dai Qing says. "It was a turning point. After that, as long as you did not have a criminal record, you could leave China. So my suffering was not in vain."

She says China has slightly eased its repression of environmentalists. She can make speeches. But she can't publish articles or books except, strangely enough, abroad. She notes that the lack of press freedom in China has a direct, deleterious impact on the environment. Because environmentalists are muzzled, Dai Qing says, there is widespread ignorance about the water shortage facing the capital. My classmate Future was the only person I knew of in Beijing trying to conserve water.

In Mao's time, people were restricted to one shower a week at their workplaces. Today, with Beijing's population more than doubled, the consumption of water is astounding. While one in every four Chinese still lacks piped water, many Beijingers have bathtubs, showers and washing machines at home. The city has planted gardens, grass and flowerbeds, many with continuous-trickle sprinklers, others watered daily by white-gloved workers in blue cotton suits. Beijing has at least twenty-four golf courses and thousands of spas, restaurants and health clubs. Three million automobiles need washing. Meanwhile, to reduce particulate matter in the air, Beijing has ordered each of the city's eight thousand construction sites sprayed with water several times a day to keep down the dust.

Some experts are so alarmed that they have advocated water rationing. The water table beneath the city has been in serious decline for years. One of Beijing's two main reservoirs, the Guanting, is already dry. "A huge dry basin is developing underneath 60 percent of the North China Plain," Dai Qing says. "People don't know every year the water level is dropping several meters. They're unaware of the shortage. There's no sense of crisis. The rich are digging swimming pools. We're using artesian water for golf courses.

"When the Olympics open in 2008, the ordinary people of Beijing will have to drink water drawn from the Yangtze River, thousands of kilometers away," she warns. Indeed, China is building three 1,100 kilometer channels that will divert 45 trillion liters of water a year from the South—the biggest water project in human history.

Her voice turns sarcastic. "Meanwhile, the beloved leaders and their families, and others with power and wealth, have started enjoying water taken from deep aquifers where it has been stored for millions of years."

In the 1970s, the skies were crystalline blue. This August, the sky is blue only twice the entire time we're here. So one morning, when the television weather person announces, "Today is a Blue Sky Day," I rush to the window. The skies are dun, as usual. A Blue Sky Day, it turns out, doesn't mean the sky is blue. It's an Orwellian air-quality index based on three primary pollutants. To qualify, the air must not exceed, per cubic meter, 150 milligrams of sulphur dioxide, 100 milligrams of nitrogen dioxide or 300 milligrams of particulate matter of 10 microns or less. Using this by-no-means-stringent standard, Beijing recorded only nine Blue Sky Days in April. In July it rained for twenty-seven days. Although the skies were overcast, the rain rinsed away the pollution, so the capital scored twenty-nine Blue Sky Days, an eight-year record.

Beijing's air-pollution problems didn't begin with the Communists. When the Great Wall was built, a ten-kilometer-wide swath of forest was cut down on each side so that enemy troops could not hide within. For similar security reasons, no tall-growth trees were planted anywhere in the vicinity of the Forbidden City. In the fourth century BC, the Chinese philosopher Mencius decried desertification, blaming massive tree-cutting and overgrazing. Through the centuries, the burgeoning Chinese population deforested the country for fuel and building materials. By 1900, Gobi Desert dust clotted Beijing's atmosphere. Bertram Lenox Simpson, a twenty-two-year-old Briton employed by the Imperial Customs Service, wrote in *Indiscreet Letters from Peking* on the eve of the Boxer Rebellion, "The Peking dust, distinguished among all the dusts of the earth for its blackness, its disagreeable insistence in sticking to one's clothes, one's hair, one's very eyebrows, until a gray-brown coating is visible to every eye . . . has become damnable beyond words, and there can be no health possibly in us. The Peking dust rises . . . in clouds and obscures the very sun at times."

Today, a million tons of Gobi Desert dust descend on Beijing annually, according to the New China News Agency. Scientists say the dust contains minerals such as aluminum, zinc and iron, all of which affect the respiratory system. Fallout from the dust has been detected as far away as South Korea and even Hawaii. North Korea, South Korea and Japan have all registered formal complaints. Desertification has destroyed grasslands a hundred and fifty kilometers north of Beijing. Severe sandstorms now shut down the Beijing airport for days at a time. And the European Satellite Agency recently named Beijing as having the world's highest levels of nitrogen dioxide, a gas spewed from exhaust pipes; levels are up 50 percent from a decade ago, and rising.

In the last few years, I have developed a persistent bronchial cough every time I've spent more than two weeks here. This time, right on schedule, I start hacking and wheezing again. Ben develops a bad cold and nagging cough too. Sam's theory is that many people spit on the sidewalk because of the dirty air. He starts trying it out himself, with great gobs of success. I have no idea how the athletes at the 2008 Olympics will manage. Perhaps they will be like Fat Paycheck, who seems impervious.

When I meet my friend Kathy Wilhelm for lunch, she says that living in a heavily polluted environment is like being in a sensory-deprivation tank. "You can go two or three weeks without seeing a blue sky," she says. "The smog reduces the sense of the four seasons. It's always gray. You don't feel it's summer or spring. And it's more humid."

We covered Tiananmen Square together back in 1989. She was a dedicated, workaholic reporter at the Associated Press who worked so hard that she collapsed and had to be hospitalized. We've kept in touch, and she has agreed to meet me for a lunch of tuna-fish sandwiches and lattes in the coffee shop of one of Beijing's newest office towers. Despite her legal career, Kathy hasn't lost her reporter's instincts for trends.

I tell her that the other day I bought three perfect peaches. We ate the first two right away. I left the third one on a shelf in the living room at Beautiful Lodging. In less than twenty-four hours, the peach had turned moldy and putrid. I'd never seen anything decompose so quickly. In the 1970s, no one had a refrigerator, and the food didn't go all sci-fi on us like that. I ask Kathy if I'm hallucinating.

"No, you're not crazy. The weather *is* different," she says. "The air is horrible. It's the worst it's ever been. The air used to be bad in the winter when everyone burned coal. Now it's all year round. But there's no discussion about the car problem because it's not a problem in their minds. The Chinese see cars only as a sign of progress. They keep thinking: if we build more roads, widen the roads, it will be fine. They're making the same mistake as we made in the West."

We finish our sandwiches. A middle-aged woman in a neat blue uniform is mopping the floor nearby. Despite her lowly job, she has indulged in one vanity: her hair is dyed orange. Once upon a time, China was derided as a nation of blue ants. Czeslaw Milosz, the Polish Nobel laureate, pondered the impact of collectivism on the human aesthetic. He could have been describing Maoist China when he described Eastern Europe in the grip of Stalinism in his book *The Captive Mind:* "The liquidation of small private enterprises gives the streets a stiff and institutional look. The chronic lack of consumer goods renders the crowds uniformly gray and uniformly indigent . . . Fear paralyzes individuality and makes people adjust themselves as much as possible to the average type in their gestures, clothing, and facial expressions. Cities become filled with the racial type well-regarded by the rulers: short, square men and women, with short legs and wide hips. This is the proletarian type."

In a post-Mao hunger for pizzazz, men and women alike are tinting their hair orange, yellow or burgundy. Even among the twenty-four members of the ruling Politburo, most of whom are pushing seventy, only two show gray. The Confucian ideal that age equals wisdom is fading faster than a bad dye job.

19

The Ten Commandments in English and the Lord's Prayer in Chinese

Spring Plum has not called me back. She *must* remember me. And, as the Communist Party secretary of the history department, she would be obligated by protocol to call me, an alumna, back. I could call her again—that's what reporters do—but I decide her silence must mean something. Exactly what, I haven't yet figured out.

In the meantime, as a history graduate, I want to see the newly opened Capital Museum on the far west side of the city. It's second in size only to the National Museum of China in Tiananmen Square. An old friend, Xie Jianping, has offered to accompany me there, partly because it's right beside her home. Jianping suggests I take the subway from Beautiful Lodging, the fastest, most efficient way to go across the city. But it isn't very pleasant.

The air in the subway car is fetid and hot. The feeble air-conditioning can't combat the furnace-like body heat of the crowds. Strangely, an old woman across from me is wearing gray Lycra gloves in the humidity. My eyes fall on a middle-aged man sitting near her. He's wearing neat trousers and a pale yellow polo shirt. He is also picking his nose. With the index finger of his right hand, he digs around and excavates a big gray gob, which he flicks on the ground. Then he roots around some more. As a reporter, I am used to examining human horror, but this is too much. I avert my eyes.

A one-legged beggar on crutches bangs his way into our subway car. With a grandiose gesture, he thrusts a small canvas bag in front of various passengers, who do the New York thing and pretend he is invisible. Only one person gives him money.

When I get off the subway, Jianping is waiting. She is handicapped herself, her spine twisted by scoliosis. I tell her about the nose-picker, the beggar and the old lady, whose gray gloves now make perfect sense. "The city is filthy," says Jianping. "The first thing we do when we come home is wash our hands. And those beggars—they're part of professional gangs. I once saw a team of them dropped off by a van. They changed into their rags in a public toilet. No one gives them money now."

Jianping's name means "Constructing the Peace." I met her in the 1970s through some American friends in Beijing who were associates of her father, a senior Communist official. Her parents called her Peace because she was born after Mao's victory, when China stopped being in a state of war for the first time in half a century. She's kind-hearted, smart, wise and, well, a true Communist at heart. She cares about others, about the public good, about morality.

At the museum entrance, she flashes her handicapped ID. Free admission, she tells me, is a disabled benefit. "What other benefits do you get?" I ask.

"That's the only one."

The Capital Museum is five stories high and takes up an entire city block, which is why, as per my pre-trip pledge, Ben and Sam haven't come. (Fat Paycheck, who also dislikes museums, immediately volunteered to keep an eye on them.) The museum took four years to build and cost more than one billion yuan ($130 million). Peace thinks that's extravagant. Worth it or not, the museum sure beats the dusty exhibits I visited during the Cultural Revolution. It has imaginative displays on Peking opera, wedding rituals and the Yuan-dynasty canal system. I spot a crib sheet seized from a candidate who tried to cheat on the imperial exams. There's a flashy jade thumb ring belonging to Li Lianying, the most powerful eunuch in history.

The museum gift shop, though, is bizarre. It has nothing to do with Beijing or its history. It sells needlepoint portraits of Jesus with a halo, and another needlepoint of Mary, Joseph and Baby Jesus in the manger. There are framed scrolls of the Ten Commandments, in English, and the Lord's Prayer, in Chinese. There are ties with the Christian fish symbol and Jesus, with the heart icon for "Jesus loves." A set of plaster angels costs twenty-five yuan. For good measure, there are Buddhist sutras and prayer-bead bracelets too. But there's not a Mao badge in sight. In its religiosity, the gift shop reminds me of the one in the Vatican. This officially atheist country will now do anything to make a profit. And yet, consider this: Dai Qing says that while authorities have eased up on environmentalists, they are cracking down on the Falun Gong, pro-democracy advocates and underground Christian churches—officially sanctioned churches under Communist Party supervision, however, are fine.

"Lots of people believe in Buddhism and Christianity," says Peace. "It's very common nowadays. Maybe they are spiritually starved. Also, we're allowed a lot of freedom."

We stop at an exhibit on doors and gates, really a display about conspicuous consumption. In feudal China, one's status determined the exact ornateness or plainness of front doors. Only a high government official could have golden knobs in his doors. A merchant, no matter how rich, could not. The doors with the most rows of golden knobs, of course, were the massive front gates to the Forbidden City.

Peace and I both fade after a couple of hours. After some investigation, we figure out that there are only two food options. We can buy microwaved hamburgers in a bag and eat on a bench. Or we can spend a lot of money at the museum restaurant, hidden in the basement. It offers a dismal-looking "Mexican and Russian" all-you-can-eat buffet. I suggest we escape and find something nearby. Peace agrees. "I should invite you to lunch, but I don't have any money today," she says, looking embarrassed. Yesterday she emptied her wallet to help the child of a migrant worker pay for tuition. I tell her that lunch is on me. I'm so glad to have had her company at the museum.

You'd never know from her unassuming manner, but Peace, like Dai Qing, is part of the elite. Her father was governor of Shanxi province. Peace is one of six siblings—nine if you include three orphans, all offspring of revolutionary martyrs—adopted by her parents. When her father was called to the capital in 1964, the nine children were sent to boarding schools, but Peace's mother missed them so much that the government finally allotted the family three apartments in Beijing.

During the Cultural Revolution, Peace's father was denounced but survived. His political problems hindered her chances of getting into university, but as a disabled person, she would have been barred anyway. Chinese authorities considered higher education wasted on the handicapped. Peace never married either; prospective husbands weren't interested in a hunchback. After she finished high school, she worked on a factory assembly line making radios. Now retired, she lives off her factory pension of 900 yuan ($115) a month, the same amount the steel-worker-turned-crossing-guard at Panda Circle gets. She also inherited one of the family's original three flats, which she rents out for extra income. "Otherwise my pension wouldn't be enough."

After lunch at a nearby restaurant, Peace invites me home. I've never been before, but now that I'm in the neighborhood, I'm curious how the Party elite once lived. Since 1984, Peace has lived with her widowed mother, a brother and his wife in a sprawling block-long building as famous in Beijing as the Watergate Apartments are in Washington, DC. Buzhang Lou, which means "Ministerial Apartments," was built in the 1980s for senior Chinese officials. Before he became premier, when he was head of the Ministry of Hydroelectric Power, Li Peng had a flat two doors over. Li Ximing, the Communist Party secretary of Beijing, lived in one just west of Peace's. These apartments were once the grandest housing in Beijing, with glassed-in porches, terrazzo floors, bookshelves and more than one bathroom. Today they're nothing compared to Jianwai SOHO.

"Now not even a rural county chief would deign to live here," says Peace. "The only people left are retired officials who have no more power, or the family members of officials who are dead."

Despite the nobodies living there now, security remains tight. We pass a line of People's Armed Police goose-stepping around the perimeter. At the gate, an alert guard lets me pass only after Peace vouches for me. The elevator in her building is automatic, but it has an operator, also for security reasons. All these precautions must be holdovers from the days when Communist Party officials might have feared attack by disgruntled citizens. Nowadays, who cares?

Peace's mother, an elderly, birdlike woman, is just getting up from her nap when we arrive. The apartment is a throwback to Mao's time, plain rectangular rooms without a hint of design or flash of color. The rooms themselves, though—a living room and three bedrooms—are unusually large, the only way luxury was expressed before a Bentley dealership opened in Beijing and villas began having his-and-hers saunas. There are two full bathrooms, another unheard-of extravagance in the 1980s. But what passed for posh two decades ago seems so spartan today. Scarlet's rented condo is so much nicer, so much more comfortable, than the building where the powerful Communist Party secretary of Beijing once lived. My roommate's new home will be even better, and will certainly have more bathrooms, a testament to how far Beijingers have come in such a short time.

I have another reason for wanting to see Ministerial Apartments. In 1989, any students marching to Tiananmen Square from the university area would turn here, at Muxidi, to head east along the Avenue of Eternal Peace. "The first marches started that spring," says Peace. "I awoke one morning at 5 a.m. I heard people singing 'The Internationale.' I thought I was dreaming."

When the army rolled into the city on June 3, 1989, Muxidi was a key entry point. Many protesters were killed here. "We had a clear view of the troops," says Peace. "The cloverleaf overpass wasn't built at that time, so we could see everything. We saw them shooting at people." The apartment above her belonged to a Supreme Court judge. When the gunfire erupted, his son-in-law became enraged. He leaned out his window and began hurling teacups at the troops below. Suddenly Peace saw a sharpshooter on the street below taking aim.

"He's aiming at us!" she screamed to her brother. "Duck!"

Shots rang out. Trembling, Peace stayed crouched. And then she heard screaming in the hall. The judge's son-in-law had been shot. "The sharpshooter shot him in the forehead. The bullet exited the back of his head. The family was hysterical. They dragged him into the elevator, trying to get him to the hospital. But he was already dead."

All that night she watched the carnage from her kitchen window. "I remember people on both sides of the street, screaming, 'Down with the People's Liberation Army!'" Li Ximing, the Party secretary of the City of Beijing, was also home that night. Peace says he must have spent the evening taking photographs from his kitchen window. "He took the best photos of the soldiers on the bridge," she says. "They were later published in magazines."

20

Women Hold Up Half the Sky; I Never Thought Their Arms Would Get Tired

This really is a mission impossible. I'm getting nowhere in my search for Yin/Yan. If Kathy Wilhelm lost touch with people after the Tiananmen crackdown, then how will I find someone from the middle of the Cultural Revolution? I've decided I don't trust Honest Han, the detective. And I'm still waiting to hear back from Celebrating Virtue Pan, who is supposedly hunting down Yin's new cellphone number. Without trying to look desperate, I've already called Pan again to remind him, ever so casually, that I would like to find Yin/Yan before I leave—in twelve days. At least he hasn't changed his cellphone number on me.

In the meantime, I'm hot and crabby. My fan has broken; the pin binding the bamboo ribs snapped. Even though a fan doesn't do much good in the smog, flapping it around helps calm me down whenever I panic about how little time remains. I decide to buy a new fan. Fat Paycheck says that would be a waste of fifty cents. Also, he wants to conduct an experiment. In Mao's day, Beijingers were so frugal that craftsmen could and would repair anything. If a collar was frayed, the tailor would flip it inside out and sew it back on. A rusty enamel bowl would be soldered and patched. Fat Paycheck wants to see if it's still possible to repair a paper fan in this shiny, new consumer era.

I think he's nuts, but half an hour later he returns triumphant. He tells me he went straight to the migrant-worker neighborhood behind Beautiful Lodging and found a shoe repairman sitting by the edge of the road. When Fat Paycheck showed the young man the broken fan, he gestured to a small stool he provides for customers while they wait.

"I asked him how much," my husband says. "He didn't say anything. He just examined the fan."

Using shears, the man cut out a small disk from an old tin can and hammered a nail through it, creating a washer. Inserting a new pin in the base of the fan, he riveted it in place using the homemade washer.

"How much?" Fat Paycheck asked again.

"Where are you from?" the repairman asked.

"Canada," Fat Paycheck said, bracing himself for a Canadian price. Instead the repairman complimented Norman on his Chinese and said there was no charge. "I suppose he felt sorry for me. I'm not terribly well dressed and I'm this old guy with a beat-up old fan that I'm trying to repair."

"I'm downstairs! Sorry I'm late!" says Luna Lee. She is calling from her car. Her father has invited us for dinner and insisted she pick us up. They live in the suburbs, just north of Beijing University, but the afternoon traffic turned the drive downtown into a three-hour nightmare. The boys begged off; they'd rather stay home and eat take-out spicy chicken from the 7-Eleven. Fat Paycheck and I hurry down without them. Luna waves gaily from the road. She couldn't figure out how to get across the sidewalk blocking Beautiful Lodging's drive.

Luna is thirty-two but looks like a teenager, with a round face, glasses and a ponytail. Her father, Li Shuyi, was Fat Paycheck's colleague at the Institute of Computing Technology. He's retired now, but he was a brilliant electronics engineer. He was also a founder of Lenovo Group, which bought IBM's personal-computer business in 2005 and became the third-largest PC maker in the world.

It's safe to say Li, now seventy-one, is a very rich man. He and his wife divide their time between Beijing and Australia's Gold Coast. Luna, who has immigrant status in Australia, flies there several times a year. Her older sister has a coffee shop in Melbourne and her brother-in-law is developing townhouses there. In Beijing, Luna and her husband live with her parents and her sister's children together in a traditional extended-family setup. But they don't live in a Four Harmonies courtyard home. They live in a monster home in Shangdi, Beijing's new Silicon Valley, five minutes from her husband's office.

Luna was born during the Cultural Revolution. I first met her when she was five and her family was living in a ramshackle courtyard home near the Forbidden City, along with twenty other families. Little Luna, her older sister, and their father, mother and nanny shared a single small room. Like Future's, their kitchen was a lean-to. They had to use public latrines down the lane.

The family's housing history tracks the arc of economic progress of China. Even that cramped single room was possible only because the hospital where Luna's mother worked as a doctor assigned it to them. In 1986, a decade after the Cultural Revolution ended and the government began building more housing, they moved into a new two-room flat, the first with their own toilet. They were so house-proud that Li Shuyi invited us one Sunday for dumplings.

We couldn't keep the date. It was June 4, 1989. Beijing was a war zone with armored personnel carriers smoldering in the streets. The next day the Tank Man would leap in front of a convoy of tanks. Soldiers were still randomly firing AK-47s, but Fat Paycheck was determined to bicycle across town for lunch. He told me he would wear his bike helmet. I insisted he call Li, who'd recently had his first residential phone installed. "A nine-year-old girl was killed, and they've just brought her body back," Li told him. "I don't think it's a good idea to make the trip out here."

Luna is driving a made-in-China Volkswagen Jetta. She also owns a Buick. Each month, she spends twice as much on gas for the Buick as Peace receives from her factory pension. "I never thought when we met years ago that I'd be driving a car and picking you up," says Luna, beaming. "All my husband's friends can afford BMWs and Audis, which cost one million yuan [$130,000 U.S.]. Now we think an Audi isn't that great. A Porsche is better. It costs two million yuan."

She reminds me of Scarlet, except that Luna is fearless on the road. "I really am a Beijing driver," she says, passing on the right. "The first time I took the driving test in Australia, I failed. I didn't signal a turn. I cut in front of other cars. I didn't signal a lane change."

Her cellphone rings. It's the carpenter who is building custom cabinets for her new condo. Despite a regulation against talking on the phone while driving, Luna takes the call—that's another rule for others. Like many Beijingers, she bought her new condo as a concrete shell. So far, she has spent 300,000 yuan installing doors, plumbing, bathrooms, a kitchen and floors. A few days earlier, she bought a side-by-side refrigerator with a built-in ice machine. Like everyone I meet, Luna has real estate fever. "You can't *not* buy a home," she says. "Real estate prices keep going up." Her condo has already appreciated 15 percent in four months, and she has yet to move in.

"No matter how expensive the houses, they sell out so fast. The coal-mine owners from Shanxi province and the merchants from Wenzhou buy them as investments and leave them empty." The other day, she was in a panic. The condo management notified her that the parking spaces were up for sale. She had one day to cough up 90,000 yuan. "I ran around borrowing from everywhere. I used my credit card. I'll worry about paying it off next month. I had no choice—there aren't enough parking spaces." She and her husband, a Lenovo executive, have a thirty-year, 5.8 percent mortgage, a new financial product in China. Their monthly payment is 10,000 yuan ($1,300 U.S.), one-third of his salary. Since then, mortgage rates have jumped to 6.2 percent. Banks lend only to those thirty-five or younger, Luna says. The combined years of the mortgage and your age can't exceed sixty-five, the age of retirement.

Her husband is in charge of Henan province, which has 100 million people. Because his *hukou,* or residence permit, is in Beijing, Lenovo gave them a choice of a free apartment in Henan or eight round-trip plane tickets for Luna. She chose the plane tickets, and now travels back and forth with her husband to Henan.

The computer company also pays Luna to stay home. "Lenovo is paying me three thousand yuan a month not to work," she says. "It was their proposal, not mine." I assume this is a kind of non-compete payment. Luna used to work in sales at Fang Zheng Corp., Beijing University's high-tech company. Perhaps Lenovo dislikes spouses working for the competition.

Luna sets me straight. "It's so my husband can concentrate on his job. It's supposed to preserve the stability of our marital relations." In other words, Lenovo pays Luna to stay home and keep her husband happy. I am stunned. I can't decide whether this is horribly retro—paying women to stay home—or wonderfully cutting-edge—putting a cash value on running a household. After Scarlet, Luna is the second person I know who just wants to be a housewife.

"What do your parents think?" I ask.

"My parents don't have the old thinking. They don't think I have to work and be independent."

Funny how "old" thinking is defined in the post-Mao era. "What do your friends think?" I press.

"They said, 'Why are you idle?' When I quit working, I slept until ten every morning. I had nothing to do. My husband was embarrassed at first when people asked what I did. Now he's proud of me. It means he's so macho he can take care of me."

To me, feminism has always meant having a career and financial independence. But now I understand that women's liberation has no allure without freedom of choice. Under Mao, all the women of Luna's mother's generation were forced to work, like it or not.

"I think the direction in China is for women to stay home," Luna adds. "About one-third of my female friends don't work." One-third? I'm shocked anew. The Maoist era, then, was a blip. Now China is going through a belated industrial revolution, experiencing the same problems as the West—pollution, exploitation, long working hours—telescoped into two frantic decades. During the Industrial Revolution in Europe and America, from about 1780 to 1830, women didn't work either.

Luna tells me she is trying to get pregnant. Besides taking care of her husband and the house, she chauffeurs her nephew and niece to school in the city. "I call my husband, *ye* [my lord] as a joke. He doesn't lift a finger at home. He doesn't even know how to get money out of the bank machine."

I mention my visit to the private detective agency. "The detective said most of his business was spying for suspicious wives," I say.

"Extramarital affairs are common," she says. "A wife doesn't make a fuss unless the husband is too obvious. Lots of men now have *er nai* [second set of breasts]. Flight attendants are always looking to become someone's mistress. They can't stay in their jobs past thirty."

"The detective said they can check phone records," I say.

Luna snorts. "If someone is checking your cellphone records, the company automatically sends a message informing you. There's a really popular movie called *Cellphone,* all about extramarital affairs. The husband secretly calls his girlfriend from the bathroom. When he sneaks off to see her, he doesn't turn off his phone. That would look too suspicious and could still be traced through global-positioning satellites. He just takes out the battery. All it shows is he's 'out of the service area.'"

The drive to Luna's home takes nearly two hours, even though Shangdi is just north of Beijing University. As we turn off the expressway, I confess, "I keep getting lost in Beijing. I can't recognize anything."

"My father doesn't recognize Beijing anymore, either," says Luna. "I drive him around, and he says, 'Where are we?' He says the maps in Australia never change. In Beijing they change all the time."

She pulls into a driveway outside a white stucco home. It's a relief finally to get out of the car. The air feels cooler. Luna confirms what I've suspected—the concrete and cars make the city hotter. "It's always three or four degrees cooler in the suburbs," she says. Li Shuyi is waiting for us beside his tiny yard landscaped with ornamental shrubbery. His face wreathed in smiles, he opens his garage door for us as nonchalantly as if we were in California.

"Are you afraid of dogs?" he asks, just before we are assaulted by two tiny yapping ones and a prancing Irish setter. The fluffy purebred Pomeranians, one white, the other golden, are cute. But the purebred Irish setter, the first bred in Beijing, apparently gets all the attention. "CCTV came to film it," says Luna. "I got on television, too."

In his expansive living room, Li snuggles the big dog and proudly tells us he spends a thousand yuan a month on Purina dog food. That turns out to be a hundred yuan more a month than they pay a migrant woman to clean and cook for them daily. Last winter, Li says, they spent two thousand yuan on vet bills when one Pomeranian caught pneumonia. He bought the Irish setter six months ago. "We paid four thousand yuan. Now it's worth fifteen thousand yuan." He's the second person, after the mahjong gambling-den owner, to tell me how much he paid for his pet and how much its value has increased. Dogs really are like real estate. Everybody wants to talk about how much they paid and what the animal is worth now.

When I lived in the grip of Maoism in the 1970s, I couldn't imagine a China free of the Great Helmsman's influence. When he said women hold up half the sky, I never thought their arms would get tired. When he banned dogs, I thought the Chinese would never have pets. But like the First Emperor of Qin, Mao's legacy did not last. Four years after the Qin Emperor's death, his dynasty ended. Mao's ended one month after his, with the arrest of Jiang Qing, his widow. Ten months later, Mao's arch-enemy, Deng Xiaoping, was back in power. Today, it's glorious to get rich, people can leave the country whenever they want and anyone can own a dog.

To be sure, now and then, the government shows its roots. China is launching an old-fashioned all-out Maoist campaign to limit the time teenagers spend online. Parents are paying substantial fees to lock up their teenaged Internet addicts in military facilities and treat them with drugs, hypnosis and mild electric shocks. The tactics include opening eight "rehab clinics" around the country, including one just south of Beijing, on the site where Future and I once planted rice.

August is the month for harvesting peaches in Beijing, and Li has bought some perfect specimens for us. Luna slices one and feeds it to the dogs. "Have some peaches," Li's wife, Huang Xiaomao urges. Dr. Huang, who is now retired, met her husband when they were both learning Russian at the Beijing Language Institute. After studying in the Soviet Union, Li was back at the Language Institute in 1966, this time concentrating on English, on his way to Cambridge University. Fat Paycheck, newly arrived, was also at the Language Institute, learning Mandarin. They were both digging a swimming pool during "voluntary" labor when Li spotted him. "I wanted to speak English," he recalls. "I sought you out."

As Norman's field was also computer science, the two hit it off. Unfortunately, the Cultural Revolution aborted Li's

Cambridge plans. He spent the next four years hauling pig manure in the Chinese countryside. Years later, he and Fat Paycheck both ended up at Chinese Academy of Science's Institute of Computing Technology. Li became part of the team managing the institute on behalf of Lenovo, then called Legend. The company introduced its first laptop in 1996. By 2000, it was listed on Hong Kong's Hang Seng Index.

"That's when my financial situation changed. Legend became Lenovo. I was treated well," says Li, who retired in 2000 as company controller. The same year, he bought this house. At nearly three thousand square feet, it has five bedrooms, three bathrooms, a living room, den, media room, kitchen, dining room, loft and attic. "Some of my neighbors use their homes only on weekends," he says. "By the time the Olympic Games open, there will be a subway right to our house."

He and Dr. Huang, now seventy, spend May through October in Beijing. From November to April, they live in Australia. They've traveled to Hawaii, Russia, Scandinavia and much of China. They plan to visit Africa next. Luna and her husband vacation all over China, too, and recently, they toured Turkey, Egypt and Greece. Timing is everything. Dai Qing was detained merely for winning a Nieman Fellowship to Harvard; now Luna and her parents leave on a whim. Despite her immigrant status, Luna has no plans to become Australian. Her husband, who doesn't speak English, won't consider leaving his position at Lenovo, where his territory is equal to one-third the population of the United States. "He doesn't want to work in Australia. He can't get a good job there."

As old friends, we can't help talking about old times. Li remembers exactly how much everyone made during the Cultural Revolution, including Fat Paycheck. Dr. Huang earned

56 yuan a month. Li earned 62 yuan. "And you made a bit more than a hundred yuan," Li says to Norman.

The yuan was worth much more in those days, but money was still very tight. "I used to get off the tram one stop early to save two fen (three one-hundredths of a cent) when she was a baby. And I had to carry her," says Li, pointing at Luna and grinning.

"I remember when Mom once paid 25 fen for a bottle of Coke," Luna recalls. "It was so much money then. I thought it was no good. It tasted like Chinese medicine."

Dr. Huang laughs. "Now people drink Coke like it's water."

Lenovo, for them, was the equivalent of hitting the jackpot. But even without the computer company, Li and his wife believe they could manage on their state pensions and still indulge in their passion, international travel. "If we were careful, we could get by," he says. "Clothes are very cheap as long as we don't wear designer labels. If we spent two thousand on food a month, we'd still have three thousand yuan left for travel [a year], enough to buy a basic package tour to Europe or Australia."

"Now the gap between rich and poor is not just a multiple of two," Li adds, alluding to Fat Paycheck's fat paycheck. "It's huge. It's hard to create a harmonious society. People hate the rich. They don't distinguish between the kinds of wealth. Some have worked hard for their money. Others are corrupt." He thinks Australia is more stable because incomes aren't so disparate. A bricklayer there, he claims, can earn nearly as much as a doctor.

"Just like in the Cultural Revolution," Fat Paycheck quips.

Like many Chinese, Li can't joke about the Decade of Disaster. He shakes his head. "There was no reason to criticize everyone, struggle against people or put them to death. You were considered a traitor just for wanting to go abroad. The crime was called *panbian zuguo* [betraying the motherland]."

That was Yin's crime. For wanting to taste life beyond the borders, for claiming the space for her own ambitions and desires, she was labeled a traitor. And a traitor would be executed. Yet Celebrating Virtue Pan says she survived. Is he just weaving another lie into the narrative, the narrative of collective amnesia? I'm afraid it would be so simple for him to tell me he simply can't find her new cellphone number.

Li must have suffered too, for his foreign education. He does not want to talk about those bitter times. Yet he still thinks like a socialist, or at least a liberal democrat. "I'm in favor of moderate progress," he says. "We should raise taxes and create more social services."

We go out for a lavish dinner at a nearby restaurant. Afterward, Luna insists on taking us home. It means she'll probably clock seven hours of driving by the end of the day. This time Li comes along for the ride. At the Avenue of Eternal Peace, we pass by Ministerial Flats. "No ministers live here anymore. It's too ordinary," says Luna, echoing what Peace has told me. "Not even a rural county chief would live there."

As we drive through Tiananmen Square, Li remembers the first Tiananmen Incident, in 1976. Premier Zhou Enlai had died, and the masses had spontaneously gathered there to mourn his death—and to indirectly criticize Mao for the way Zhou had been attacked by innuendo in the last months of his life. "I remember the workers' militia armed with clubs. They beat the people," Li says. "I ran away and escaped on my bicycle."

On June 4, 1989, Li sensed danger. Luna was just sixteen. "No one goes out," he ordered that night. Luckily, Luna obeyed. She says one of her best friends went out that evening and narrowly escaped arrest. "When the soldiers arrived, he went south to Qianmen [Front Gate] where there are lots of alleyways. All the people who headed north got arrested."

But for Luna's generation, Tiananmen Square holds positive memories, too. "I remember the day Beijing got the Olympics," she says. "Everyone streamed down to Tiananmen Square. People were honking their horns and waving. Everyone was so proud, so patriotic. I saw a fender-bender. Normally there'd be a fight. But the two men got out, shook each other's hands, and drove off."

21

Move Out Early.
Realize Your Dream Early

pring Plum Wang still hasn't returned my call. I decide her silence means she doesn't want to go there, not now, not in the new millennium. Then Cadre Huang phones. He says he and Spring Plum have discussed Yin's case, and now he knows the details. He tells me the charge against her was insignificant.

"Yin read foreign newspapers," says Cadre Huang, giggling. "We were all ultra-left at the time," he says. "Now what she did is considered nothing." Then he gives me some unsolicited advice. "Don't worry about Yin. Spring Plum says that what happened to her had nothing to do with you. It was a problem within the history department."

Nothing to do with me? That is impossible. I know what I did. There were consequences. What does he mean—"a problem within the history department"? I sense he's trying to discourage me from probing further. And yet both Cadre Huang and Scarlet have steered me toward Spring Plum. Why? Before I can ask, Cadre Huang giggles some more and ends the call.

With all the feelers I've put out, perhaps someone has contacted Yin—and she doesn't want to be found. With only a dozen days remaining, I'm about to give up my quest. I can't think of anyone else to contact, or anywhere else to look.

After class, Fat Paycheck and I take the boys to Beijing's bomb shelters. There's no imminent threat of a NATO attack— I've simply overdosed on expressways and need a nostalgia hit. The bomb shelters are part of Beijing's forgotten past. In the late 1960s, when Mao contemplated all-out war with the Soviet Union, he ordered the population to dig tunnels beneath every major city. Fu the Enforcer taught me this pithy, and quite useless, Mao quotation: "Dig tunnels deep, store grain everywhere, oppose hegemony." (It sounded catchier in Chinese.)

The stratum beneath Beijing became honeycombed with bomb-shelter tunnels. The tunnels also enhanced security for top Chinese leaders, whose homes were connected to the underground system. Their Red Flag limos could zip beneath the city unimpeded and undetected. At the home of the late Vice-Premier Guo Moruo, now a museum open to the public, a sign marks the hidden vehicular entrance to the tunnels. The underground system also made the leadership less vulnerable to assassination attempts. Since the Communists took power in 1949, many Chinese leaders have been persecuted to death, but not one has been assassinated. Mao's number two man, Lin Biao, reportedly made several attempts on Mao's life. In 1971 Lin and part of his family ended up fleeing China in a small military plane, which crashed and burned in Mongolia.

Every able-bodied Beijinger helped dig the tunnels during the Cultural Revolution. Fat Paycheck worked on the ones beneath the Foreign Languages Bureau. The system, called the Underground City, was completed by the time I arrived in 1972. I toured it on a university outing, and remember that we emerged, blinking and disoriented, from a trap door into

Qianmen, one of Beijing's busiest shopping districts. The next time I return, the tunnels almost surely will be gone, swallowed up for condo garages. I want Ben and Sam to see this bit of Maoist madness before it's too late. The taxi drops us behind Qianmen in a *hutong* that looks as though a tornado has swept through. A sign in the rubble says, "This area is for use by the city government for a road."

Qianmen is old Beijing's last stand. Its name means Front Gate, and it was indeed the front door to the city. During the Qing dynasty, scholars from the provinces stayed in boarding houses here while preparing for the civil-service examinations (at the spot where the Citibank tower now stands). The district was famous for its theaters, opera halls and brothels, and it had more bookshops than anywhere else in the city. Its magnificent fifteenth-century gate tower still stands, the largest and most important of a trio of gates demarcating the Tartar City from the Chinese City. The tower itself is protected from demolition, but authorities want to clear the surrounding neighborhood.

As one of the last places in Beijing to be bulldozed, Qianmen residents have learned from the bitter experience of others. Three hundred thousand Beijingers have lost their homes in the past decade. At first there was little resistance. People felt they lived in slums and were anxious to move into new flats with plumbing, and the deal was simple and attractive. The government offered just enough compensation for residents to buy a place in the distant suburbs. It turned out that their new housing was built by government cronies who got sweetheart deals on the newly vacated prime downtown land. The suburban apartments the developers built were shoddy. Beijingers also found the local schools and hospitals substandard. They discovered their commute back to their city jobs took hours. Belatedly, the displaced residents protested with petitions, even suicides. A few brave lawyers took the city to court, with scant results.

Now many residents in Qianmen are refusing to leave. They have found new allies: preservationists, human rights activists, and alarmed foreigners who consider the ancient courtyard homes part of Beijing's architectural heritage. Paradoxically, the Olympic Games, the catalyst for much of the destruction, also provide protection. In the run-up to the Games, authorities are nervous about bad publicity. In 2006, they fired Liu Zhihua, the vice-mayor in charge of Olympic construction and citywide demolition. And the city no longer uses brute force and bull-dozers; it now sends in inspectors to declare the homes "unsafe."

The Underground City recently opened as a museum. As the only visitors at noon, we get our own guide. He is twenty, and wearing a trendy turquoise camouflage jacket and trousers with knock-off Nike runners. As he leads us down a broad set of stairs forty feet beneath the surface, the temperature suddenly drops. The tunnels drip with condensation. Underfoot, the red plastic mats are squishy. On the walls, framed posters of Chairman Mao are soggy and bleached with age. Military uniforms hang in tatters on blue-eyed, red-lipped female mannequins, like Miss Haversham's wedding dress in *Great Expectations*. Everything is in an advanced stage of decay, an apt metaphor for this remnant of the Maoist era. Our guide, who speaks some English, tells Ben and Sam the tunnels were built during the Cultural Revolution. Fat Paycheck blurts out that he helped dig them.

"Really?" the guide says, amazed.

I keep encountering Chinese who have no idea what their country was like under Mao. In the 1970s, no one knew how to say "generation gap" because, well, there wasn't one. I try to see my husband through the guide's eyes. Norman is sixty-two, but with his bald pate and white beard—both signs of advanced age in China—the guide must think he's at least ninety-eight.

The tunnels lead past small, barren rooms. Hand-painted signs grandly identify them as the "library," "theater" or "hospital." For verisimilitude, the last has a single pair of crutches leaning against one wall. An "old people's activity center," festooned, bizarrely, with Christmas tinsel, has only one item in it: a spinning wheel, covered in mold. The mid-tunnel gift shop, which sells silk blouses and replica Mao badges, seems authentically Maoist in its customer-staff ratio. There's us—four potential customers—and five saleswomen, including one gently snoring behind the counter.

"Are there rats?" I ask our guide as we walk through the sodden tunnels, stepping gingerly to avoid puddles.

"If there were rats, they would starve to death," he says. "There's nothing down here."

On the way out, soggy posters provide advice in the event of a chemical attack: "Take a bath." For bacterial warfare, "Wear a mask or put a cloth over your mouth." Ditto for a nuclear attack. Ben and Sam burst out laughing. Fat Paycheck says he had air-raid drills in fourth grade in New York City.

"What did they tell you to do?" Sam asks, fascinated.

"Get under the desk," says Norman.

The boys laugh again. When I translate that for the Chinese guide, he joins in.

I persuade the boys to visit the Forbidden City, which we toured on our last trip to Beijing. Technically it's a museum, so I should honor my no-museum pledge. But it's near our former driver's home, where we're going for dinner. Perhaps Sam got his phobia of museums from the previous visit. I told him then with a straight face that the Forbidden City had 10,000 rooms. After an hour of trudging through the 250-acre site, Sam, then ten, had sighed and asked, "How many more rooms?"

In fact, the Ming palace reportedly has only 8,700 rooms. As we approach the Forbidden City this time, Sam sighs loudly again. Rain is in the air. A peddler is hawking umbrellas and disposable raincoats as nimbly as a floor trader at the Chicago Mercantile Exchange. "Two yuan for a raincoat. Five yuan after it starts raining!" he shouts.

I hedge my bets and buy two. It starts raining as we reach the entrance. The peddlers do a brisk business because Chinese hate getting rained on. My theory is it stems from centuries of wearing cloth shoes. The morning after the Tiananmen Massacre, crowds gathered to curse the soldiers. Each time when fired upon, they dispersed briefly, then regrouped. But that afternoon, when it started to drizzle, everyone went home. They weren't afraid of dying, but they didn't want to get wet.

Liu Xinyong lives in the shadow of the Forbidden City. My former driver is a husky man with a graying brush cut and square jaw. He is reliable, efficient and smart. He is also a Communist Party member. He once ratted out the cook, another Party member, who was robbing me blind. I assured Liu that I knew about the theft. I did nothing, however, because I was hopelessly addicted to Cook Mu's mouth-puckering lemon tarts.

Liu helped me immensely when I was the *Globe*'s correspondent. A year after the Tiananmen Massacre, he coached me on how to recover my ancient Toyota hatchback from the thieving Beijing police. "Don't accuse them of stealing your car. Don't even use the word *steal*. Just say, 'Sorry, excuse me, but I believe you might have our car.'" I did as I was told. It worked like a charm. Later, when I returned to Beijing, I would sometimes contact my old driver. He was one of the only people I knew who did not change his phone number or move.

Usually I'd invite him out to a restaurant, but he always insisted on cooking dinner for me. He didn't like dining out. He was convinced Beijing's restaurants served adulterated products. And maybe he had a point. Chinese counterfeiters pass off diethylene glycol, a cheap industrial solvent and prime ingredient in antifreeze, as glycerin, a safe but more expensive syrup used to make cough medicine. The practice has led to at least eight mass poisonings in China and elsewhere over the past two decades, according to the *New York Times.* And China has been accused of exporting wheat gluten doctored with a chemical, melamine, that ended up in cat food, leading to pet deaths in Canada and the United States.

I love visiting Liu, because he lives in the historic heart of Beijing, in the Imperial City, on Porcelain Warehouse Alley, just down from Brocade Warehouse Lane and Bow-and-Quiver Workshop Lane. How an ordinary driver ended up in Beijing's most coveted patch of real estate was a combination of dumb luck and abuse of power—someone else's. In 1988, he was living with his wife and son in a new two-room apartment, right by a noisy overpass of the Third Ring Road in the former Chinese City. The apartment faced west and was unbearably hot in summer. At night the roar of traffic would keep them awake. Still, the flat was the nicest home he'd ever had. At 550 square feet, it was four times as big as the hovel they used to live in on the west side of the city.

This new apartment had been allotted to him by his state employer, and Liu had spent his life savings renovating it. He had installed wood flooring and expensive light fixtures, and he tiled the bathroom. When he finished after two years, a section chief in his office coveted it. Before private ownership, the only way to change state-assigned housing was to trade. The section chief pressured Liu to swap his renovated apartment for the chief's own dark, tumbledown three-room house. He would reimburse Liu for only 2 percent of the cost of the renovations.

"He said, 'You did it for yourself, not me. Why should I pay you?'" Liu could have refused, but he was a lowly driver in a work unit with many powerful people. Life would become difficult. So he looked on the bright side. The section chief's home was 60 percent bigger than the apartment. It was in the Imperial City, where the public schools were better. And his mother-in-law, who could help babysit his only child, lived a fifteen-minute walk away. So Liu swapped. He couldn't do much about the lack of natural light, but he set about renovating again. He installed laminated wood flooring and extra light fixtures to mask the gloom.

Neither he nor the section chief anticipated that China was about to allow private ownership and Beijing would become one of the hottest real estate markets in the world. Work units were about to sell off housing to employee-occupants at insider prices. The real estate mantra—location, location, location—would finally have meaning in Chinese. The location in the Imperial City was golden, worth much more than an apartment in the old Chinese City hard by an expressway.

• • •

Fat Paycheck, Ben, Sam and I sit in the dining room while Liu and his son cook. "Restaurants are too dirty," says Liu, shouting to us from the kitchen. "You never know what quality you are getting. I just read in the *People's Daily* that some peddlers were caught injecting red dye into watermelons." (Maybe I shouldn't blame the weather for that peach that turned putrid in a day.)

We always agree in advance that Liu will make something relatively simple, like dumplings. He always makes dumplings, and then he always lays on a feast. This time his son, now a pony-tailed university student, deep-fries jumbo prawns, one by one, in a wok of hot oil. Meanwhile, Liu prepares boiled peanuts, corn on the cob, poached shrimp, soy-braised ribs, stewed egg-plant, dill pickles and slices of sweet Hami melon. We sit down at his glass dining-room table. As we toast each other with China Red Wine, he explains that his wife, a schoolteacher, is away for the weekend. She flew to Shenzhen, on the Hong Kong border, to go shopping with friends. A few years earlier, a weekend shopping trip a three-hour flight away would have been an unthinkable extravagance.

Each time I visit Liu, he surprises me. This time he drops a bombshell. It starts when he tells me he has just purchased a spacious condo at Huilongguan, a huge development far from the city center. "How can you afford it?" I blurt out. (It's okay to ask about money matters in China.)

"My father and great-uncle were capitalists," he says, some-what sheepishly. And then he begins to tell me the Liu family's secret history, which is modern Chinese history in microcosm.

In the 1940s, the Liu family owned several small shops selling grain and mutton in Qianmen, the bustling commercial neighborhood where we had visited the bomb shelters. After Mao established the Communist regime, the shops were expropriated as housing for workers at a nearby hat factory. The Liu family was allowed to collect rent until the Cultural Revolution in 1966. At that point, Mao's Red Guards forced Liu's father to hand over the property deeds. In 1983, with Deng Xiaoping back in power, the deeds were returned to the family. The property was not. Due to the housing shortage, the government decreed that the workers could continue living there and the family could resume collecting rent—at the original 1950s rate. For the next twenty years, Liu's father collected monthly rent of 3 yuan (39 cents today) on each of his six tiny buildings.

"There was no money to repair the buildings. The tenants complained all the time about the leaking roof," says Liu.

With the 2008 Olympics looming, everything changed. Beijing earmarked Qianmen for wide roads, skyscrapers and green space. Anxious to avoid a public-relations debacle, the city wanted to negotiate. By then Liu's father had died. Given the 1950s-era rent controls, the family was happy to sell. The city offered the remaining six family members—Liu, his four siblings and their mother—an incredible deal: 1,200,000 yuan, plus another half million for "moving expenses," a bonus to move beyond the Fifth Ring Road, and "disconnecting and re-installing" fees for non-existent air conditioners, telephones and television antennas. Together, it totaled $225,000 U.S., and Liu's one-sixth share of the windfall was nearly 300,000 yuan.

Or maybe it wasn't such an incredible deal. "We're the only ones who took it," says Liu, sipping a bit of wine. "Everyone else is holding out for more."

After dinner, he agrees to show me his family's old properties, which are on the verge of being bulldozed. We walk out into the *hutong* and south through the former Legation Quarter. Eleven imperialist powers were once here: Britain, America,

France, Germany, Spain, Japan, Russia, Italy, Austria, Belgium and Holland. The diplomatic missions were a collection of mock Gothic, mock Tudor and mock Empire, a concentration of bad taste exceeded only by Mao's subsequent Stalinization of Beijing's public architecture.

In the summer of 1900, Yi He Tuan, the Society of Patriotic Fists (known in English, absurdly, as the Boxers) besieged the Legation Quarter for two months. That cataclysmic clash with the West at the dawn of the twentieth century would shape all future encounters with foreigners. With the Empress Dowager waiting nervously in the Forbidden City a block away, the Boxer Rebellion ended in defeat. Allied troops raped and bayoneted their way through the capital, looting princely palaces and smashing jade and porcelain in search of more readily disposable plunder. In the Forbidden City—the innermost sanctum, where ordinary Chinese had never set foot—the foreign troops made themselves at home, the way U.S. marines would a century later at Saddam Hussein's palace in Baghdad. In Beijing, American, Japanese, Russian, French and British troops staged a victory parade in the Forbidden City. Diplomats from Germany and the United States filched "souvenirs," including the emperor's jade scepter. Soldiers bounced on the Dowager Empress's silken bed, mocked her silver chamber pot and sampled her bedtime snack of rose-petal compote.

The Legation Quarter remains a politically sensitive spot. After 1949, Prince Sihanouk of Cambodia inhabited the former French mission. Rewi Alley, a New Zealand writer and un-wavering supporter of the Chinese revolution, shared the for-mer Italian legation compound with American writer and left-wing journalist Anna Louise Strong. During the Cultural Revolution, Fat Paycheck and I would sometimes bicycle there for a cup of Nescafé with Rewi, surrounded by his unparalleled collection of Chinese porcelains and brush paintings.

Today, the British legation compound is occupied by the new combined headquarters of the ministries of public security and state security. As we stroll past, Liu offhandedly confirms what Dai Qing told me. "The Ministry of State Security isn't actually here," he says. "That's just to fool people. I once had to deliver a letter to the minister of state security. The guard wouldn't let me in, and he wouldn't accept the letter. He said, 'The office isn't here.' When I asked where it was, he refused to tell me."

The downpour has cleared the smog. We stroll along a dark, tree-lined boulevard, fragrant with pink mimosa. Until 1925, when it was filled in, this was the Jade Canal, apparently named by someone with a sense of humor. The canal was in fact an open sewer that carried human waste from the Forbidden City through the Legation Quarter. Contemporary accounts of the Boxer Rebellion describe bloated corpses floating in it. Liu wants to show me the sewer's current re-incarnation, a three-stall solar-powered public toilet that cost half a million yuan.

"It's famous," says my former driver, shaking his head. He means famous as a white elephant of a public works project. It does seem an odd place to stick a toilet: the street is deserted. Few Beijingers, after all, are stupid enough to loiter around the Ministry of State Security, whether it actually is or not.

Naturally, there is an attendant. He's dressed in flip-flops, an undershirt and boxer shorts. When we arrive, he is locking up the toilets for the night. A migrant from Anhui province, he complains that people can't, or won't, read the instructions. They keep breaking the door latch.

"Why is there a toilet here, right next to State Security?" I ask.

"Go ask the city government, or the Ministry of State Security," he says with a shrug. "I guess having no toilet here would be bad. This is the face of Beijing." Liu cajoles him into letting us take a quick peek. The floors are granite, of course. There is a scale. Two toilets are squat-style. The third is a urinal, helpfully marked "urinal." They are free and, despite full-time help, they stink.

A few minutes later we reach Qianmen. Liu leads us down a twisting labyrinth of *hutongs*. The alley narrows so suddenly at one point that Ben and Sam can stand in the center and touch opposite walls. Suddenly, Liu stops. "Those were our shops," he says, pointing to a tumbledown building with six small rooms. The front door is missing. The roof has caved in. "As soon as we signed the papers," Liu says, "the government came in and smashed the doors and the roof. Otherwise squatters would move in."

I notice some handwritten posters pasted on a nearby wall. "Seize the opportunity. Move out early, realize your dream early." Another urges, "Believe the government. Don't listen to rumors." And the latest tactic: "The government loves the people and is helping the people. Avoid dangerous housing."

Liu tells me the residents are already on to that ploy. After all, why the sudden concern about safety after half a century of neglect? "People are saying, 'I want 600,000 yuan for this house. Otherwise I won't go.' No one can agree on a price. Our house got us over a million yuan. The government can't afford to pay that to everyone. It could end up costing a billion yuan for this alley alone."

The original plan was to move everyone out by year's end, but almost no one is moving. Once upon a time, the police would have stormed in, tossed the furnishings outside and summoned the bulldozers. I witnessed that in 1993 in Bengbu, a small town in Anhui, the same impoverished province the toilet attendant is from. The authorities wanted to build an office complex on the land and tried to evict the residents. When people refused to budge, the authorities used force. The residents wept and screamed, to no avail.

"You can't use force anymore," says Liu. "Now if you don't agree, you can go to court. You can hire a lawyer. Of course, the court is controlled by the government, so some lawyers are getting arrested."

Ahead I spot a leafless branch, festooned with discarded plastic bags, growing out of the middle of the road. It looks like the Grinch's Christmas tree. I walk over to look. Someone has stolen the utility cover, and some civic-minded person has thoughtfully stuck the branch in the hole so no one will fall in.

Half a century ago, Liu played soccer in the alley nearby and lived in a gray-brick courtyard house across from his family's shops. One Liu shop sold flour and cornmeal that the family ground on a millstone. Another sold mutton, raw and cooked, to accommodate the large Muslim population. Like Proust, my old driver has memories of the delicious steamed wheat buns sold by a neighboring shop. He remembers that another shop sold cooking oil and salt. On the other side was a jeweler famous for the quality of his gold rings. "This was a good commercial area," Liu says wistfully. "They're going to tear all of this down. Soon this will be a mall."

22

My Deepest Apologies.
I Have Wronged You

I t's rush hour on August 17. We have eleven days left in
Beijing before we must board the plane home. We're supposed to meet Qiu Hai for dinner this evening, but every taxi is
taken. The sun, masked by smog, is beating down. The roar of
traffic is stupendous. Suddenly my cellphone rings. Fat Paycheck
has it. He answers it and hands it to me.

"Who is it?" I ask.

"It's the person you've been looking for."

I stare at him speechless. He repeats himself. "It's the person
you've been looking for."

I grab the phone and shout over the din, "*Wei! Wei!*" (Hello!
Hello!)

"Bright Precious! This is Yin Luyi," says a low, utterly feminine voice on the other end.

My heart stops. I'm afraid she'll hang up on me if I say
anything.

"I've never forgotten you," she continues. She doesn't sound
sarcastic. She sounds pleased. She keeps talking. "I've always
thought about you. I can see your big shiny eyes."

"I'm so sorry," I blurt. "I'm so sorry for what I did."

To my astonishment, she says, "No, no, you didn't affect me at all. All that had nothing to do with you."

I didn't affect her at all? How is that possible? But Yin is still talking. She tells me Teacher Pan tracked her down and gave her my cellphone number. "I'm very hard to find," she says, laughing. "I changed my surname. It's Lu now, not Yin."

I feel like Alice in Wonderland, tumbling down the rabbit hole. Scarlet is Limpid Pool of Water, and Yin isn't Yan or even Yin, but Lu. Hesitantly, I ask if she's willing to meet with me.

"Of course," she says with a delicate laugh. "I would love to see you."

I sink to my knees, trying to wrestle a pen and notebook from my fake Prada purse to write down her phone number. Sam sees me struggling and comes over to help, holding the phone to my ear. I want to see Yin/Yan/Lu this minute, but I don't want to spook her. And I still have to meet my cousin's cousin for dinner.

"What about tomorrow afternoon, say, at 3:30?" I suggest.

"Okay," she says. "I'll wait for you at the West Gate of Beijing University."

That night, as I shower, I feel amazed, elated and nervous all at once. I can't believe I've found Yin. Actually, she's found me. After all this, I'm afraid to face her. She doesn't sound bitter or angry, but how can she *not* be? And why does she want to meet me at the scene of the crime? That night I sleep fitfully. In the morning I call Scarlet to relay the news. She's stunned that I have found Yin. She makes me promise to tell her how the meeting goes. As I prepare to leave Beautiful Lodging, Sam cautions me. "Just so you know, Mom, she might have a gang of thugs ready to beat you up. Because you ruined her life."

* * *

Chinese who live overseas are often chronically late. The opposite is true on the mainland, possibly the result of the government's Mussolini-like penchant for getting the trains to run on time. I know I can't risk being late for my meeting with Yin. (After years of thinking of her as Yin, I can't adjust to calling her Lu, not yet.)

I arrive fifteen minutes early and stand in the shade, just inside the red lacquered pillars of the West Gate. A security guard, a migrant in a rumpled uniform with silvered plastic buttons, stands impotently by as students and tourists stream past. A young Italian student dismounts from his bicycle to study a map. "Do you speak English?" he asks a Chinese male student. He doesn't. A female student stops. "I speak English," she offers. The Italian wants directions to the South Gate. She points him in the wrong direction.

"It's that way," I interrupt, waving him toward the southeast. He thanks me and rides off. The bittersweet irony of the moment does not escape me. I'm waiting for Yin, watching Chinese students interact casually, normally, with a foreign student. In Mao's time, Yin tried that, and look what happened.

I check my watch. It's 3:22. I scan the faces of passersby and try to remember what she looked like. All I remember is a vivacious young woman with glossy hair pulled into thick plaits. Her face is a blank. I check my watch again. It's so humid that I feel hotter when I fan myself. The minutes tick down. At 3:30, my heart sinks. She wouldn't be late. *She's changed her mind.*

At 3:32, my cellphone rings. "Where are you?" she shouts. I can hear traffic in the background.

"I'm at the West Gate. Right inside," I shout back with relief.

"I'm inside, too," she says. "I'm standing on the bridge right inside the entrance."

Eagerly I scan the marble footbridge bridge in front of me. There's no woman my age talking on a cellphone. "I can't see you. Where are you?" I shout, nearly hysterical.

"Are there two *shizi* outside the gate?" she asks.

Shizi? I think frantically. *What are shizi?* And then I remember. *Shizi* are mythical Chinese lions, carved of stone or cast in bronze, with stylized manes and slanting eyes that flank traditional gates. I rush outside the gate. "Yes! There are two *shizi!*"

"You're at the wrong West Gate," she says. "I'm at the *Small* West Gate. You're at the *Big* West Gate."

I'd forgotten. Beijing University, which, of course, is a walled compound, has two West Gates—a big one for pedestrians and a smaller one for vehicles. We agree to start walking toward the middle, on the sidewalk along the campus wall. Silently, I bless the gods of Chinese capitalism. Without the economic boom, neither Yin nor I would have a cellphone. We would have missed each other altogether. And maybe the second time, she'd think better of meeting me and cancel.

Twenty seconds later, I spot her. She waves excitedly. I wave back. Time stops as we rush toward each other, slo-mo, like in those sappy Hollywood movies. When I reach her, I hesitate. But Yin gives me a big, warm bear hug. I close my eyes in relief and hug her back. She studies my face, and laughs. "I've never forgotten you," she says. "You haven't changed. Such fair skin, such big, beautiful eyes." Yin has matured into a beautiful woman, with a heart-shaped face and dark, permed, Botticelli-like curls that cascade down her shoulders. Her eyes sparkle behind silver-rimmed glasses that sometime slip down her nose. Her brows are shaped, her eyelashes touched with mascara. She is wearing pink lip gloss. "I've thought of you all these years," she says. Her tone isn't accusatory. I search her face for signs of anger.

"I am so sorry," I say. In the most formal Chinese I can muster, I add, "*Hen bao qian. Wo duibuqi ni.*" (My deepest apologies. I have wronged you.)

Yin gives me a quizzical look. "Don't be sorry," she says. "What happened to me wasn't because of you."

Like me, she had gone early to our rendezvous. When I didn't show up, she figured I must have been stuck in traffic. She, too, counted the minutes. At 3:32, she could no longer resist calling.

"Where should we go for a walk?" she asks, linking her arm through mine. I suggest we head for No Name Lake. Perhaps there will be a cooling breeze. Yin agrees with a smile. Her teeth are even and white, a rarity because of the lack of dental care in China.

"I'm so glad you found me," she says happily.

I don't think she understands. I abandon all subtlety. "I'm so sorry for what I did," I repeat. "I'm really, really sorry for telling the teachers that you wanted to go abroad."

To my surprise, she shrugs. "It wasn't your fault," she says. "I don't blame you at all. You didn't understand."

Then, hesitantly, as if it's something she hasn't discussed before, she starts to talk about the Cultural Revolution. "I was accused of many, many crimes. Twenty-five, perhaps thirty crimes. You added to the weight of my crimes. But I wouldn't have been in such trouble merely because I asked you to help me go abroad."

Twenty-five, thirty crimes? I don't know what she's talking about. I apologize again, formally. "Never mind," she says. "We were all crazy in that era. I don't blame you at all. You didn't understand."

I don't think *she* understands. I snitched. I didn't have to. I wasn't, like Scarlet, under pressure to criticize her. Mine was merely the yearning of an adolescent outsider to fit in with the in crowd, in this case the Maoists of the Cultural Revolution. And even though the consequences apparently weren't as dire as I had feared, even though she does not hold me accountable thirty-three years later, the fact remains that when faced with a clear choice, I chose the wrong one. I did not have to rat her out. No one made me. No one would have even known about her desire to leave the motherland. And yet I betrayed her, casually, nonchalantly, thoughtlessly. It had been such a non-event in my life that I didn't even remember it until I read my diary years twenty-one years later. So I lay it out, as bluntly as I can.

"I *voluntarily* turned you in," I say.

Lu Yi stops walking. "I didn't know that," she says, sounding surprised. She stares at me for a moment. Her gaze is steady. Her expression is inscrutable. I wait for a rebuke, a reproach, something. She resumes walking. "Let me put it this way. You didn't have that much power. You didn't have enough influence to ruin my life." I feel a bit of the weight on my heart lift, but I still don't understand. If I didn't ruin her life, what did? She senses my confusion. She stops and takes my arm.

"I've never forgotten you," she says with genuine feeling. "It must be fate that has brought us together again." She is dressed in sandals, slim white slacks and a sleeveless black knit top, beaded at the neck with tiny spangles. On her wrist is a delicate wristwatch; over her arm, a knock-off Gucci handbag. We walk past lotus ponds and imperial-style buildings that look centuries old. In fact, they were built in 1923 by Henry Killam Murphy, the Yale architect who designed the campus for Yenching University. As an American missionary school, Yenching provided a Christian, English-language education to a small Chinese elite. Naturally, it was shut down after the Communist victory. In 1952 Beijing University expropriated the campus.

I am wilting. We both walk slower and slower in the sauna-like heat. Every stone bench is occupied by tourists. I wish there was a teahouse or a Starbucks. But except for the occasional souvenir stand, Beijing University remains as resolutely uncommercial as in Maoist times. I ask Yin if she knows any place we could go for a cool drink.

"Do you want to come to my home?" she suddenly asks. "My home is right on campus."

Yin is back at Beijing University? I'd been hunting everywhere for her, when she'd been here all along? I'm bursting with questions, but we walk in silence. We pass Shao Yuan, where Cadre Huang had the banquet for me. We walk by tennis courts and a pick-up basketball game. She leads me into a walled compound that seems oddly familiar. The brick homes are Western-style, two stories high, with double-hung windows and steeply sloping gabled roofs. Each has a big garden, a rarity in Beijing. And the front doors are off to one side, in violation of Chinese principles of *feng shui*.

"I live here. This is Yan Nan Yuan [Yenching South Garden]," she says.

How strange—Yin lives one compound over from Fu the Enforcer. The address Fu gave me for the visit to her home that never took place was Yan Bei Yuan, Yenching North Garden. Yan Nan Yuan, also built by the Yale architect Murphy, is a little piece of Americana intended as elite faculty housing. Only later when I reread my diaries, do I figure out why it seemed so familiar. I have been to Yan Nan Yuan before.

Zhou Peiyuan, the urbane, silver-haired chancellor of Beijing University, lived here. On New Year's Day in 1973, he invited Erica and me to dinner. It was my first glimpse of the privileged world of senior Communist Party officials. He had a maid, when almost no one did. She had cooked and served the holiday meal, which included unobtainable luxuries like a whole chicken and pastries with real cream. Later, when I was about to be expelled for crossing paths with my Swedish friend, I went back to Chancellor Zhou's home to plead my case, to no avail. I remember banging his American-style screen door on my way out.

Yin points to Number 66. "This is my home," she says. We go inside, where the cool darkness is an immediate relief. She flings her purse down on the sofa. The house, which must be about eighty years old, has worn wood floors painted oxblood red. The walls are pale yellow and white. The furniture is old and expensive. On the main floor are an old-fashioned parlor, a study, a formal dining room, a powder room and a kitchen that hasn't been updated since the 1930s. Four bedrooms and another bathroom are upstairs.

"*Lao Gong,*" she calls, using the respectful Chinese for "husband."

Somehow I hadn't contemplated a husband in the picture. A tall man comes down the stairs. He has thick, white hair, horn-rimmed glasses and an impish, Cary Grant–like charisma. "This is my *lao gong,* Professor Yao. Yao Xiushen," says Yin. We shake hands.

"Please forgive me," he says courteously. "I wasn't expecting guests. I apologize for being so informally dressed." In the heat, he is wearing gray shorts and a white sleeveless undershirt. He has been reading upstairs in a bedroom, the only room with air-conditioning.

"Lu Yi," he says affectionately, "you two take the bedroom. It's cooler there."

She tells him we'll be fine in the living room. When we sit down, Professor Yao hospitably switches on an electric fan for us. "I'll make you some green tea," he says. He goes into the kitchen to put on the kettle.

"We registered for marriage last January," she whispers.

"How did you meet?" I whisper back.

"Someone introduced us," she says mysteriously.

Professor Yao reappears and sets out a plate of sliced watermelon. When the water boils, he scalds a small terra-cotta teapot, empties it, puts in the tea leaves and refills it with boiling water. She smiles at him as he pours the tea for us. "Oh, Husband, you spoil me," she says, with a happy laugh. Professor Yao beams. He's obviously besotted with her. When I compliment him on his American-designed home, he tells me it's a university perk commensurate with his status. He's a professor emeritus of physics. He's sixty-six, a decade older than Yin, and has just retired as vice-chair of Fang Zheng Corp., the university's profitable high-tech company. Coincidentally, it's where Luna worked before Lenovo paid her to take care of her husband.

"This house once belonged to Bing Xin," says Professor Yao proudly. "Have you heard of her?"

Yin and her husband live in a heritage house, akin to living in Hemingway's home, or F. Scott Fitzgerald's. Bing Xin, or Icy Heart, was the pen name of Xie Wanying, one of modern China's most prominent writers, whose friends included

Virginia Woolf. Bing Xin published her first novel at nineteen, while still an undergraduate in literature at Yenching University. She translated Rabindranath Tagore into Chinese, and wrote prose and poetry until her death, at age ninety-nine, in 1999. Her works available in English include *Spring Waters* (1929) and *The Photograph* (1992). After earning a master's degree in English literature from Wellesley College, Bing Xin returned to Yenching to teach in the 1930s. The circle that binds me to Yin is growing tighter. Never mind that Luna worked at Fang Zheng Corp—I met Bing Xin in the 1970s, and I know the writer's daughter, Wu Qing, today a prominent Beijing feminist and politician.

Yin tells her husband that we were both students at Beijing University at the same time. She doesn't elaborate. I take her cue and keep quiet. We sip tea until she shoos him, tactfully, back upstairs. Then she begins to tell me her story.

23

They're All Crazy

Lu Yi refills my teacup. Now that I've heard her husband call her Lu Yi, it doesn't sound so strange. She confirms what I had already learned. She was part of the first class to enroll at Beijing University during the Cultural Revolution. She was two years ahead of Scarlet's class, and there was no class in between. She majored in Chinese history and, like Scarlet, was on the varsity women's volleyball team.

"We became good friends. We were the only history-department students on the team. That year we were city champions. We spent a lot of time together. We were very close. I knew she was roommates with you."

What Lu Yi didn't know was that I was a True Believer. Scarlet never gossiped, and she wouldn't have talked about me. Lu Yi would never have dreamed that someone from the West would be a Maoist. She confirms that she wangled an introduction through Scarlet. Soon she was pouring out her heart to Erica and me as we strolled around No Name Lake that summer's evening in June 1973.

All these years, it never occurred to me we weren't the only ones she told. But Lu Yi told anyone who would listen about her dream of going to America. Of course, once she says this, it makes sense that if she told us, she would tell others. I don't know if I was the first to turn her in, or the third or the seventeenth or the twenty-fifth or thirtieth. She doesn't know either. Perhaps I set the juggernaut in motion. Did anyone else voluntarily rush to report her, hoping to enhance their application to join the Party? In the end, it really doesn't matter who went first, because everyone ratted her out.

Lu Yi also criticized the Communist Party, the Chinese government and Chairman Mao himself. She declared out loud that China was too radical, too ultra-left. "Others agreed with me, but they kept their mouths shut," she says. "They kept their thoughts to themselves. I'm the only one who talked about it openly. I didn't understand. I was very naive."

She spoke freely because she felt invulnerable. She had been raised in a cocoon of privilege. Her parents had joined the Party before the 1949 Communist victory, which gave them impeccable revolutionary credentials. Her mother was chief of personnel for the Ministry of Railways. Her father was a political commissar in the General Political Department of the People's Liberation Army. The oldest of three children, Lu Yi attended Number Eleven High School, an elite school for the offspring of high-ranking cadres. "If I had been the child of a worker or a peasant, I wouldn't have had such thoughts. But both my parents were educated. I was interested in the world."

Lu Yi also loved to write, which became her downfall. Like me, she began keeping a diary at Beijing University. Just as I wrote down all my struggles to conform to the bizarre world of the Cultural Revolution, my ambivalence to my bourgeois upbringing, my yearnings to be accepted by Chinese society, she wrote down all her doubts and questions about Communism, her passion for a better life, her burning desire to see America.

A month or so after our brief encounter, I left Beijing and returned to McGill University for my final year. Lu Yi remembers Communist Party officials calling her in for her first information session that fall. They told her they only wanted to know what she was thinking. "If you come clean with us, you won't have any problems," the history department's Communist Party secretary said.

Lu Yi took them at their word. After all, she had been raised to trust the Communist Party. When the Party secretary promised there would be no reprisals, she did not sense a trap. Like young people everywhere, she believed she was invincible. She had it all. She was born in Beijing in 1950, the first generation to be raised under Mao. She was the eldest child of senior Party officials. She was also a star athlete earning top marks at the best university in China.

She thought she understood Marxism. She'd spent hours reading Marx, Engels and Lenin. With the hubris of a young person, she shared her epiphanies with her classmates. "I said that Marxism could not possibly be a belief system. That would make it tantamount to a religion, and Marxism was opposed to religion. I also thought world communism wasn't possible without coercing people. If you had communism in only one country, that couldn't really be communism. You needed a worldwide system for communism to work."

All this was heresy, of course. Religion was the opiate of the masses. Marxism would save them. And coercing people into world communism? How insulting. The authorities kept asking what Lu Yi was thinking, and she kept telling them. She also kept writing everything in her diary. That fall, she noticed someone was rummaging through her things while she was in class, but she still didn't get it. "They were secretly reading my diary," she says softly. She keeps her voice low.

"Doesn't Professor Yao know?" I ask.

"He knows there was some trouble during the Cultural Revolution, but I haven't told him much."

Lu Yi's maid arrives through the back door. She's a migrant worker who comes every afternoon to clean house, wash laundry and prepare dinner. Three decades ago, I was shocked that Chancellor Zhou had a maid. He called her *ayi*—"auntie." Now one-third of Beijingers hire migrants as maids, and no one keeps up the auntie charade. In capitalistic fashion, everyone calls them *xiao shi gong,* or "hourly worker."

Lu Yi's class had entered Beijing University in 1970. Graduation was scheduled for January 1974. Officials assured her she would graduate without incident if only she confessed more. They pressed her for new details, more heretical thoughts, fresh revelations. Confident this was all benign, she provided them. "They duped me," she says, staring down at her teacup.

As autumn turned to winter, Lu Yi still had no worries. She had scored A's on every essay and assignment. If Beijing University had had a valedictorian in the history department, she would have been it. Her marks were the best in the class. She joined the class photo and had her individual picture taken for her diploma. She awaited her job assignment with anticipation. Brimming with confidence, she hoped to be hired on at Beijing University, an honor equivalent to a Harvard grad's being recruited directly onto the faculty.

The day before her graduation ceremony, the sky fell in. The knock on the door came in the middle of the night. It was Spring Plum Wang, her classmate and the class Communist

Party secretary, who had come to her dormitory to arrest her. Suddenly I understand why Scarlet suggested I look up Spring Plum. I see why Cadre Huang gave me her phone number. Both Scarlet and Cadre Huang pointed me in the right direction without ever once acknowledging what they must have known: Spring Plum's key role in Yin/Lu's disgrace. Fu the Enforcer, as a Communist Party member, also must have known; she would have been privy to confidential dossiers. Yet all of them insisted that they remembered nothing, or almost nothing.

At that moment, I realize Spring Plum will never call me back. The convenience of collective amnesia is clear. None of them wants to engage in Cult Rev soul-searching. Yet how can I judge them? Perhaps, like me, Fu the Enforcer sincerely believed in the revolution, at least at the beginning. And when she no longer did, she could not simply discard her ideology, as I did, flying back to North America, donning panty hose, and reinventing myself as a banking reporter at the *Wall Street Journal.* I cannot calibrate their unwillingness or inability to make brave choices in such a politically repressive culture. Pretending nothing happened is perhaps the only way to cope.

Lu Yi says that Spring Plum burst into her dorm very late that night. She came with reinforcements, several other classmates. They sternly ordered Lu Yi out of bed, then bundled her off to the Number Three Classroom Building, the magnificent gray-brick building with graceful eaves designed by the Yale architect. All night, Spring Plum and the others took turns interrogating her. The departmental Party secretary, a history professor, joined in. Lu Yi had once criticized his pedagogical technique. "If I hadn't got him mad at me over that, I might have been better treated. But he really had it in for me," she says.

"They took turns interrogating me continuously all night and all the next day. I couldn't endure it. I collapsed."

The next day, Spring Plum staged a department-wide "struggle meeting." This was not like the mildly annoying one-on-one criticism sessions I had with Cadre Huang or Fu the Enforcer. This was class warfare—vicious, cruel Maoist bullying, the mob unleashed. Attendance was compulsory for every student, faculty member and administrator in the history department. So Scarlet was there, together with all the young female students who lived with me in Building Twenty-Five. Lacking Virtue Pan, as Lu Yi's classmate, was front and center. Since this was not a university-wide rally, Fu the Enforcer and Cadre Huang would not have participated. But afterwards, as Party members, they would certainly have seen the documents concerning Lu Yi's case.

A Maoist struggle session was like a kangaroo court. Guilt was a foregone conclusion. The rally was part of the punishment. It was also a way to keep others in line. The Chinese had a proverb for it: "killing the chicken to frighten the monkeys." There was never an opportunity for the accused to speak. Lu Yi stood alone at the front as her classmates read aloud a list of her crimes.

"They had gone around to everyone to ask for dirt on me, even one of my childhood playmates. I saw the report that I had asked you and Erica for help in going abroad," she says.

Her voice falters. "I thought they had approached you. I didn't know you had told them on your own."

"I am so sorry," I murmur, apologizing again.

"Yours was just one of about thirty charges against me," she says wearily. "Everyone who knew me denounced me."

I realize that every time I point out my responsibility and

apologize, I force Lu Yi to exonerate me over and over again. That isn't fair. I can't keep unloading my guilt on her. But I do tell her what Cadre Huang told me—that I had nothing to do with what happened to her. I tell her because I want to know if that's true.

"It is true," she says instantly. "It wasn't because of you. You added to the weight of my crimes, but I wouldn't have been in such trouble just because I asked you for help in going abroad."

When her maid passes through the living room, Lu Yi falls silent. I sense that if she had planned on inviting me home, she might have told her maid to stay away, as Scarlet did. Lu Yi pours more tea and urges me to eat some watermelon. "My biggest crime was the thoughts I expressed in my diary. I said I thought China was too left-wing, that things were in a mess. That was unacceptable. They were secretly reading it all. In the end, they confiscated my diaries." She sighs deeply. "I really wish I had them now. They would be so precious to me. That is my biggest regret."

I tell Lu Yi that I've seen Scarlet. Her expression doesn't change, but I know she remembers that Scarlet denounced her too. I try to make excuses for my roommate. "Scarlet didn't want to denounce you," I say, the words tumbling out. "She had no choice. Someone else wrote her speech. She had to read it." I stop talking. It sounds pathetic, evasive, like the Nazi death-camp guards who said they were just following orders.

In her book, *Extraordinary Evil, A Brief History of Genocide*, Barbara Coloroso describes the "slow descent" of the German people into the "trap of comradeship." By introducing comradeship from the earliest age, through the Hitler Youth movement, the Nazis destroyed the sense of personal responsibility for their actions. Coloroso quotes from Sebastian Haffner's 1939 memoir, *Defying Hitler*: "They do what their comrades do. They have no choice . . . Their comrades are their conscience and give absolution for everything, provided they do what everybody else does."

Lu Yi doesn't say anything bad about Scarlet. Slightly changing the subject, she asks, "Has she gained weight?" Lu Yi is fifty-six now, a year older than Scarlet and two years older than I. She is still slim-waisted and curvaceous. Back when we all wore Mao suits, no one could, or dared, show their shape. "I swim every week to keep fit," she says. "I must get Scarlet to exercise with me."

One of Lu Yi's most enthusiastic attackers at the denunciation meeting was Lacking Virtue Pan. He got the job Lu Yi coveted: a faculty position directly after graduation. When I mention his name, Lu Yi grimaces.

"He told me he often sees you," I say.

"I have very little to do with him," she says abruptly.

That makes sense, but why would Pan have said otherwise? I suppose it's just another example of a persecutor's self-delusion, of people just wanting to pretend the Cultural Revolution never happened.

"He told me you weren't expelled. He said you had 'left' the school."

"No, I was expelled," she says, betraying a flash of anger. She's upset that people are still trying to cover up what happened. "I was *expelled*," she says, spitting out the Chinese word. She recites the formal language of her punishment: *Kaichu xuexiao, qiansong hui nongcun* (expulsion from school, forcible deportation back to the countryside). "I was dealt the gravest possible punishment. In hindsight, I'm lucky they didn't shoot me."

Lu Yi had already cried her eyes dry during the overnight interrogation. By the time of the departmental struggle meeting, she was numb. "I didn't cry. I just stood there. I told myself, *They're all crazy.* I was very strong."

After the meeting, Spring Plum ordered her to pack up her belongings. From that moment on, no one spoke to her again. The betrayal by her classmates, her teachers, her roommates was absolute. Only one young professor in his thirties tried to comfort her. "Teacher Wang approached me in the Big Canteen. He told me, 'Keep your chin up. Don't let them get you down.' I'll never forget his kindness."

Lu Yi was a Red Guard too, of course. She was a Beijinger, but during the Cultural Revolution, she had been deployed to rural Jilin province. Toiling among the peasants, she had made such a good impression that they had endorsed her application to Beijing University. The university had been her ticket out of the countryside. Her *hukou,* or residence permit, remained there, pending her new assignment upon graduation. But now that Lu Yi had committed thought crimes, the university was sending her back permanently to rural Jilin. It was a kind of internal exile, a lifetime sentence of backbreaking labor.

That night Lu Yi tried to kill herself. In the latrine, she found a small bottle of DDV, a pesticide. She went into a toilet stall and drank it. "I went back to my bed and fainted." She says this calmly. I close my eyes. Ingesting pesticide is the suicide method of choice in rural China. She could so easily have died. "In the morning, they shook me awake. I thought, *Why am I still alive?* I didn't want to live." Then her voice turns steely. "After that, I never tried to commit suicide again."

"They" were Spring Plum and a nasty cadre from the Foreign Students Office named Cai Heshen. It's strange that the Foreign Students Office was involved, but Fat Paycheck later tells me that anyone working there would be, by definition, an

ultra-reliable Party hack, hard-core enough to resist any temp-
tation involved with foreign contact and hard-hearted enough to
escort Lu Yi back to the countryside. It means, too, that Cadre
Huang had also been involved, if only peripherally, and would
have known exactly what happened.

The sun is setting. In the kitchen, Lu Yi's maid is chopping vegetables for dinner. Lu Yi keeps talking, as though she is finally
unburdening herself. That cold January morning, while the rest
of her class was preparing for the graduation ceremony, she
was bundled into a black prisoner's van. The windows had been
covered. She remembers shivering as the van pulled out of
Beijing University. She passed by, but was unable to see, the
huge beige concrete statue of Chairman Mao, his right hand
raised, accepting the adulation of the masses. The van went out
the South Gate heading downtown. When it reached Muxidi, it
turned onto the Avenue of Eternal Peace, passing Mao's compound at Zhongnanhai and then crossing Tiananmen Square.

Spring Plum and Cai, as Communist Party officials, were
escorting Lu Yi back to Manchuria. I remember Cadre Cai
well. He was a puny guy, with a greasy combover and a small,
pinched face that he would scrunch up into an insincere smile.
He looked like the stereotypical class enemy in Chinese propaganda films. He was odious. I would have hated to be under
his thumb.

At the Beijing Railway Station, Lu Yi's stern escorts and
her own hopeless demeanor drew attention. "I remember people staring at me, wondering what I had done wrong." She was
not in handcuffs—only those convicted in a court of law were
handcuffed. Yet a conviction would have been better. Without

a formal sentence, her exile to the farm fields was effectively a life sentence.

On board the train to Jilin, she drifted in and out of consciousness. The pesticide made her groggy and incoherent. She hadn't been allowed to contact anyone, including her family. Her parents had moved from Beijing to Manchuria, because her father had become the political commissar for Jilin City Military District. Someone informed her parents that people from Beijing University were coming to see them. They were excited—they thought the university was going to tell them that their daughter had been hired on as faculty.

Instead, Lu Yi showed up, pale, sick and escorted by Spring Plum and Cadre Cai. Spring Plum informed them of their daughter's disgrace. When Lu Yi's parents went into shock, Cadre Cai turned on them. "My mom and dad were distraught. They wept and moaned. Teacher Cai accused them of political vacillation, of failing to resolutely support Chairman Mao and the university's policies. He said that by their behavior they were implicitly criticizing the way the school had taught me."

It is the only time Lu Yi sounds bitter. She was not allowed a private moment with her parents. And they could do nothing to save her. Her father was under political attack himself, as was anyone who had had any power at all at the start of the Cultural Revolution. Spring Plum and Cadre Cai took Lu Yi back to the village that had sent her off with firecrackers, red banners and crashing cymbals when she had been accepted at Beijing University. Now the same peasants became her parole officers. Cadre Cai and Spring Plum Wang informed them that Lu Yi had committed unspecified "counterrevolutionary" crimes. In true Orwellian style, they forbade her even to tell anyone what she had done. (What if other people started thinking about going to America, too?)

People imagined the worst. After all, Lu Yi was very pretty. "Everyone—the peasants, the other city youth—treated me like dirt. They all looked down on me and assumed my *zuofeng you wenti* [that I was a slut]. Or that I had stolen something."

Although ostracized, Lu Yi was forced to share a dormitory with those who shunned her. It was solitary confinement, Maoist style. When she ate, no one would speak to her. When she fell sick, people ignored her. Nobody chatted with her in the communal washroom. All day she worked beside the others, planting rice and wheat. But she was invisible, a ghostly presence. Lu Yi falls silent. I don't press her for more. I have done enough to her already.

24

Stepping into Heaven

Two years later, Lu Yi's father was back in power as political commissar of the Jilin City Military District. He had just enough influence to get her out of the countryside. But given the serious nature of her crimes, the best he could muster was a job in a Manchurian oil field. She had to work rotating swing shifts. The work was grueling. And she was paid starvation-level wages commensurate for someone with a political problem. Lu Yi subsisted on meals of coarse grain and salted turnip. Her dossier followed her like dark cloud. People were told she had committed a crime so terrible that it was, quite literally, unspeakable. Just as in the village, everyone at the oil field shunned her.

One young man was different. Like Lu Yi, he was a Red Guard from Beijing. He was dazzled by her beauty and obvious intelligence. He provided a sympathetic shoulder for her to cry on. When she finally confided in him, he told her he didn't think what she had done was so horrible. Instead, he asked her to marry him. Instantly she said yes. "We had nothing in common," she says. "But my life was such a shambles then, I wasn't thinking straight."

Scarlet was right. Lu Yi was originally Yin Luyi. Her surname, Yin, means "silver" and is extremely rare. It was so unusual—the way Rockefeller is, or Giscard D'Estaing—that as soon as she told people her name, they connected her with the Jilin political commissar. To avoid besmirching her father's reputation, she decided to drop Yin. With his anguished permission, she became known just as Lu Yi, with Lu as her new surname. Scarlet was wrong about the characters, though. They don't mean "Road of Friendship." They mean "Delightful Land."

One day Lu Yi's foreman needed a document copied by hand. Most of her co-workers at the oil field were barely literate. Lu Yi, of course, could write. She volunteered, and impressed everyone with her elegant calligraphy. "After that, I was promoted to the Jilin Oil Fields Propaganda Team. It was like stepping into heaven. I only needed to work the day shift."

On September 9, 1976, Chairman Mao died, setting off a seismic chain of events. Newly married, Lu Yi digested the shocking news that Mao's widow, Jiang Qing, and her radical Gang of Four had been arrested. Mao's policies were dismantled one by one, but there was no national soul-searching, no reflection on personal responsibility. Examining the excesses of the Cultural Revolution was dangerous. Very few cadres had clean hands. The Communist Party was too thoroughly implicated.

In 1978, Lu Yi gave birth to a daughter. She named her Jianing, which means "Beautiful Peace." Other young mothers might have settled into domesticity. Lu Yi wanted exoneration. For two years, she had watched enviously as thousands of "counterrevolutionary" verdicts had been reversed. Cradling her newborn baby, she took the train back to Beijing. At Beijing University, she tracked down Spring Plum Wang. Like Lacking Virtue Pan, Spring Plum had won the great honor Lu Yi had hoped for: a faculty job right after graduation. Despite her youth, Spring Plum had even been promoted to Communist Party secretary of the history department. Now that she was in power, she was not interested in second-guessing the past, certainly not a case in which she had played a key role.

"I asked her to reconsider my case," Lu Yi remembers. "She turned me away."

Lu Yi did not give up. The next year, 1979, she made a second trip to Beijing University. Again she asked Spring Plum to clear her name and expunge the damaging accusations from her dossier. Again Spring Plum refused. But this time, Lu Yi did not go away. She had already made inquiries and had learned that a certain Professor Hao had been persecuted under the Gang of Four and had since been promoted to vice-chancellor. He outranked Spring Plum. Lu Yi went to see him.

"He said right away that I had been wronged. My verdict was overturned and I was exonerated."

Her life changed immediately. Beijing University wiped her dossier clean of thought crimes. It changed its records to say she had indeed graduated in 1974. Her personnel file at the oil field was similarly corrected. Now that she was officially a university graduate, she leapfrogged into a much higher pay category. The oil field gave her five years of back-pay differential. After years of subsistence living, she was rich.

"I was the first person in the factory to buy a television. And I bought furniture. Oh, I had furniture in every room," she says, laughing. "People would come to visit me and tell me, 'It looks like a furniture factory!'"

Some young women might have been content to lounge in their new bed and watch Chinese propaganda movies on their new television set. Not Lu Yi. She made up her mind to become a lawyer. She applied for graduate studies at the Central Institute of Politics and Law in Henan province. She correctly figured that, as China began rebuilding its economy and developed rule of law, there might be a shortage of legal experts. Her husband was not a go-getter, but Lu Yi persuaded him to follow her to Central China. He could help look after their one-year-old daughter in Henan. She also arranged a job for him, buying books for the Institute's library. At law school, her marks again were at the top of the class. And after graduation, she was hired on as faculty, the honor that had eluded her at Beijing University.

"My timing was right. China was just beginning to build a legal system after the Cultural Revolution. They needed teachers badly."

All that remained was the last element of her punishment: exile from Beijing. In the diaspora of the Cultural Revolution, millions of Chinese had been sent to rural villages, state farms and labor camps. Now everyone wanted to return. But restoring a Beijing residence permit was virtually impossible. Lu Yi turned the problem over in her mind and found a loophole.

The People's Liberation Army operated under its own rules. If it wanted to transfer someone to Beijing, it could override the city's Draconian *hukou* restrictions. In 1985, Lu Yi was thirty-five, well past the age for military recruitment. But she figured the army would want her legal expertise. That year she took the national exam for officers and aced it. "Dozens took the exam, but only three of us were chosen," she says.

In 1988, as she had hoped, a new assignment brought her to Beijing. She would teach law at the Military Prosecutors Institute in Badachu, on the western edge of the city. The military assigned her a campus apartment and provided residence permits for her, her husband and her daughter, now ten. Fourteen years after she had been forcibly deported, Lu Yi was back.

She and I happened to return to Beijing at the same time. In 1988, I had just arrived as the *Globe*'s thirteenth Beijing correspondent. In the previous eight years, I too had gone to graduate school and had changed cities several times. A year later I was covering the massive protest marches that paralyzed Beijing. That April and May, tens of thousands of students, journalists, police officers, bankers and steelworkers demanded human rights and democracy. After a dramatic hunger strike, the government imposed martial law. And then the protesters erected the tall white statue of the Goddess of Democracy in Tiananmen Square. On June 4, 1989, the army shot its way into the square, killing perhaps thousands.

Lu Yi had been an officer in the People's Liberation Army. I asked what she had done at the Military Prosecutors Institute. Had she canceled classes? Had she joined the hunger strike? To my surprise, she had done . . . nothing. "I stayed put at the Institute. I wasn't afraid. But I didn't march," she says.

It wasn't that she felt conflicted as a PLA officer. She was beyond protest. She had already expressed her dissenting views when she was a student, and she had paid the price. "I felt I had done my bit to change China. I didn't need to join the protesters. Now it was up to someone else."

Lu Yi's maid has left for the day. Supper is cooling on the table. We are sitting in shadows. Professor Yao has been downstairs several times. Now he is rattling around in the kitchen. I know I should leave, but I want to find out more. I want to ask what happened to her first marriage. I want to know if she ever made it to America.

Before we met this afternoon, I had no idea how Lu Yi would react. If it went well, I had a vague plan to invite her to dinner at Jade Garden, where we'd taken Fat Paycheck's former boss. Now, sitting here in her living room, the electric fan whirring in the corner, I'm afraid to break the spell by inviting her out. I guess it's obvious that if they don't invite me for supper, they won't eat any time soon. "Would you stay for supper?" says Lu Yi. "It's just a simple meal."

She calls to her husband. He must be hungry, because he's over in a flash. When he sees I'm still glued to the living-room sofa, he bows slightly and expresses the ritual apology of a proper Chinese host. "My deepest regrets," he says. "We have nothing to eat."

"I apologize for this *turan xiji,*" I say, dropping a Beijing colloquialism for "ambush."

"Our supper is too plain," Lu Yi frets, as we head for the dining room.

Even a simple meal in Beijing in these affluent times means four main dishes, plus rice and soup. The maid has left Chinese rapini flavored with the saline crunch of tiny dried shrimp; spicy whole green chili peppers, cooked until tender and tossed with crisp bits of Chinese pancetta; a salad of marinated sliced cucumber; clear consommé with fish dumplings; and shrimp, their heads still attached, sautéed with ginger and a touch of sugar and soy sauce.

The food is delicious, but I eat little. In my mind's eye, I keep stepping outside the scene, as in a Woody Allen movie, and marveling: *I can't believe I found her.* Lu Yi has no such problem. The freshwater shrimp are her favorite. She concentrates on them, greedily sucking on the heads, daintily spitting out the shells. She giggles when the mound of detritus reaches an embarrassing height. "I adore shrimp," she says.

"When I knew you would be staying for dinner, I bought shrimp," Professor Yao says, beaming.

"You're a model husband," she coos.

"And when are you going to be a model wife?" he coos back, grinning at her.

I must look confused because they explain that she doesn't spend every night with him, even though they are newlyweds. For the moment, she stays about half the time with him, the other half with her daughter, now twenty-eight. They registered at the marriage office eight months earlier. By Chinese tradition, however, the paperwork is only the first step. They won't fully be considered husband and wife until they have a wedding feast. But they are waiting; Professor Yao tells me his first wife died one year and nine days earlier. Over the past week, the house has been filled with white flowers, the color of mourning. Many friends dropped by to pay condolence visits on the first anniversary of her untimely death. During this sensitive period, Lu Yi has tried to keep a low profile.

"My wife died last August ninth in Moscow," he explains. "She was on a trip with Beijing University. She fell outside Lenin's tomb and hit her head."

I remember the bruises on Cadre Huang's head and think: *another uncanny coincidence.* He told me about this woman, whose death made it possible for Lu Yi to marry Professor Yao and move back to Beijing University. The irony is that while I have been searching all over for Lu Yi, she was back where I first met her thirty-three years ago. After all her humiliation, she had returned to Beijing University, married a rich and eminent professor and was living in the best housing on campus, in a house built by a Yale architect, next to her persecutors. When they turned on her in 1974, I'm sure Fu the Enforcer, Spring Plum Wang and Lacking Virtue Pan never dreamed that years later they would end up as her neighbors.

I look up at a framed piece of calligraphy on the dining-room wall. It's a quotation from Mao: "We must believe in the masses. We must believe in the Chinese Communist Party." Professor Yao, who speaks Russian and English, tells me he was born in wartime Chongqing. His father worked in Chiang Kai-shek's education ministry, disbursing funds to schools and universities. During the Cultural Revolution, his father came under attack for his Kuomintang ties. Professor Yao himself was considered "salvageable."

"I was *keyi jiaoyu hao de,*" he says, with a small laugh that suggests he is embarrassed. The phrase means "possible to educate well." What it really meant was that he could save himself only by betraying his father. He would have been forced to *hua qing jiexian*—"draw a clear demarcation line"—between himself and his father. Everyone had to delineate themselves from the politically suspect, especially from a person they loved. To prove his own revolutionary fervor, Professor Yao would been under pressure to denounce his own father.

I can still sing a ditty popular during the Cultural Revolution: "Daddy is dear, Mommy is dear, but neither is as dear as Chairman Mao." In 1994 I told Zeng Lin, who had briefly been roommates with Erica, what we had done to Yin. "We all would have done the same," she reassured me. "We were all reporting on each other." When I looked doubtful, she confessed that in

1966, when she was fourteen, she had denounced her father, the deputy minister of propaganda.

"We plan to have our wedding feast on October 1," says Lu Yi, eating another shrimp. They chose the date, not because it's the day Chairman Mao proclaimed the People's Republic of China, but because it's the first long weekend after the anniversary of Professor Yao's wife's death.

Beijing now has Internet dating and speed-dating, but Lu Yi and Professor Yao met the old-fashioned way, through a match-maker. From the way she avoids certain topics in his presence, I surmise they are still getting to know one another. Professor Yao tells me he just finished a five-year term as a delegate to the Chinese People's Political Consultative Conference. That's the prestigious rubberstamp body headed by Jia Qinglin, the co-developer of the Great Mall of China just down the road and the fourth most powerful man in China. Professor Yao represented Haidian, the high-tech district encompassing Beijing University.

"Really?" Lu Yi says. "I didn't know that."

The talk turns, as it does in Beijing these days, to real estate. Between them, Lu Yi and Professor Yao own five properties. He has this house and a country villa in the mountains. Lu Yi has three properties: a new 1,900-square-foot condo that she shares with her daughter, her old flat at the Military Prosecutors Institute and a small investment property in a hot section of downtown Beijing. She bought the last one, a pied-à-terre southwest of Tiananmen Square, in 1994 for 58,000 yuan. In twelve years, it has appreciated 700 percent. When I ask how they travel between their five properties, they laugh. They each own a Volkswagen Jetta—his is silver, hers is white. "I never expected I'd be driving or owning a car," he says.

Lu Yi serves us more watermelon for dessert. When we finish, Professor Yao goes back upstairs to his study. I'm still bursting with questions, but I understand that Yin must tell her own story in her own way. I can see that some parts are difficult for her, and she glosses over them. Other parts are cathartic. As a reporter, I normally ask many questions, but this time I suppress my instincts. I sense Lu Yi is recounting her story for the first time and, as such, is engaged in an act of re-creation. I will let her tell her story in her own way. I will not press her on inconsistencies, or on silences. It is the only gift I can give her now.

"Let's go for a walk around the campus," Lu Yi says impulsively. "The air is cooler now. We'll go back to the history department, for old time's sake."

Darkness has descended, but the air remains still and hot. The tourists have left. The campus is quiet, but not like when we were students and China was in the throes of the Cultural Revolution. Then there were only a few hundred students. Today, Beijing University has fifty thousand. "Let's find Building Thirty-Six," says Lu Yi, referring to the charmless brick dormitory where Spring Plum once knocked on her door in the middle of the night. We walk past the basketball courts where students are playing sweaty pick-up games.

Lu Yi resumes her story. In 1992, she became the first person at the Military Prosecutors Institute to *xia hai*—literally, "jump into the sea." It meant she took the plunge and quit her state job, giving up the cradle-to-grave security. She became a capitalist, which, in hindsight, I suppose was inevitable. "I started a wine and tobacco wholesale business," she says. "I also went into business with my brother. He owns a purse and luggage company in New York. My job was to manufacture semi-finished products in China and ship them in containers to him. He'd have the suitcases and purses finished there, put on a 'Made in the U.S.' label and sell them in America."

In 1994, when she was forty-four, she acquired her own car and learned how to drive. That icon of the American dream changed her life, giving her mobility, freedom, status, everything she craved. "I was the first person in my compound at the Prosecutors Institute to buy a private car. I was so proud." The economic freedom of plunging into the sea and the joy of having her own wheels lifted Lu Yi's spirits. She only had to look around her to realize the whole country was validating what she had written in her diary so long ago. Everything she had believed in and dreamed about suddenly was not only acceptable, but desirable. "Until then, I couldn't talk about what happened to me without crying," she says. She recites a line of classical poetry: "Many things occurred in the past; we can laugh about them now."

I think of all her tears, her isolation, her feelings of betrayal. For more than two decades, from 1973 until the 1990s, Lu Yi suffered terribly. Millions of Chinese victims did. For Lu Yi, expunging the damaging material from her dossier in 1979 was only the first step. All these years, she had had no one to talk to. She had already learned what would happen if she confided in friends.

Professional help was, practically speaking, nonexistent. At the time of the Cultural Revolution, China had a handful of psychiatrists, psychologists and psychotherapists, all trained before the Communist takeover. During the Maoist era, they were more likely to be victims than enforcers. During the Cultural Revolution, clinics were shut down en masse. The entire field was denounced as bourgeois, self-centered and unneeded in a proletarian paradise. Even now, psychiatry in China remains the lowest rung in the medical hierarchy. Only four thousand qualified psychiatrists are available to 1.3 billion citizens, according to a report in *Psychiatric Times* by Dr. Alan A. Stone, a Harvard professor who visited Beijing in 2005 on behalf of the World Psychiatric Association. If New York City had the same ratio, it would have just twenty-five psychiatrists for the entire city.

Except for some abuse of Falun Gong practitioners and other dissidents, China does not generally practice malevolent Soviet-style psychiatry. But supposing Lu Yi could get help— and more than 90 percent of schizophrenics in China don't, for instance, for lack of trained doctors—what possible treatment is available for a survivor of the Cultural Revolution? Anti-depressant drugs? Talk therapy? The latter would only point the finger at Mao and the Chinese Communist Party, and that remains unacceptable.

Suddenly Lu Yi turns to me and takes my arm. "You wouldn't have found me before 1996. Nobody knew where I was. I didn't dare show my face anywhere."

Despite the brave front she puts on, I sense she was deeply traumatized. The Communist Party, which she trusted, lied to her. Her classmates and teachers betrayed her. The peasants who had once embraced her ostracized her. Even her father, albeit reluctantly, allowed her to change her surname. And she had been gagged: she was not allowed to talk about what had been done to her or why.

Lu Yi couldn't shake her feelings of shame. "I didn't tell anyone about my past. I became a recluse." Even after she returned to Beijing to teach law at the Military Prosecutors Institute, she stayed low.

One injustice remained. Beijing University had changed its records to show she had graduated, but it had never issued her diploma. In 1997, she went back to the university to ask for it. After a two-month wait, she obtained it—nearly a quarter century late.

I never received my diploma either. When I graduated in 1977, I clashed with the university administration. For three years, our Chinese history program had been packed with ditch-digging and Marxist studies. But nine months after Mao's death, the university abruptly announced that everyone had to write final exams. The hypocrisy outraged my classmates. No one had cared whether we learned any history when they sent us to work in the fields. Now the administration was belatedly trying to restore the trappings of academia. My demoralized classmates boycotted the exams and, of course, I joined them. They all received their diplomas, but I didn't. (In 1994, Cadre Huang informed me I had in fact officially graduated. But considering that there are no records, how would anyone know?)

For Lu Yi, having her diploma—holding the little forest-green plastic booklet in her hands—was like a talisman, a healing amulet. It was tangible proof that she was finally whole. The next year, 1998, Beijing University marked its one-hundredth anniversary. Like a debutante, Lu Yi came out. She took part in a whole week of centenary activities. Most of her classmates had returned to the campus for the anniversary and were overjoyed to see her. These were the same people who had attended her denunciation rally, and many of them would have made speeches attacking her. But Lu Yi ignores those details, and I don't push. I let her tell me how much fun the reunion was. "Those with space put up out-of-towners," she says, smiling. "Those with money picked up the bill for our parties. Those with influence got things done."

Scarlet also attended the centenary celebrations. I know because in 1999, when I dropped by to visit her, she gave me her commemorative mug from the event. But neither she nor Lu Yi spotted the other. Or maybe they did, and pretended they didn't.

Lu Yi and I have trouble finding Building Thirty-Six. We find a building with the right number, but it isn't the dusty brick building we remember. This one is taller and bigger and has a front door made of glass that requires a swipe card. The door on our Building Thirty-Six had peeling paint and hung askew on squeaky hinges. This must be a new Building Thirty-Six. We peer through the glass and decide there is no point in talking our way in.

As we walk to the gates, Lu Yi tells me that she actually made it to America. In 1999, her brother invited her to stay with him in New York City. Her daughter, Peace, had turned twenty-one and was at university. It was time to realize her dream. Lu Yi applied for a visa at the U.S. embassy, and was successful. When she knew she was finally leaving, she decided to cut all ties. "I divorced my husband. We had been married more than twenty years, but we had nothing in common. I never intended to return to China."

By the time we reach the campus gate, it's very late. I still have so many questions. What did she do in America? And why did she come back?

"Can we get together again?" I ask. I wonder if she will decline, if this evening has been her one obligation to someone who came so far to see her.

"Of course," Lu Yi says instantly. "I want to meet your family. On Tuesday. Come to my new condo."

25

Straight to Heaven

When I get back, Sam and Ben are watching a bootleg copy of *The Devil Wears Prada*. Sam pauses the DVD player. "How was it?" he asks, examining me for bruises. "Was she mad at you?"

I tell them we're all invited to her condo in a few days. They hug me and go back to watching the movie.

Fat Paycheck is relieved. He let me go alone to the rendezvous because that was what I wanted, but he was worried the whole time I was gone. I tell him I had dinner at her house and met her new husband and learned that so many others had turned her in too.

"You were the least of her problems," he says, nodding. "Even if you hadn't done anything, she was already in deep trouble. You don't have to feel so guilty."

Norman believes she wasn't angry with me because I hadn't been the sole cause of her troubles. Yet he points out that she also assumed I had been interrogated about her. Until I told her, she did not know that I had scurried to Fu the Enforcer of my own accord. "But she also realized you had no idea what you were doing."

Having lived through the entire Cultural Revolution, he's heard many tales of betrayal and suffering. He says that for years he figured I might not have been Yin's only problem. Now, when he shares that thought with me, I'm upset. Why didn't he tell me this before?

"I didn't want to speculate," he says. "But she obviously was disenchanted with China. Why would this be the only problem she had?"

On Tuesday, August 22, Ben's pollution-induced cough has turned into a full-fledged cold. He has a runny nose and sounds fearsome when he sneezes. We have one week remaining in Beijing, but Fat Paycheck thinks it's the perfect opportunity for the boys to experience traditional Chinese medicine at its best. He takes Ben to Tong Ren Tang, the most famous herbalist in Beijing. The building is big and modern, with dusty marble floors. A balding, bespectacled doctor examines Ben the traditional way. He doesn't peer down his throat. He doesn't take his temperature.

"He felt my pulse," says an unimpressed Ben. "Then he told me I had a cold."

That afternoon, we head to Tiantong Yuan, which means "Straight to Heaven." In Mao's time, Tiantong Yuan was a labor camp for class enemies in rural Changping county. Now it's one of Beijing's biggest residential developments, part of the city's rapid urban sprawl. The road to Straight to Heaven was only recently finished. In a few months, a new elevated monorail will whisk its residents into downtown.

Like Scarlet, Lu Yi is convinced I'll never find her condo on my own. And she's probably right. It's like the Bronx, with condo towers as far as the eye can see. There are fountains, supermarkets and recreational facilities. When the cab drops us off beside a park inside the development, I phone Lu Yi as she instructed. Within minutes, she's pulling up in her white Jetta. "Jump in," she says gaily. "I didn't bring Professor Yao because . . . you know, we're not really . . ."

I nod. They're not officially out as a married couple. I don't mind. It's easier to talk when he's not around. In China there are too many secrets, too many proscribed topics, so that as soon as there are more than two people around, everyone clams up. Perhaps because I'm a history major, or because I'm a journalist, I do want to talk about the past. I do not want to leave it buried.

I asked Lu Yi if she felt like meeting Scarlet. She said of course. When I asked Scarlet if she wanted to meet Lu Yi, she readily agreed. I got the feeling that both were being polite, superficially agreeable about something they would never have done on their own. To refuse would be an acknowledgment of the pain of the past. Neither is prepared for that.

I didn't press either of them for their true feelings. Selfishly, I wanted to bring them together as part of my own search for redemption. I thought that if they could meet with one another, perhaps the wounds would heal and we would all feel a little better. And so I've arranged for all of us to meet for dinner later. It will be the first time the two will see one another since Scarlet denounced Lu Yi in Building Thirty-Six in 1973.

Lu Yi lives in Building Thirty-One, District Six, Straight to Heaven. She wedges her Jetta in a sliver of space beside some garbage cans. Inside her building, the stairwell is unfinished concrete. The walls are smudged and there is trash on the ground.

But when Lu Yi opens the door to her condo, I realize she *has* gone straight to heaven. Her vast living room looks like a glossy ad for Maurice Villency furniture in the *New York Times Sunday Magazine*. A lemon-yellow L-shaped sofa faces a large flat-screen television. Sheer drapes are printed with black calligraphy and ink-wash landscapes. The floors are hardwood, stained almost black. By the window, a white chaise longue, wide enough for two, is positioned to watch the sunset.

"I want to build a screen wall here for privacy," she says, pointing to a spot just inside the front door. I'm puzzled. Then I realize Lu Yi wants a spirit wall to shield her home from prying eyes. She is absorbed in redecorating her new condo. For two months, she ran her air-conditioner with the windows *open,* to rid the apartment of toxic smells. She takes me on a quick tour. Her condo has three bedrooms, two bathrooms, a dining room, a living room and an airy all-white kitchen with white lacquered cabinets and Corian-type countertops. When I admire her home, she smiles. "People's thinking has changed. Before, people saved money. Now they think, 'What else is money for, but to enjoy?' Why save it for your kids? That would be like turning paper money into *fei zhi* [waste paper]. So people spend it on themselves."

A fluffy white cat proudly stalks across the floor. "That's Precious," she says. The cat has the same name as the cat in the mahjong parlor, but Lu Yi does not tell me how much she paid for it. She cradles the cat, which has deep blue eyes. "She's deaf from an overdose of antibiotics at the pet hospital. Now, that's another change. People spend more on their pets than some people spend on their children."

That reminds me of my sixteen-year-old's visit to the herbalist. "Ben has a bad cold," I warn Lu Yi.

"I have some Chinese medicine for him, good stuff. It's expensive, very hard to find," she says, rummaging through the kitchen drawers. She finds the bottle and pours several dozen brown capsules into a thick white paper napkin from IKEA, the same kind I hesitate to buy in Toronto because they're expensive. "He should take eight of these a day. They really work."

The boys and Fat Paycheck are sitting in the living room on the yellow sofa. Lu Yi turns on the television and flicks the remote until she finds a channel of Chinese cartoons for them. Looking pained, Fat Paycheck closes his eyes. He hates television in any language. Back in the kitchen, as Lu Yi slices some watermelon, I think about Dai Qing. Her 1991 battle to leave China smoothed the way for Lu Yi eight years later. Her only delay was the two-month wait for her diploma, which the U.S. embassy required before issuing a visa.

"I had always wanted to see America, and now my wish came true," Lu Yi says, grinning broadly. She was forty-nine when she landed in New York in 1999, but she felt like a little kid as she walked, wide-eyed, through the streets. She could hardly believe she was there. "I was in America at last. America was so beautiful." At first she stayed in Flushing, with her brother, the luggage entrepreneur. Later she found an apartment of her own and earned a living teaching Mandarin to the children of Chinese immigrants.

She missed her daughter terribly and, over the next two years, flew back to Beijing several times. In honor of the Big Apple, she gave her daughter an English name: Apple.

In America Lu Yi was free to reinvent herself. This was a country that looked forward. No one there cared about her past. "I decided to stay permanently in America, even if it meant going underground as an illegal," she says. Lu Yi tried her best to learn English, but new vocabulary just didn't stick in her middle-aged brain. This was the one missed life opportunity even she couldn't remedy. She stayed close to Chinatown, where she could shop, buy newspapers and talk to people.

"I couldn't get a good job in America because I didn't speak much English and I was illegal. In Beijing, I don't do menial work. There I was a second-class citizen. I could do only minimum-wage work. And I was bored out of my mind."

She began noticing signs in Chinatown shop windows advertising bargain bus tours, in Mandarin and Cantonese, to Boston, Philadelphia, Washington, DC, and other destinations. Incredibly, the bus to Atlantic City was free—in fact, better than free: passengers were paid twenty dollars in cash. "They told us you have to tip the guide one dollar each way. Some people would take the trip every day, wait for the bus home and live off the eighteen dollars," she says, laughing.

Lu Yi recalls the bus was luxurious, with plush seats, a toilet in the back and a television screen every third row. She went five times to the casinos. "I brought two hundred dollars each time. At first I was timid. I put money only where others did. I lost it all."

Lu Yi didn't care. Her whole life, after all, had been one high-stakes gamble. On her fifth and last trip to Atlantic City, she decided to go for broke at the craps table. But when it was her turn to be shooter, she was too shy to roll the dice. "Everyone said, 'C'mon, c'mon.' So I tried," she says, with a huge grin. She rolled the dice forty times without once throwing an unlucky seven. "Everybody was winning. They clapped for me all the time!" she says, her eyes shining. That day she won a thousand dollars, exactly breaking even on her five gambling trips.

In the summer of 2001, Lu Yi went back to Beijing to visit Apple. She was planning to return to the United States when terrorists attacked the World Trade Center. Glued to her television set in Beijing, she watched scenes of the twin towers collapsing again and again, and began to reconsider her American dream. "After 9/11, I didn't want to go back anymore."

Lu Yi finishes cutting the watermelon. She opens her refrigerator and takes out a plastic container filled with creamy yellow lobes of durian. A funky odor pervades the kitchen. "This is my favorite fruit!" she says.

I've had durian as often as I've had donkey penis. I prefer penis.

Speaking of which, durian is considered to be an aphrodisiac in Thailand and Indonesia, where some 7-Eleven stores sell durian-flavored condoms. In Southeast Asia, the yellow and tan spiky fruit is so stinky that it's routinely banned in hotels, subways and airports. Anthony Burgess, the English novelist, famously likened the smell of durian to "eating vanilla custard in a latrine." Richard Sterling, the principal author of the Lonely Planet food series, put it this way: "The odor is best described as pig-shit, turpentine and onions, garnished with a gym sock." On *Fear Factor,* the reality-television series, competitors sipped durian juice while chowing down on a stew of ground-up pig brains, rooster testes and cow eyes. My own opinion is that durian smells morbidly sweet, like the decomposing bodies in the Capital Hospital after the Tiananmen Square Massacre.

"The children will love it," says Lu Yi. She carries a heaping platter of durian and watermelon out to Fat Paycheck and the boys. Ben and Sam help themselves to the watermelon. "Try the durian!" she says. None of them has previously tasted the tropical fruit, which is already flooding the living room with the smell of sewage and stale vomit. Norman takes a tiny bite. At Lu Yi's behest, Ben and Sam reluctantly swallow a mouthful.

"*Hao chi*," Sam says politely, practicing his newly acquired Chinese word for "delicious." Lu Yi laughs and claps her hands.

"*Hao chi*," his older brother echoes, not to be outdone.

I know neither of them wants to eat another bite. When Lu Yi urges them to have more, they look to me for cultural guidance. Accompanying me to visit the person I ratted out is, well, right up there with anything on *Fear Factor*. I nod, and the boys suck up another lobe. I look at my watch. I could save my children from death by durian by pointing out that we're late for our dinner with Scarlet. Lu Yi's daughter will be joining us too, and given the endless traffic jams, we really need to get going.

"I think we'd better hit the road," I say. Sam and Ben smile in relief. I am not such a terrible mother after all.

Lu Yi is driving when her cellphone rings. It's Apple, who is in her own car and wants directions to the restaurant. "Baby, I can't talk. I'm driving. I'll call you later," Lu Yi says.

"Apple has her own car?" I ask.

Lu nods. "Does everybody have a car in America?" she asks, glancing sideways at me as she navigates through the late-afternoon rush hour. Suddenly the two of us are back at No Name Lake, a lifetime ago, and Lu Yi is asking me if everyone has a refrigerator. She interrupts my thoughts with another question. "Are there any poor people?"

What an odd question. New York is full of homeless people. Didn't she stumble across them? I'm about to answer when Sam pipes up from the back seat. "There is no place without poor people," he says.

Scarlet has booked a private room at Xizi Renjia, a restaurant specializing in the delicate cuisine of Hangzhou, the southern capital Marco Polo may (or may not) have visited. The restaurant is a favorite of hers, partly because it's within walking distance of her rented condo and partly because she doesn't need a reservation. Three times a week, a buyer in Hangzhou, 1,500 kilometers to the south, air-freights local specialties to Beijing.

My old roommate is waiting for us in a private room. She and Lu Yi do not hug. They stand a few feet apart. They are both smiling. I sense the strain.

"Traffic was bad," says Lu Yi.

"Did you have trouble finding the restaurant?" Scarlet asks.

After some chitchat about the weather, they discuss what kind of tea best suits the cuisine. If I didn't know Scarlet felt used by Lu Yi and Lu Yi felt betrayed by Scarlet, I would never guess by observing them. They look like two middle-aged women getting together for a pleasant meal. The odd thing is the disconnect between their respective memories. Scarlet recalled very little about Lu Yi. She wasn't even sure of her correct name. Lu Yi, on the other hand, remembers being close to Scarlet and spending a lot of time with her. Whose memory is correct? Does it even matter? I have discussed the issue of betrayal, separately, with each them. I have reunited them, but I feel as though I am forcing them on each other. Neither wants to revisit the past. Everyone ratted out everyone else, and now all the participants prefer to walk away and pretend the Cultural Revolution never happened. At least Scarlet remembers what she did. Fu the Enforcer professes complete amnesia, but after learning how actively involved Spring Plum and, indeed, the Communist Party structure at Beijing University were, I have doubts about Fu's faulty memory. She had to have known something.

During the Cultural Revolution, Fat Paycheck was publicly condemned by his section leader at *China Reconstructs* for insulting Chinese womanhood. Norman commuted by bike forty-five minutes to the office. In winter, upon arriving at the chilly office he shared with others, he'd remove his outer trousers, don a pair of padded pants, and then put his outer pants back on. Section Leader Li Zongren framed this daily disrobing as something only a lewd, rude American imperialist would do. Even though Norman was always wearing at least three other layers: underpants, cotton jersey long underwear, and thick, knitted woolen long johns, he was exiled to a brutally cold office down the hall. Three months later, Li was overthrown by another faction and sent to hard labor in Qinghe, ironically the current location of Lu Yi's new Straight to Heaven condo. In the 1970s, after Li returned to *China Reconstructs,* he pulled Fat Paycheck into the stairwell and apologized. "He said he had been completely wrong. I thought he was sincere."

In his remarkable book *The Captive Mind,* Czeslaw Milosz discusses the "beguiling allure" of totalitarian rule: "Informing was and is known in many civilizations, but the New Faith declares it a cardinal virtue of the good citizen . . . It is the basis of each man's fear of his fellow men. Work in an office or factory is hard not only because of the amount of labor required, but even more because of the need to be on guard against omnipresent and vigilant eyes and ears." In East Germany, the Stasi paid informants. When cash wasn't enough, the Stasi would unearth incriminating information about prospective informants and blackmail people into snitching on others. China was different. No one was paid to turn in others. No one was blackmailed. Perhaps Europe had a stronger history of individualism and free will that only force and cold cash could overcome. Certainly, the Iron Curtain produced great dissident thinkers, such as Sakharov and Solzhenitsyn.

In a feudal, hierarchical Confucian culture such as China's, a sense of duty to the collective was ingrained. Scarlet had felt the pressure of that "cardinal virtue," as Milosz describes it. As my roommate, she was also terribly vulnerable for having introduced a dissident to me, an outsider, a foreigner. Under Mao, everyone felt pressure. Lu Yi's husband had to *hua qing jiexian*— "draw a clear demarcation line"—from his own father. Those who didn't would stand accused of allowing bourgeois sentiment to obstruct their revolutionary duty.

At first, Chinese betrayed each other for idealistic reasons. They were motivated by ideology. They were True Believers. Later, with no individual will or choice in a police state, people became frightened; they turned in others to save themselves. And when cynicism set in, people became more like the East Germans and the Soviets, and snitched to get ahead. Today, people still apply for Party membership as a career move. "Upwardly mobile young lawyers join the Party while they're at Beijing University," says my friend Kathy Wilhelm, the American lawyer. "They know nothing about politics. It's all about networking, burnishing their résumés."

• • •

Apple arrives at the restaurant, out of breath, with the catch-all Beijing excuse for tardiness. "Traffic was terrible," she says, apologetically. She's slightly taller than her mother, in strappy black high-heeled sandals, a white knit top and a frilly skirt. Over her wrist is a pink and white fake Dior purse, with dangling gold letters, D-I-O-R. It's hard to imagine she was born in the oil fields of Manchuria and bundled to Beijing University as a babe while her mother sought exoneration.

Apple is, well, the apple of her mother's eye. At twenty-eight, she works as a web designer. "She earns more than I do," says Lu Yi, proudly.

Our waitress sets out half a dozen appetizers on the lazy Susan turntable. Scarlet has ordered all her favorite dishes and mine: a pyramid of crisp, deep-fried stinking bean curd (its actual name); candied sesame walnuts; whole braised fish; chicken hacked in bits and stir-fried with blackened chili peppers; boneless fillet of yellow-croaker fish sautéed in a rice-wine sauce of fresh bamboo shoots and white cloud ear fungus; *jiwei* greens cooked with minced garlic; stewed lionhead meatballs (minced pork, said to resemble the heads of *shizi,* like the ones standing guard outside the West Gate of Beijing University); cubes of braised pork belly, served in individual terra-cotta bowls; clear consommé with baby lotus leaves.

The food is delicious. However, I haven't brought my old roommate up to date on everything Lu Yi has told me. I can tell Scarlet is dying to ask questions, but she doesn't. And even if she had the courage, I doubt Lu Yi would say much. She wouldn't talk in front of Professor Yao, so I'm sure she wouldn't now, not with so many people sitting around the table. I don't ask Scarlet anything of significance, either. I don't challenge the half-truths she told me. It would only embarrass her, and it wouldn't be fair.

We settle on Lacking Virtue Pan as a safe topic. "He's deputy chief of joint ventures for Beijing University's international division," I tell them.

LuYi suddenly reveals a side of herself I haven't seen before. "He's still a 'deputy,'" she says contemptuously. "He'll never become a chief. He'll never get to the top."

I mention my own bitter experience with him over my wedding invitations. Not that my classmates missed much. During the Cultural Revolution, austerity ruled. Chairman Mao had died only three weeks earlier and the country was still in mourning. We offered our guests only tea, peanuts and a few foreign luxuries like pâté, brown bread and dill pickles plus shots of Maotai, the sorghum-based white lightning that Nixon used to toast Premier Chou Enlai. Our wedding presents included a cleaver, a chopping board and a tin kettle.

Apple says that today the wedding gift of choice is cash. Ordinary friends give 200 to 300 yuan. Good friends give 999 yuan. Nine, pronounced *jiu,* is a homonym for "eternal," and is also the highest digit, signifying the male side of yin and yang.

Apple, who attended a high school classmate's wedding two days ago, says that Western-style weddings are big in Beijing. Her friend was married at the East Cathedral, a Catholic church in the Imperial City. "They're not Christians," she says. "They just wanted to get married in a church. They rented a stretch Cadillac and ten Audi cars for the convoy. Afterwards, there was an open-air Western-style buffet lunch in Chaoyang Park."

Sometimes Western customs are interpreted in interesting ways. In this case, Apple says, the bride and groom both wore white, more appropriate for a Chinese funeral. The bride adhered to Chinese conspicuous-consumption norms by switching gowns three times. Two were bridal gowns, and the third was an evening gown, even though the reception ended at two in the afternoon.

Trendy young people like these newlyweds must be the ones who patronize the religious gift shop at the Capital Museum. They don't wear the Jesus Loves tie because they are Christian and believe Jesus loves; they just want to look hip. Although Western weddings have become popular only in the last decade, the Capital Museum already feels compelled to explain Chinese wedding traditions.

At a display, a Chinese sign explains that guests sometimes hid dates, sunflower seeds and peanuts in the nuptial bed. "The characters for dates, seeds and peanuts are puns for the phrase 'giving birth early to a son,'" it said.

"What about you? Are you planning to get married?" I ask Apple, in that annoying way your mom's friends always have.

"I want to go to America," she says, sipping some coconut juice. She adds that U.S. visas are much harder to get since 9/11. "So I've applied to go to Canada. That's not easy either, so I'm applying to the province of Quebec. I think fewer people try to get into Quebec."

Suddenly I see a way to make amends. I can help Lu Yi's daughter get to Canada. The immigration process is strictly an arm's-length process and her application has already been submitted, but at least I can advise her from the sidelines. And when she finally arrives, I can help her settle in. "I applied two years ago for an immigration visa to Quebec," she says. "I'm applying under the category of 'educated technician.'"

I tell Apple I will try to help her. Lu Yi bursts out, "I just want to make friends with you, not because I want your help . . ."

"I thought you *were* friends," Apple interrupts, looking mystified.

"Baby, it's a long story. I'll tell you later." I realize that not only has Lu Yi not told her new husband about her past, she has never told her daughter either. Perhaps there is solace in silence. Holocaust survivors typically do not tell their children much. World War II and Vietnam veterans rarely discuss the horrors they experienced. Survivors of the Rwandan genocide are mostly silent.

My father will not discuss what happened to him, either. He was nine during the Great Depression when his father sent him from Montreal, where he was born and raised, to China, a country he had never seen before. His responsibility: to grow enough sweet potatoes to feed his mother and three younger siblings. Two of them died. My father has never eaten a sweet potato since, not even at Thanksgiving dinner. When I was writing *Red China Blues* and pressed him for details about our family history, he could talk for no more than ten minutes at a time. His words would grow more halting, and then he would end the session and leave the room.

Lu Yi tries to tell her daughter what happened without actually saying anything. "Things were tense because Bright Precious was a foreign student," she says.

"She's a foreigner?" Apple says. "I thought she's Chinese."

I try to help. I tell Apple that the Cultural Revolution was a very . . . unusual time. "When your mother and I were at Beijing

University together, I was very 'left,'" I say stumbling over the lack of a word in Chinese for "Maoist" or "Maoism."

Apple looks more confused. "What is 'left'?" she asks, genuinely puzzled.

I am astonished. Lu Yi's daughter—this bright young thing who does web design, who lives in the People's Republic of China, run by the Chinese Communist Party, who was born just two years after the death of Chairman Mao—does not know what "left" is. Seeing my face, Apple quickly explains that she has studied only one book about Marxism, at university. "I forgot it right after."

As I stumble around trying to explain leftism, Lu Yi tries to help. "I was right-wing," she tells her daughter.

Apple looks perplexed. "Were you a counterrevolutionary?" she asks slowly.

Scarlet, Lu Yi and I shudder simultaneously. Being labeled a counterrevolutionary is still serious enough to get you shot. The three of us try to explain the political spectrum to Apple, but she quickly loses interest.

"I like French," Apple says, turning to Ben and Sam. She's been taking night classes in preparation for moving to Quebec. She tries out a few sentences. "*Ou allez vous a l'école?*" she asks. Ben and Sam applaud. Apple beams.

26

Lu Yi's Revenge

As Lu Yi says, it must be fate that has brought us together. What were the odds that I would find her? There were so many coincidences, so many tenuous connections. She was expelled from Beijing University, where the trail ran cold. Even if she had graduated, the school has no records from that era. She moved many times, from a village in rural Manchuria to the oil fields near Jilin to Henan province to Beijing to New York City and, finally, back to Beijing. She even changed her name.

If that Chinese journalists' delegation had not come to visit the *Globe and Mail,* I would not have found Scarlet. I wouldn't have contacted Future, who coached me on how to approach Lacking Virtue Pan. Cadre Huang had already retired, but at least he was still living in university housing and easily found. He provided a phone number for his neighbor, Spring Plum Wang. Cadre Huang probably knew she wouldn't return my call, but he still provided two invaluable bits of information. He told me there was no intake class in 1971, which meant Lu Yi had to be in the 1970 intake class, the first since the Cultural Revolution began. At that point, I realized that she had to be in

the same class as my own Party secretary, Lacking Virtue Pan.
Cadre Huang also provided me with Pan's cellphone number.

By all logic, I still shouldn't have found Lu Yi. The alumni
office couldn't even trace Scarlet and Future. But because Lu Yi
wanted to go abroad, she needed her diploma. That forced her
to return to Beijing University and renew contact with those
who had tormented her. China's dramatic transformation also
played a role. By the 1990s, Lu Yi no longer felt ashamed of her
dream. She emerged on the centenary of Beijing University
and reconnected with classmates who included people she
didn't particularly like, such as Lacking Virtue Pan. Beijing's
cellphone penetration rate played a critical role, too. Without
cellphones, it might have taken me weeks to contact people,
and then I would have run out of time. I certainly would have
botched that first meeting with Lu Yi, when we went to different campus gates.

By chance, my timing was just right. Lu Yi had returned
from America. She had just remarried and had moved back
onto the campus of Beijing University. Had I searched any earlier, I would not have found her—she still would have been in
seclusion. If 9/11 hadn't happened, she might still be living in
the United States. But if I had waited any longer, Cadre Huang
might have been too old or too ill to help. Scarlet and Future
would have retired, and both surely would have moved yet
again and changed phone numbers too. When I think about it,
finding Lu Yi was a miracle, as improbable as her dream in 1973
of going to America.

Five days before our departure, Lu Yi invites Scarlet and me,
along with Ben, Sam and Fat Paycheck, to a special meal: Ma La

Xiang Hot Pot. *Ma* means "numbing," *la* means "spicy" and *xiang* means "fragrant." I've never had Numbing, Spicy, Fragrant Hot Pot before, but it's the rage in Beijing right now. The restaurant Lu Yi chooses—it's actually called Ma La Xiang—is so trendy that when you phone to book a table, it's invariably busy, like Nobu in New York.

When we arrive, the restaurant is packed. A line of customers snakes out the door. Apple has managed to book a tiny private room. It is whitewashed, bare and cell-like. There are exposed wires overhead. A fretted screen over the door makes it appear as though we're behind bars. "It looks like an interrogation room," says Ben, laughing. Stupidly, I translate that for Lu Yi. As someone who has actually been interrogated, she doesn't find that funny.

"Why did you translate that?" says Ben, embarrassed. Scarlet smoothes over my tactless moment. She presents Ben and Sam with gifts—ornate seals carved with their English and Chinese names. The top of Ben's is sculpted with a horse, his Chinese zodiac year. Sam gets his zodiac year too, a rooster.

This meal will be called Lu Yi's Revenge. The waitress brings an enamel washbasin brimming with chunks of leek, nuts, garlic cloves, bay leaves, blackened chili peppers and herbs I've never seen before. These are just the seasonings. She sets the basin over a gas burner sunk in the middle of the table. We're supposed to order the raw ingredients to cook in the basin. I defer to Lu Yi, a Numbing, Spicy, Fragrant aficionado.

"You choose," I say.

"Absolutely no tripe," Scarlet interjects nervously.

Lu Yi is disappointed. "The tripe is delicious," she says.

Scarlet is adamant. "No tripe."

Lu Yi orders: squid bodies and tentacles, sliced chicken, bamboo shoots, lotus root slices, enoki mushrooms, shiitake mushrooms, a can of Spam, shrimp with the heads attached and cow esophagus. "That's disgusting," says Sam, who isn't talking about shrimp heads. "Why'd they put Spam in it?"

To accompany our *Fear Factor* stew, Lu Yi orders deep-fried slices of *wotou,* the coarse steamed cornmeal bread that we all dreaded in the university canteen and that she ate for years while she was being punished in Manchuria. "You'll like it," she promised. "*Wotou* is delicious deep-fried. Very crisp." For cold appetizers, she chooses shredded half-raw potato, boiled soft peanuts, blanched Chinese celery with radish, and lotus root stuffed with glutinous rice. I hate them all, especially the half-raw potato, which my health-food cookbooks say will destroy all the Vitamin B12 in your system and give you scurvy or rickets or some dread disease.

I'm worried Lu Yi is about to order durian juice to wash down our Numbing, Spicy, Fragrant Hot Pot. Instead she orders chrysanthemum dried-lemon tea. I'm allergic to chrysanthemum, but she looks so happy I say nothing. At worst I'll just get dizzy and pass out.

"Can I have a bowl of rice?" Fat Paycheck asks the waitress. He turns to Lu Yi. "I can't eat anything spicy," he explains. She looks mortified. All the food here is Numbing, Spicy and Fragrant. Norman concentrates on his rice, with a clove of raw garlic or two. Ben eats sparingly too. Unlike Sam, he declares Spam superior to esophagus.

Despite his visit to the famed Chinese herbalist and several doses of Lu Yi's special medicine, Ben still has a very bad cold. He swallows a chili by mistake and starts coughing so violently he has to get up and walk around. Meanwhile, Sam has rudely fished through the entire washbasin of chilis and filched every single bit of chicken. "Tastes like chicken," he says with a grin. Suddenly his nose starts bleeding profusely. He excuses himself to go to the washroom to hemorrhage in private. Nosebleeds must be a common hazard at Numbing, Spicy, Fragrant Hot Pot, because the attendant knows the drill; she immediately advises Sam to splash his forehead with cold water.

"I did. The bleeding stopped," he says, returning to the table amazed.

Scarlet pushes squid tentacles around on her plate. "I can't eat spicy either," she confesses.

Unlike everyone else, I like spicy. But Numbing, Spicy, Fragrant Hot Pot is off the capsicum charts. As the cayenne pierces the back of my throat like a poisoned dart, I too succumb to a fit of coughing.

"Oh, you don't like it," says Lu Yi, looking disappointed. "I've failed."

"No," I lie, chewing on a piece of cow esophagus. "This is fabulous."

After dinner, Ben and Sam plead to go back alone to Beautiful Lodging. After what they've just endured, I relent. Scarlet stops several taxis to take a hard look at the drivers' faces. Finally she finds one she thinks looks honest. Norman gives the driver the directions and writes down the license plate number. We wave goodbye to our heir and spare. "Do you think this is a good idea?" says Lu Yi, looking doubtful.

Apple escapes too. She says she has to work on the weekend.

"Let's go back to my place," says Scarlet. "There are four of us. Perfect for playing mahjong." We pile into Lu Yi's white Jetta.

The aboveground lot at Scarlet's condo is full. We drive around and around the underground parking garage until Scarlet finally tells one of the guards to lead us to an empty space. He trots ahead of us to point it out. Maybe the parking attendant at Alfred Peng's office was actually doing his job.

Mao Mao has just put her toddler to bed. She comes out to greet us, looking sexy in loose trousers and a sleeveless silk top, exactly what her mother wouldn't have been caught dead in during the Cultural Revolution. While we set up the table, Mao Mao cuts a ripe Hami melon from Xinjiang into chunks for us to snack on. We set up our tiles. Then we roll the dice to see who goes first. Scarlet rolls a three. I roll an eight. LuYi rolls a nine, and Fat Paycheck a seven. "I win!" LuYi shouts.

Mao Mao prompts Norman from behind him. Scarlet coaches me. I never dreamed that my Red Guard roommate would morph into a housewife addicted to a game Chairman Mao banned. Every Sunday, Scarlet says, she hosts her siblings for an afternoon of gambling. "I never bet less than fifty yuan," says Scarlet. "Otherwise it's not exciting." Since neither Fat Paycheck nor I know how to play, no one bets any money.

"I win!" Lu Yi suddenly screams. "Give me silver! Silver! Silver!" she shouts, waving her arms and curling her fingers in the universal gesture of "gimme." She wins, theoretically, all evening long.

Scarlet's son-in-law, the army man, was supposed to join us for Numbing, Spicy, Fragrant Hot Pot. At the last minute he had an emergency. "So he had to deal with it, which meant throwing a banquet," says Scarlet. The army apparently needed to smooth over a public-relations problem. The *Beijing Evening News,* a muckraking tabloid, reported that two army trucks fled after police had stopped them for running red lights. The army already had an image problem: it frequently uses its sirens and flashing lights to muscle its way around the clogged expressways. Scarlet's son-in-law had to placate senior municipal officials with a long, boozy, expensive dinner.

When he gets home at ten o'clock, she orders him to drive Fat Paycheck and me home. He meekly agrees.

"You didn't drink alcohol, did you?" she demands of him as we're leaving.

"Not much," he says.

27

Lu Yi's Revenge II

We are leaving Beijing on Tuesday, the day after tomorrow. Lu Yi has invited Scarlet and me and my family to a farewell Sunday lunch. I have just dragged the boys out of bed when Lu Yi calls to switch it to dinner. "Something's come up," she says. "Special situation. I'll explain later."

The boys and I spend the morning shopping for presents. For lunch, we stop at the awkwardly named Sichuan Provincial Office in Beijing Restaurant, run by, yes, the Sichuan Provincial Office in Beijing. The office, like an embassy, represents Sichuan's political and economic interests in the capital. Happily, that includes showcasing its best chefs. The restaurant is packed when we arrive. We order Sam's favorite, chopped-up chicken with dry-fried whole chilis. Ben has beer, but Sam has a Coke. Now that booze isn't forbidden, it has no more allure for a thirteen-year-old. At a noisy table nearby, a drunken, red-faced man has his arm around a very young waitress. She cringes at his touch.

"He's sexually harassing the waitress," says Ben in disbelief, shaking his head. A beer bottle crashes to the floor. A scene like

that would silence diners in a Toronto restaurant. Here everyone ignores the incident, which must be commonplace given
how fast the cleaner arrives. With a blank expression, she mops
up the foaming beer and shards of glass.

After lunch, I hunt for a florist. I went empty-handed to my
first meeting with Lu Yi because I couldn't think of an appropriate gift for someone whose life I had ruined. For our second
meeting, I brought her a brick of fine black Pu Er tea from
Yunnan province. For our final meeting, I want to bring her a
huge bouquet of flowers. The restaurant staff assure me there's a
florist down the *hutong*. Stuffed with tea-smoked duck and
other Sichuan delicacies, we stagger down the alleyway.

Suddenly we see a Tudor-style mansion. Seeing us stare, a
middle-aged woman, clutching shopping bags, stops to explain.
"This was the home of Shi Liang, the lawyer," she says proudly.
Shi Liang was a feminist pioneer, the first justice minister of the
People's Republic of China. In the 1930s, she was one of the few
female lawyers practicing in Shanghai. In 1936, the Kuomintang
government arrested her for leading protests against Japan's
invasion. She died in 1985 at the age of eighty-five.

"And the Panchen Lama used to live here," the woman
adds, pointing to a nondescript Western-style house next door.
She's referring to the tenth Panchen Lama, Tibet's second highest spiritual leader, after the Dalai Lama. The Panchen Lama
was held under house arrest—probably here—until 1982. In
1983, he married a Chinese woman, a highly controversial
move for a Tibetan monk. The Panchen Lama died in Tibet in
1989 at fifty-one, shortly after criticizing the presence of
Chinese troops there.

"Soong Chingling lived just across the road." Madame
Soong, of course, was the widow of Sun Yat-sen, the founder of

republican China. Seeing how intrigued we are, the woman offers to show us the neighborhood. "I'm a schoolteacher," she says, leading us down a tiny *hutong*. "I live just over there."

We squeeze by a flatbed truck onto which three workers, their bare chests glistening in the sun, are shoveling rubble. As we walk past a humble courtyard home with a plain red door, she says, "This is my home. Even if they give me enough compensation, I'd still rather live in a courtyard home in the city than a high-rise in the suburbs."

On several walls, I notice the character *chai*—"demolish" —crudely painted in red, then obscured with a splash of whitewash. Like the neighborhood in Qianmen, the schoolteacher's neighborhood has been reduced to rubble. "This will all be gone in two months," she says, pointing to what seems to be a vacant lot with three homes still standing in it. A black tarp covers a mound of dirt, complying with city directives to reduce dust. On a half-collapsed wall, someone has spray-painted two linked hearts and, in English, "I love U." Ben, a budding photojournalist, spots a brown plush dog propped on a pile of loose bricks in front of a banner heralding the Olympics. He thinks it would make a neat photo. As he raises his camera, a security guard materializes.

"No photos," the guard orders roughly, stretching out his hand to block the lens. He is wearing a green shirt, knock-off Nike runners and a black insignia on his sleeve. Ben is surprised. I explain that in Beijing rubble is political; many people are upset that the city's architectural heritage is being demolished for the Olympics. As the government destroys the *hutongs,* it wants no record. The guard must have been given orders. That would also explain why the *chai* character has been whitewashed. It's quite literally a cover-up.

The guard sticks close to Ben, who keeps trying to sneak a few shots. Suddenly Ben succeeds. When he tries to take another, the guard gets angry. I warn Ben that the guard might smash the camera. We need to get out of there. Surprisingly, the schoolteacher is unruffled. In Mao's day, she would have been quaking. Why isn't she afraid now? Then I get it. She's a Beijinger, and the guard is a migrant worker. After all, who else would be guarding *rubble?* She ignores him as if he's invisible. Taking our cue from her, so do we. We chat for a few minutes about nothing much, just to show our contempt for his authority. And then we thank the schoolteacher and head back to the main *hutong.* Ahead, I finally spot a sign: "Flowers and Fruit."

"What kind of flowers do you have?" I ask.

"No flowers. Only fruit," says the shopkeeper, sounding like a Cultural Revolution relic. There's no other flower/fruit store in sight, so I resign myself to buying Lu Yi fruit. Wiping the sweat from my face, I am tempted by the gorgeous peaches. They're pale pink and at their peak and, therefore, far too cheap for a gift. I spy a pile of spiky durian.

"How much?" I ask.

"Ten yuan a catty," he says, citing the traditional Chinese measure that equals half a kilo. That's expensive, which is just what I want. He chooses one on top of the pile. It's bigger than a football. He weighs it. It's nearly seven pounds. I examine it carefully, hoping to fool the vendor into thinking I'm a sharp Beijing buyer. In fact, I haven't a clue how to pick a durian. The tan exterior looks unblemished. I sniff it. It doesn't smell like pig shit. Anyway, why should I worry? I'm giving the durian away. I nod, and the vendor slips it into a red plastic bag.

The vicious spikes poke right through the thin plastic. The durian looks like a medieval instrument of torture. Its name comes from the Malay word *duri,* meaning "thorn." In Vietnamese, its name, *sau rieng,* means "private sorrow." Durian pickers wear hardhats because a falling durian can cause serious injury, even death. I hail a taxi. Unsure of the durian-in-a-Beijing-taxi fatality rate, I sit in front, the durian gingerly nestled between my bare legs. The boys and Fat Paycheck stay safely in the back seat.

The ride to Beijing University is collision-free. Inspired by Lu Yi, I drop off a letter to the Foreign Students Office asking for my diploma to be issued retroactively. (They will ignore my request.) Then, holding the seven-pound durian with an outstretched arm to keep the thorns from stabbing me in the calf, I successfully lead everyone to Yenching South Garden. But where is Number 66? The houses are in no particular order. Twelve is here, and 28 is beside it. Again, the cellphone comes to the rescue. "I'm standing by an outdoor latrine," I tell LuYi. "Which way do I go?"

"I'm stuck in traffic," she shouts. "I'll be there soon. Call my husband at home."

Before I can, Professor Yao has already rushed out to hunt for us. LuYi had him on speed-dial. He makes us a pot of green tea and puts out a dish of small red grapes, each already plucked off the stem and set out like a bowl of candies. "These are rose grapes," he says. "They're not big, but they're very sweet and they taste like roses."

He pours us small cups of tea. "Did LuYi tell you what happened?" Professor Yao asks. "Apple called. She was having a bath this morning in their condo. She left the bathroom to fetch something, and the door accidentally locked, with the tap running."

The only key to the bathroom door was inside the bathroom. Why builders install bathrooms locks that require keys is a mystery I can only attribute to the Chinese passion for walls and gates. When we lived in Pagoda Garden, every room and closet in our flat came with a lock and key. (Yet now that I think about it, our 1938 Toronto home has locks on most of the doors. And our Yamaha piano comes with a lock and key, too. What's up with that?)

Professor Yao says that Apple has to work, even though it is Sunday. She was already late, so Lu Yi dashed over to handle the crisis. Lu Yi drove madly around Straight to Heaven hunting for a locksmith. The first one couldn't get the door open and damaged the lock. The second locksmith succeeded. Meanwhile, the bathroom had flooded the condo below. It seems there *are* advantages to dilapidated state housing after all. In Mao's time, no one had private bathrooms. And if the communal one flooded, it was always someone else's headache, usually some poor sap of a class enemy.

Lu Yi arrives, looking quite cool in a short-sleeved dark green sweater and white trousers, a purse daintily slung over her wrist. She's wearing iridescent fuchsia lipstick. She throws her purse down on the sofa. "The traffic is horrible," she says. Rushing back from Straight to Heaven, she got stuck in the Sunday-afternoon traffic pouring out of the West Gate.

"Beijing University now offers MBA weekend courses for CEOs," Professor Yao explains. "The school makes a lot of money from this. It charges very high tuition, and all the CEOs come in their fancy cars with their chauffeurs. This is exactly the time when their classes let out."

"Scarlet can't make dinner," Lu Yi says. "She had to go to a baby shower. She was on her way here this morning when I called her to cancel the lunch."

I give Lu Yi the durian. According to Chinese etiquette, she should barely acknowledge it. She should put it aside, as a sign of humility, an indication that she is far too humble to even consider that this fabulous item might be meant for her.

"I have something for you, too," she says with a huge smile, handing me a red silk box.

"Should I open it?" I ask uncertainly. She nods happily. It's a teapot hewn from a solid piece of milky white jade, its handle and spout carved to look like bamboo. I run my fingers over the smooth, cool stone. It is beautiful. I shake my head in embarrassment. "I give you fruit, and you give me jade," I say.

Lu Yi brushes off my protest. "It's ornamental," she warns, assuming I'm an idiot. "You can't actually use it for tea."

Then, to my horror, she takes the durian out of the red plastic bag. "My favorite! We must eat it together!" she declares, as Ben and Sam shoot me dagger glances from the couch.

Call it Lu Yi's Revenge II. She marches into the kitchen with the fruit of death. Professor Yao gallantly gets out a paring knife and tries to cut it open. The fierce brown husk refuses to yield. He gives up and joins the boys on the couch.

"Do you like sports?" he asks Ben and Sam. When they nod enthusiastically, he turns on the television to CCTV's all-sports channel, where the Brazilian women's volleyball team is beating the crap out of the Chinese women's team.

"I've never opened a durian before," says Lu Yi.

That makes two of us. "Save it and eat it after we leave," I urge.

"No," she says, beaming. "It's delicious. We must eat it together."

She rummages in a drawer and finds another small knife. It too bounces off the durian's spiky hide, like a plastic fork against a rock. Lu Yi is clearly not the type to surrender, either to political persecution or to thorny fruit. She gets out three more knives, including a ferocious-looking Chinese cleaver. Raising it high above her head, she brings it down with all her might. Peering at the durian, I think I see a superficial nick.

Lu Yi tries several more slashes. She ends up impaling her hands on the thorns. Bloody but unbowed, she gets out another, bigger cleaver. Fat Paycheck, who isn't interested in women's volleyball, wanders into the kitchen. He gives us moral support but refuses to touch the durian. Professor Yao comes back into the kitchen too. About now, I'm thinking a chain saw might do the trick. Instead I suggest a hammer. Professor Yao brightens. He reappears with a metal box, from which he extracts a small hammer. Positioning the cleaver between the spikes, I slam the hammer onto the top of the cleaver. The blade goes in a couple of millimeters.

"Let me try," says Lu Yi, dabbing her bleeding knuckles. She takes the hammer from me. This has now become a two-woman job. While she pounds and hammers and chops, I grip the durian. Professor Yao, who I am beginning to notice is a fairly helpful husband, gets out an oven mitt. Using that and a folded dish towel, I manage to hold onto the durian while Lu Yi chops. It occurs to me that she might have been faking forgiveness, waiting for just the right moment to take revenge.

But Lu Yi's chopping is accurate and non-vengeful. After twenty minutes of determined work, she splits it open. Inside are half a dozen big lobes of pale, creamy yellow fruit. Its distinctive, rotting fragrance fills the kitchen. It takes more chopping around the tough membranes to free the soft lobes, then Lu Yi begins scooping out mounds of fruit.

"Enough," I say weakly.

"The kids can eat this," she says, triumphantly carrying a heaping bowl of durian into the living room.

"No thank you," Sam says politely.

"No thank you," says Ben, less politely.

"Eat, eat," Lu Yi urges, thinking I have two of the politest kids in the world. According to Chinese etiquette, you always refuse when someone offers a treat. The host then ignores you and gives you what you just said you didn't want, on the assumption that you really want it. LuYi piles some slimy yellow chunks onto their plates. She gives me a plateful, too. I eat it because, well, I deserve it. It tastes better than it smells, which is to say it tastes horrible.

As I swallow a lobe of durian, I think to myself, *LuYi and I are finally even.* But, of course, we aren't, and we can never be. I can never make up the lost years to her, the humiliation, the pain and suffering, the damage of a mismatched marriage. I understand now that what happened to her wasn't entirely my fault. I was only one-twenty-fifth, one-thirtieth responsible. Yet I bear a heavier burden than the others who persecuted her. I was different. I wasn't a Chinese citizen. I was just a stupid, wannabe Maoist from Montreal, trying to prove I was as stalwart and tough as the next guy. I was under no pressure to turn people in. No one made me snitch. I didn't have to do it. I think LuYi is letting me off far too easy. She is a better person than I.

"It's delicious," she says, wolfing down a mouthful. She glances at the television set. A Chinese volleyball player has just bungled an easy setup by the net. "Oh!" she exclaims. "She shouldn't have missed that." When she leaves the room for a moment, Sam quickly picks up a gooey lump of durian from his dish, and then another, and another and throws them back on the serving plate. Ben glares at me, and does the same.

28

A Grain of Sand,
Helping China to Change

Professor Yao heads over to a campus restaurant to make a reservation for dinner. "You take them on a walk," he suggests to Lu Yi as he leaves. She demurs. Like me, she can no longer find her way around her alma mater. "Husband, we'll wait for you to come back."

When he leaves, I finally have a chance to ask Lu Yi what she did after she returned from America in 2001. "I really have a lot of energy and drive," she says. "I wanted to make something of myself." She says she started two businesses. One was a high-tech consulting firm. The other, with three partners, produced medicinal wolfberry wine.

"Do you regret not staying in America?" I ask.

She shakes her head, and eats a bite of durian. "That was my dream. I wanted to see America, and I did. I supported myself there, but I came back." She smiles and looks around her comfortable home. "In fact, my life here is better than there." The boys are studiously ignoring the piles of durian on the coffee table. Lu Yi concedes defeat. I follow her as she carries the remaining fruit back into the kitchen.

"I would have returned to America," she continues, "but then I got married. And now my new husband prefers that I spend time with him during his golden years. I gave up my companies. I'm retired."

So Lu Yi is like Scarlet and Luna. The keenly independent young woman who, through sheer grit, became a law professor, then a businesswoman and then an undocumented alien in the United States, is now . . . a housewife. She quit working to devote herself to her husband. Her days are filled with plumbing problems and decorating her condo. After dinner, she and Professor Yao have an appointment with someone who is making slipcovers for their sofa.

Lu Yi seems very happy now. But I can't help but wonder: is this what the revolution was all about? There I go again. When Lu Yi wanted to go to America, I judged her. And now that she wants to be a housewife and decorate her condo, I'm judging her again. Even at this late date, I still need remedial help to recover from Maoism. Come to think of it, writing this book is tantamount to a Maoist self-criticism.

Professor Yao returns, reporting that we have an hour before our reservation. We all troop out for a tour of the campus. He leads us past the history department's administrative offices, with delicate cinnabar latticework over the windows and a curved gray-tile roof. In 1973, this was the Number Three Classroom Building where Spring Plum interrogated Lu Yi. Now, as departmental Party secretary, Spring Plum's office is in the same building. "I hate that place," Lu Yi whispers, with a shudder.

Professor Yao points out the university library. "It's the biggest in Asia," he says. "No, wait. It can't be bigger than the China National Library. It must be the biggest *university* library in Asia." I feel a small surge of pride. I tell Ben and Sam that I helped dig the foundation. I'm happy that Beijing University finally has a modern library. In the 1970s, the old one had closed stacks. If you wanted a particular book, you had to know the author and exact title, hope the library had it and pray it wasn't on a banned list. And then you had to beg for it. The librarians were curt. But then, what kind of librarian would smile in the midst of the Cultural Revolution?

Professor Yao heads for No Name Lake. I doubt he knows about the stroll Lu Yi and I took there in 1973. From the way he treats me—courteously, but neutrally—I am sure she has not told him. "This was the bed of the Yongding River in the Ming dynasty," says Professor Yao, pointing to the lake. "The river later changed course, leaving behind these hills and the valley. The water now is pumped in from a reservoir near the Great Wall."

A villa on the highest hill is almost hidden behind a copse of bamboo. "It's called 'Veranda by the Lake,'" he says. "The university uses it for receptions. It was once the home of Situ Leideng." John Leighton Stuart—Situ Leideng—a missionary educator, was the last American ambassador to China before Mao's armies took Beijing. Born in 1876 in Hangzhou of missionary parents, Stuart was also the first president of Yenching University. In an essay published in the *Collected Works of Mao Zedong,* the Great Helmsman sardonically dispatched him with a polemic titled "Farewell, Leighton Stuart!" Back in America, the hapless missionary-educator was condemned by critics who accused him of having "lost" China to Communism. In 1972, Erica and I inherited Stuart's chef, who made the best apple pie, donuts, potato chips and hamburgers. At least, he did until Erica insisted that we had to renounce privilege and potato chips, and eat slop in solidarity with Scarlet in the Big Canteen.

Professor Yao points out the tomb of Edgar Snow on the next hillock. Snow first arrived in China in 1929 as a twenty-three-year-old correspondent for the *Chicago Tribune*. In 1933, he taught journalism at Yenching University. Three years after that, he became the first American reporter to interview Mao and other Red Army leaders in their caves in Yanan. His glowing account of Mao in *Red Star over China* was a key reason I became a True Believer and journeyed to China in 1972.

At the height of the Cold War, Snow was one of China's staunchest friends. Mao invited him to Beijing in 1960, during one of the worst famines in Chinese history. Snow's editors at *Look* barraged him with queries, but he filed nothing. Instead he blamed the persistent reports of famine on "cold-war press indoctrination." After he left, Snow wrote this in *The Other Side of the River: Red China Today:* "I diligently searched, without success, for starving people or beggars to photograph."

Some have called him a willing dupe. But it is entirely possible that Snow saw no evidence of famine. The Chinese escorted him everywhere and let him see what they wished him to see. China could and did create a convincing Potemkin world that could fool a foreigner, even a seasoned American journalist with excellent sources who worked for *Life* and *Look*. I know I truly believed, in 1973, that China was such a wonderful society that anyone who wanted to leave had to be saved.

In 1970, Beijing rewarded Snow with the biggest scoop of all. In *Life,* he broke the news that Mao was inviting President Richard Nixon to China, a turning point that would lead to the normalization of Sino-American relations. When Snow was dying of pancreatic cancer in 1972, Beijing sent a round-the-clock medical team to care for him. He died on February 15, the same week President Nixon traveled to China. One hundred days later, I arrived in China, alone, on my summer vacation from McGill University.

Lu Yi and I study Snow's tombstone. The granite is carved in Chinese and English with the words "Edgar Snow, American friend of the Chinese people." Sometimes friends fall out. When Snow's widow, Lois Wheeler Snow, visited the grave in 2001, she noticed a man on the nearby bench "ostensibly reading a newspaper, but in actuality filming us through a lens in the briefcase on his knees." Lois Wheeler Snow, then seventy-nine, had already been tailed by an unmarked car and two motorcycles when she tried to meet Ding Zilin, a professor whose seventeen-year-old son had been killed during Tiananmen, fatally shot by Chinese soldiers right outside Peace's home at Ministerial Apartments.

"Plainclothes police jumped out, and we were filmed from briefcases which we discovered contained concealed video cameras. It was an ugly scene, one I could have imagined only in a third-rate spy film," she wrote in an essay posted on the website Human Rights in China.

Professor Yao points to a beautiful gray pagoda rising by the side of No Name Lake. "It's an exact replica of an ancient pagoda in Tong county just east of Beijing," he says proudly. He bristles when I inconsiderately add that an American architect from Yale conceived of building the pagoda to encase an unsightly water tower .

As we stroll around No Name Lake, Professor Yao shows us a large stone boat in the water beside a small island. "That belonged to He Shen," he says. "He was copying the Empress Dowager's stone boat at the Summer Palace. It became one of the crimes for which he was executed."

"They never taught us that," says Lu Yi. "We majored in history, but we never learned any history. We were history students, but they never even mentioned the history of Beijing University."

Indeed, no one told us that our revolutionary campus had been the summer retreat of He Shen, the richest, most powerful mandarin of eighteenth-century imperial China. Professor Yao's other information is half-right. He Shen did get into trouble for copying a stone boat, but not the Empress Dowager's. He copied his patron's, the Qian Long Emperor. He Shen predated the Dowager by a century. Perhaps our history professors never mentioned He Shen because of his homosexuality. Although historical records about homosexuals date to the Shang dynasty (1600 to 1100 BC), the Communists persecuted gays. They decriminalized homosexuality only in the late 1990s and finally removed it from an official list of mental disorders in 2001.

The Qian Long Emperor was sixty-five when He Shen, then a twenty-five-year-old imperial bodyguard, caught his fancy. He Shen's feminine features were said to resemble those of a favorite imperial concubine who had committed suicide. He became the emperor's preferred catamite. Within a year, He Shen gained control of the powerful Board of Revenue and the Civil Office. Two months later, he was promoted to grand councilor. A month after that, he became minister of the imperial household, a post usually filled by a venerable, meritorious official. In 1777, when He Shen was just twenty-seven, the emperor granted him the privilege of riding on horseback within the Forbidden City, a favor normally bestowed upon the highest officials too elderly and frail to walk.

In 1790, He Shen married his son to Qian Long's tenth and favorite daughter. Openly corrupt and untouchable as Qian

Long's lover, He Shen amassed great wealth. He built a magnificent home here beside No Name Lake. When Lord Macartney arrived in Beijing in 1793, hoping to open China to British trade, He Shen received him in a pavilion here by No Name Lake. But when the emperor died in 1799, Qian Long's son, the Jia Qing Emperor, ordered his father's lover put to death "by a thousand cuts." He Shen was forty-nine. His friends at court managed to see that he was merely hanged.

After imperial auditors broke into his warehouses, they found thousands of solid gold bowls, dishes and washbasins; 6 million ounces of gold; 10 large pearls, each the size of an apricot; and 14,300 bolts of fine silk. His assets included 600 concubines and 8,000 acres of land. In all, auditors confiscated property estimated at 800 million taels of silver. Its value was one and a half billion dollars—and that in eighteenth-century dollars—making him, quite possibly, the richest man in the world. At the time of his execution, He Shen's assets exceeded more than ten years of China's entire state revenue.

As we walk around No Name Lake, Lu Yi and I have come full circle. Professor Yao senses we want to be alone, and he joins Fat Paycheck and the boys. While we retrace the steps we took together so many years earlier, I realize that Lu Yi symbolizes the upheaval, the pain, all the cataclysmic changes that have transformed this eternal city. She must be reading my thoughts. She suddenly turns to me. "My destiny and China's destiny were inextricably linked. Everything I suffered is branded onto my body. Everything I suffered is a scar," she says. "I was a trailblazer. I had the idea of going abroad before anyone else. Now everyone congratulates me on my foresight. I suffered so much, but I was just a grain of sand, helping China to change."

• • •

A day later Lu Yi calls to say goodbye before we leave for the airport. "You know, the day after our first meeting, I was *shang xin* [wounded in the heart]," she says. "I didn't know you had told them about me on your own, without anyone asking you. I felt very sad. But now I'm so happy we have found each other."

She doesn't press me for an explanation of why I chose to turn her in. And I have stopped apologizing. It's not fair, really, to keep forcing her to exonerate me over and over again. So I stay silent. Yet I feel so lucky to have found her, and to have received her forgiveness. I finally feel at peace. It makes me wonder why, in a nation as vast as China, so few people try to come to terms with their past.

In its journey from communism to capitalism, Beijing has reinvented itself in ways that leave it unrecognizable—physically, culturally and emotionally. As the past disappears, I keep getting lost. But at least I found Lu Yi. There are millions more like her, the walking wounded of China. She has survived and thrived. But I have glimpsed beneath her self-assured persona. Superficially, she resembles the effervescent woman I met briefly so long ago, but I know she has changed.

I have changed too. When I was young, I believed that ideology trumped everything. I thought I should save people from themselves. Now I understand the sheer arrogance of that stance. Having lived in China under Mao, having witnessed the massacre at Tiananmen Square, I now believe in human rights for all. I have raised my boys to respect others, to fight prejudice wherever they see it, to speak out about racism, sexism and homophobia. In my workplace, I am ferocious about freedom of the press and the responsibility that goes with it. I try never to be an innocent bystander—because there is no such thing.

I haven't told Lu Yi that she has changed my life. Over the telephone, I only tell her I am so very happy to have found her too. And then we end our brief conversation, promising to stay in touch. Will we? As I head to the airport, I keep thinking about her. I am thrilled that she got to America after all. And I am even more thrilled that she has come home. Beijing is where Lu Yi belongs.

We board Continental flight 88 back to Newark. Sam settles in next to me. "Thank you for taking me to Beijing," he says. "I had a really good time."

I'm momentarily speechless.

Sam keeps talking. "I just knew you were going to find her," he says, giving me a quick kiss. "I thought you would be able to do it. But then when she was so excited about seeing you, I was afraid she would kill you. I'm surprised she didn't hate you. She's a nice person."

As the plane takes off, I try to catch a last glimpse of the new Forbidden City. Through the smog, I can see the faint outlines of building cranes and expressways. Somewhere below, Fu the Enforcer must be heaving a sigh of relief that I've left, Scarlet will be playing with her grandchild and Lu Yi is planning a feast of shrimp with Professor Yao. The plane gains altitude and breaks through the smog. Soon the sky really *is* blue.

Acknowledgments

At Doubleday Canada, Maya Mavjee commissioned the book. Martha Kanya-Forstner inspired, shaped and edited it, pushing me to dig deeper in all the right places. Stephanie Fysh did a masterful and meticulous job of copy-editing. My agent, John Pearce, provided crucial encouragement throughout.

I thank Stevie Cameron, Edward Carter and Joyce Johnston for believing in me. Colleen Parrish provided support and wisdom through a very difficult period in my life. My sister, Gigi, and my father, Bill, were there for me, as always.

In Beijing, Kuang Ling helped me reserve Beautiful Lodgings. Geoff York provided a contemporary perspective. Rich Herzfelder pointed out how colorfully Beijingers were dressing nowadays and suggested I take a look at the writings of Nobel laureate Czeslaw Milosz.

Talin Vartanian had the idea of emailing me news articles to test the extent of Chinese Internet censorship. Margaret MacGregor, who studied at Beijing University in the 1970s, kept the letters I sent her and kindly forwarded me a copy of one from 1972. Zhou Lei patiently answered my queries about exit permits and Chinese slang. Elinor Reading, John Saunders and Lori Scopis helped me brainstorm titles.

I especially thank my husband, Norman, and our sons, Ben and Sam, for accompanying me to Beijing. They kept my spirits up. Back in Toronto, Ben designed and drew the maps. Norman read and corrected the manuscript, and was always available for a quick consultation or memory check.

Finally, I thank Lu Yi. Without her friendship, forbearance and forgiveness this book would not have been possible.